Fighti
in th

Fighting Viet Cong in the Rung Sat

Memoir of a Combat Advisor in Vietnam, 1968-1969

BOB WORTHINGTON

McFarland & Company, Inc., Publishers
Jefferson, North Carolina

All photographs are from the author's collection unless otherwise noted.

Library of Congress Cataloguing-in-Publication Data

Names: Worthington, Bob, 1937– author.
Title: Fighting Viet Cong in the Rung Sat : memoir of a combat advisor in Vietnam, 1968-1969 / Bob Worthington.
Description: Jefferson, North Carolina : McFarland & Company, Inc., Publishers, 2021 | Includes index.
Identifiers: LCCN 2021045793 | ISBN 9781476679419 (paperback : acid free paper) ∞
ISBN 9781476643960 (ebook)
Subjects: LCSH: Worthington, Bob, 1937- | Vietnam War, 1961-1975—Personal narratives, American. | United States. Army—Officers—Biography. | Vietnam War, 1961-1975—Campaigns. | BISAC: HISTORY / Military / Vietnam War
Classification: LCC DS559.5 .W678 2022 | DDC 959.704/3092 [B]—dc23
LC record available at https://lccn.loc.gov/2021045793

British Library cataloguing data are available

ISBN (print) 978-1-4766-7941-9
ISBN (ebook) 978-1-4766-4396-0

Front cover image: The author driving one of the advisor team's Boston Whalers (author's collection); *background* © 2021 Shutterstock

Printed in the United States of America

McFarland & Company, Inc., Publishers
Box 611, Jefferson, North Carolina 28640
www.mcfarlandpub.com

To my companion, best friend, and partner
of almost 65 years, my wife, Anita.

To the great staff at McFarland for providing me
the opportunity to share my stories and to allow me
time to overcome several obstacles.

Acknowledgments

The story you are about to read begins almost 55 years ago. I believe that my memory is excellent and many events I can recall like they happened yesterday. My quest to recall and accurately describe events, locations, situations, and people I interacted with in the late 1960s compelled me to seek all kinds of help to ensure the words I have used appropriately record the truth. Often opinions and perceptions are voiced by me alone. At other times I relied on help to portray my story as correctly as possible.

To describe what happened as precisely as I am able, I used several hundred pages of studies, after-action reports, official documents, decoration citations, academic theses and dissertations, my own letters to family, my own photographs, my own used combat maps, and diaries and photographs of other veterans where our persons may have intersected in Vietnam. Additionally, almost 200 books were consulted to describe vehicles, boats and planes, combat operations, medical units I spent time in, and background on the military leaders I worked for.

Lastly several people devoted many hours to help me author this book. Professor James B. Wells, PhD, of Eastern Kentucky University, provided detailed diagrams, maps and photos depicting the combat airfield at Boa Trai. Retired Brigadier General Jerry Laws, an army aviator (both plane and helicopter) with two tours in Vietnam, discussed the ins and outs of flying low and slow in Vietnam.

Mary Iadicicco was my first reader of the original manuscript and provided valuable feedback on what worked and what did not. Back to the drawing board, and then more people read edited versions. Ted Spitzmiller, an award-winning author in his own right, spent hours reading every word of every chapter, correcting errors, pointing out confusion or problem areas in what I wrote, and aiding to make my writing better.

To Margie Graham, a community college computer teacher and

master of word processing who possesses the magic of taking my cobbled together manuscript and turning it into a polished book.

To Natasha Nunez, a young lady and college art student who drew all the maps. She deserves thanks for drawing the originals and then accommodating all my revisions.

Last is Anita, who read several drafts many times and spent hours ensuring my writing reflected what was real and pointing out better ways to depict what I wanted to say.

To everyone, I thank you very much for devoting so much time to make my story better.

Table of Contents

Preface

The Vietnam War was not going well for the U.S. in 1968. This is my story of how the conduct of this confusing, and often contradictory, war impacted my second tour as a combat advisor.

Our politicians were divided as to what they wanted. The hawks, favoring General Westmoreland's strategy of how to fight the war, fervently believed that adding more combat soldiers would win the war. The doves wanted to pull our troops out at any cost. General Westmoreland prevailed, receiving more U.S. forces than ever before.

Lyndon Johnson became president after John F. Kennedy was assassinated. President Johnson inherited a war not of his making and refused to run for another term to avoid making decisions regarding the war. Richard Nixon, campaigning for president, promised to withdraw U.S. troops and return the war to the South Vietnamese. Many Americans believed this to be an unwinnable war for the U.S. military. Others said no, do not let South Vietnam become another communist victory.

During 1968 General Westmoreland was promoted to Army Chief of Staff and we elected Richard Nixon president. A change in leadership foreshadowed change in how this war would be carried out. Requiring the Vietnamese to assume more control of the war became the political goal.

The U.S. entered World War II because the Japanese attacked Honolulu on 7 December 1941. We responded with a vengeance by pushing west across the Pacific with the goal of destroying Japan. Similarly, we joined the war in Europe with the objective, shared by our allies, to drive the Germans back into their country and obliterate it. On both fronts the solution to end the war was to take the fight into the heart of the enemy's homeland and demolish it.

Then came the Korean War, frequently described as a police action. At the end of World War II, Russia and the United States divided Korea into two countries at the 38th parallel. Then on 25 June 1950, 75,000

1

North Korean troops attacked South Korea with the objective of unifying the two under communism. This action forced the UN to intervene. Russia and China supported North Korea. Military strategy to destroy North Korea was viewed as inciting another world war—unthinkable. A political solution was reached in July 1953: the continued division of North and South.

This same stalemate confronted the Vietnam combatants in 1968. Taking the fight into North Vietnam could initiate a world war because of its support by China and Russia. As American military forces continued to engage main force units, there was renewed emphasis by the South Vietnamese and their U.S. advisors to attack the North Vietnamese and Viet Cong infrastructure within South Vietnam.

In early 1965, the influx of American combat troops began, and it was no longer just an advisors' war. When I arrived for my first tour as an advisor in January 1966, South Vietnamese combat units and American forces did most of the fighting (see my award-winning book, *Under Fire with ARVN Infantry*, McFarland, 2018). The strategy was to find, fix, and destroy the enemy utilizing the massive firepower and strength of the U.S. military. This was my job as a combat advisor with a Vietnamese Army infantry battalion.

Returning to Vietnam after 19 months, I found the war had changed dramatically from my first tour (1966–67) as 1968 became the bloodiest year of the war, beginning with the battles of Tet in January.

For American military ground units in 1968, the combat emphasis was locating and annihilating major NVA and VC units. But that was not where most of the fighting took place. It was among the Viet Cong infrastructure. South Vietnam had 44 provinces, 250 districts, with thousands of villages and hamlets as well as its power center, Saigon. All these geopolitical jurisdictions had their own South Vietnamese governing entities. Unfortunately, most had an identical, secret, underground, parallel Viet Cong organization. Both systems were vying for the loyalty of the local population.

To counter this escalating threat, the U.S. State Department and the advisory leadership focused on two issues: eliminating the VC infrastructure and pacifying rural areas by reinforcing the South Vietnamese local civil government. This was overseen by a new command structure created in 1967, Civil Operations and Revolutionary Development Support, or CORDS. It brought together, under a single command, personnel and resources from both U.S. and Vietnamese military and civil organizations.

The CORDS structure and strategy focused on conducting military operations using reinforced Vietnamese Regional and Popular (territorial) Forces to secure villages and hamlets for the rural Vietnamese to live in.

A primary focus of CORDS was the enhancement of the Vietnamese territorial forces, to equip and train the Regional and Popular Forces to take on the VC infrastructure. From under 200 American RF/PF advisors the number was increased to over 2,300. At the same time the territorial forces were raised from 300,000 to over 500,000 soldiers by drafting more men.

Another major program introduced as part of CORDS was the Phoenix program, based on previous CIA methods used to destroy VC organizations. Through the combined efforts of Vietnamese national police, Vietnamese military, provincial reconnaissance units, and U.S. Intelligence specialists, Phoenix was designed to identify, locate, and detain or destroy the leaders of the Viet Cong infrastructure.

Once intelligence was confirmed as authentic, the dangerous work was carried out by Regional and Popular Force units and other Phoenix assets. When an enemy target was identified, a small force was tasked with apprehending or annihilating the target using the unconventional strategy that would best lead to success.

During the Vietnam War, guerrilla warfare and insurgency were typical means employed by the Viet Cong. Countering these tactics is best accomplished using what is known as unconventional warfare. I studied this in the mid–1960s as a student in the U.S. Army Special Warfare School. Today this type of combat is known as special operations.

Unconventional warfare consists of small, highly trained units conducting military missions to delay, harass, capture, or destroy specific military targets through speed, surprise, and the avoidance of friendly casualties. Typically, these operations involve assisting a friendly government to fight a guerrilla or insurgent force operating inside their borders.

During my second tour, I served in a dual role. I was advising soldiers of district Regional and Popular Force units, conducting military operations, often using unconventional warfare tactics. As a CORDS member I also advised the civil district government regarding refugee resettlement, agriculture, health care, education, and the overall welfare of the district citizens.

My background in unconventional warfare was a major key to our achievements. Frequently, before the civil district government could safely work in a village or hamlet, the military would first have to eliminate the VC in the area. Our operation plans were to go in swiftly, surprise the enemy, do our job, and just as swiftly depart. Our missions were not to seize terrain but to catch or destroy the VC.

This was a dangerous and sometimes bloody assignment for an advisor. Most unconventional warfare missions were quickly planned and executed, since timely intelligence often came with a limited opportunity for success. If a raid was not immediately executed, the chance was lost. On the other hand, a lack of comprehensive planning quite often led to unexpected surprises, sometimes funny, other times deadly.

This was my year of practicing unconventional warfare; this was my war in 1968 and 1969.

Note: Names of some Americans in this book have been changed.

1

Cambodian Border, November 1968, Second Tour

I am sitting by the open right door of a command and control Huey flying on the South Vietnamese side of the Cambodian border. We are loitering, slowly searching for our target on the ground below. It is pitch-black, moonless, and calm this night of 14 November 1968, on my second tour as a combat advisor in Vietnam. I have been back in-country for three months now.

The South Vietnamese I advise have a secret agent in Cambodia observing the North Vietnamese Army units positioned on the Cambodian side of the border. Earlier today, we were notified when and where an NVA transport company would be moving rockets across the border to Saigon. Our mission: locate the transporters and destroy them and their rockets.

We are a team (called Firefly) of three helicopters maneuvering in a stack of three layers. Closest to the ground is a gunship, also armed with rockets. The helicopter in the middle has a powerful searchlight, with command and control in the high ship. We are tracking the path of several water buffalo which have been carrying the rockets from a North Vietnamese Army supply depot in Cambodia.

We locate where the unit has entered South Vietnam and where it crossed a shallow river. While we can see where the buffalo exited the river and climbed up the riverbank, we quickly lose their trail where they entered the jungle.

A brief time later we find the transport animals, grouped together in a corner of an open area surrounded by heavy jungle growth. The gunship closest to the ground shoots and kills the buffalo, and reports the enemy rockets are not visible. It then radios that there are several camouflaged underground bunkers hidden in the field. I tell the pilot to destroy them with his rockets. Calling back, he explains the field is too small for a safe rocket run as he would be too low and close to the explosions.

5

I ask my pilot to fly down in front of a bunker. He does and we see an opening into a bunker. I am armed with an M-79 grenade launcher which shoots a single 40 mm grenade. I have a vest full of grenades. Hovering a couple feet off the ground in front of a bunker, I fire a grenade into its opening, detonating with a bang, followed by another greater, secondary explosion. This, I guess, must be the rockets blowing up.

The pilot swings to another bunker where I repeat the process, resulting in another secondary explosion. Instantly we realize our intel from the agent is accurate. Then we come to the last bunker but someone inside opens fire on us. Now we are engaged in a firefight. Once again, I dispatch a grenade through the low opening.

I sense a sharp stab in the back of my upper right thigh. It feels like the rapidly spinning bit in an electric drill has just been rammed into my leg. I ask the pilot if he is flying into our shrapnel and he replies no. Reaching to the back of my thigh, I feel warm blood and the end of a hot piece of twisted metal embedded in my leg. I tell the pilot I have just been shot!

And I am just starting my second tour in Vietnam as a combat advisor.

2

January 1967, Back Home from First Vietnam Tour

Leaving Vietnam, just before noon on Wednesday, 18 January 1967. The temperature is in the high 80s with the humidity in the low 60s. I am wearing a wrinkled short-sleeve khaki uniform and sweating. Departing Saigon, I am homeward bound in a dull gray air force C-141A Starlifter. Our flight stops for fuel and crew changes at Wake Island and Hawaii; even with favorable tailwinds, it is over 21 hours until we touch down at McGuire Air Force Base in New Jersey. The outside temperature is below freezing as we exit the plane to enter a large room with empty tables, customs agents and air force NCOs telling us what to do.

My baggage is checked, papers processed, and I am cleared for my leave. I am pointed toward a door which opens into the main terminal, filled mostly with screaming young females and children. These are the wives, parents, and families waiting for their loved ones returning from a year's separation.

Glancing around the room I quickly spot a slim brunette wrapped in a warm coat, holding a warm field jacket, recognizing me. Anita and I rush to meet each other. Our daughters are at my parents' home in Roxbury, Connecticut, about four hours away. It is now around 9 p.m., which would mean a long drive on a very cold snowy night, putting us home after 1 a.m. Besides, I am bushed after the long ride in an uncomfortable air force plane packed with 130-odd other sweaty bodies. Anita tells me she already has reservations at a motel just outside the McGuire main gate.

Early the Next Morning We Leave for Roxbury

Our two daughters have changed so much. I have not seen them for over a year, and we cannot stay away from each other. After all, I have

7

missed one third of my youngest, Julie's, life. The other, Suzi, is now six and in first grade.

The days in Roxbury pass quickly. My sisters and assorted aunts and uncles visit as well as friends from high school.

When I met Anita in Hawaii, she brought our 8 mm home movie camera so during my last couple of months in Vietnam I could film everything a combat advisor did. I have about three hours of footage, but it needs editing and arranging in sequence. I buy an 8 mm editing kit which includes a film viewer and slicer. Thus, I spend many nights viewing hours of footage, discarding footage which didn't provide a clear picture and splicing together suitable footage. I now have about an hour and twenty minutes of a documentary film (but no sound) which depicts what a combat advisor did.

Christmas, 19 January 1967. Anita, Bob (holding Julie), Suzi.

Before leaving Roxbury, I show this movie to diverse groups of people (both adults and children) while I narrate what they watch. Their concept of the Vietnam War is mostly colored by the scenes shown on the evening TV news, where the images almost always depict young American soldiers and marines fighting in jungles, with dead bodies in evidence somewhere in the pictures. Most of the Vietnamese shown are either captured Viet Cong or dead Viet Cong. None are smiling.

My movie presents an entirely different picture of Vietnam. Most of the film depicts how American combat advisors help the Vietnamese people. There are scenes of kids playing, running around, yelling, and smiling, images of family pets, medical clinics where American military medical personnel are treating sick Vietnamese people. The film shows Vietnamese people working in their fields, tending to their livestock, and building refugee homes. A night segment clearly displays, during a night combat operation, the Viet Cong stopping the war so the American advisor (me) could bring in a military med evac helicopter to save the life of a small Viet Cong baby, which I did.

The viewers' comments are notable in that virtually everyone viewing the movie remarks that it presents an image of the war and American involvement they had never seen before. (In 2019 this film became commercially available as *Combat Advisor in Vietnam*.)

My time in Roxbury is ending. I am to report to the Army Armor School at Fort Knox, Kentucky, on 23 February to attend the Armor Officers Career Course. Anita, our daughters and I will return to our home in Columbus, Georgia (where they lived during my first tour in Vietnam), and determine what to do with our house while I am on my six-month temporary school assignment.

It is time to head south. We have less than a month to decide what to do with our house, pack up and move the four of us, two vehicles and one travel trailer, in the winter, over 500 miles to Fort Knox. Then we must find a place to live and put Suzi in school. First, though, we face the journey to our home in Georgia, which is almost 1,100 miles. We have a lot to do, and bidding farewell to my parents and other relatives, we begin the trek south. En route we stop in Washington, D.C., spending a few days with Anita's parents.

Back Home at Fort Benning

In Columbus, we don't know what to do about our home. We will be gone over six months, and financing two homes exceeds the pocketbook of an army captain. We discuss this with a real estate expert, and he points out that Fort Benning, especially because of the Vietnam War, is a temporary home to a vast amount of military people needing a place for their family on a short-term basis. The agency has a property management office which helps us find a qualified family for a temporary lease of our furnished property. An army pilot with his family is to be assigned to Benning for the same period I will be gone. When we move out, he will move in.

By mid–February, we have packed our small travel trailer with all the household items we think we will need at Fort Knox. Departing for Knox now will permit us to arrive before school starts for me and allow time to find a place to live and to get Suzie back in first grade. We had planned to spend our first days after arriving with a family we know from our days at Fort Benning. We clearly don't have a clue as to what is really happening at Fort Knox, but, unfortunately for us, we will soon learn.

Fort Knox

School starts for me on Monday, 27 February, but I must report in on Thursday, 23 February, to process in the Armor School at Fort Knox. I have less than a week to find a place for us to live. In our experience in the past when I had a TDY (temporary duty) assignment and brought my family to be with me, finding a place to live was never a problem.

What I learn is that Fort Knox is an overcrowded base. It is a major training base and with the build-up to send troops to Vietnam, the local area faces severe rental housing shortages. I already knew that there would be no military quarters available for married officers with families.

As soon as we settle in with our friends, Anita and I acquire a local paper and a phone book. We make a list of all apartments and rental properties in the area surrounding Fort Knox and begin making calls. Nothing is available to rent. So, we decide to look further away, into Louisville, about 30 miles north of Fort Knox.

We have a Louisville paper and the Yellow Pages, so we spend the morning visiting some of the larger apartment complexes in the city, being told the same thing: "we do not have any apartments available."

Flipping through the pages of the paper, I see a half-page ad offering almost new mobile homes for sale by just taking over the payments. This could be the solution to where to live, together, as a family.

We agree on an almost brand-new ten-foot-wide by sixty-foot-long, three-bedroom, two-bath mobile home. The sales guy tells us that delivery is free, and the only cost is a nominal fee for transferring the title and the loan to us. Now we own a home to live in, so we need to find a trailer park to place it.

Army posts are noted for having an abundance of trailer parks just outside the base. The next day I am on the phone, talking to owners or managers of area trailer parks. No one has any vacant space for a mobile home. The morning after not finding a lot for our mobile home, I receive a call from a recently retired master sergeant who says he has bought a large area of wooded property next to his trailer park so he can expand. He has heard about an army captain, a just returned Vietnam vet, who needs a trailer parking place. While his expansion is not completed, he does have a new place we could rent. A few days later we move into lot number 7 and spend our first night in our new home, all together again for the next six months.

Our home at Fort Knox, March 1967.

The army has a prescribed series of schooling for its officers. Upon being commissioned, every officer attends the basic course for his or her branch. New army lieutenants learn to be officers via OCS, ROTC or a military academy. The basic course teaches the new officer how to function in the army and within the branch. Next comes the career course for captains. This course prepares officers for a variety of higher-level command and staff positions, focusing on careers within the branch. There are two more stages of officer military education, the Command and General Staff College (CGSG) and the War College. Both are designed to train field grade officers (majors, lieutenant colonels and colonels) for serving successfully in higher command and staff positions. The War College is the senior education for potential general officers. CGSC and the War College attendees are by selection only, although an officer can complete either via correspondence or by attending a reserve school which teaches each course.

Interestingly, the career course can be attended by a branch different from yours. Toward the end of my tour as a combat advisor in Vietnam, I received orders to the Armor Officers' Career Course, not Infantry.

There are two rumors regarding my selection for the Armor Course, instead of Infantry. The first says that all infantry officers who are not considered as effective infantry officers would be assigned to attend either the armor or artillery career course, but not infantry. On the other hand, the other rumor is that only the best infantry officers will be selected to be cross-trained in a branch other than infantry.

I am guessing that when my leave from Vietnam ended, I was a prime candidate for a career course and a slot was available in the Armor school, so I was sent there with no lost time waiting for a slot in the Infantry school.

The Armor Officers' Career Course is a 19-week educational program to provide captains with the training to serve, successfully, in positions of command and battalion and brigade staff. My class begins with over 140 students. While most are U.S. Army Armor officers, there are also several army Infantry and Artillery, as well as a very few officers from other branches of our military. Additionally, the course hosts several foreign officers, predominantly from countries which have ample armor units, mostly from the Middle East and Western Europe. We are a very eclectic group of military officers from remarkably diverse backgrounds and military experience. In the end, 136 of us will complete the course and graduate.

The curriculum consists of six primary areas of instruction: Automotive (i.e., the care and feeding of armored vehicles), Communication (radio), Weapons, General Subjects (military), Command and Staff, and Employment of Nuclear Weapons. The course of instruction was interesting and informative. Because of our involvement in Vietnam, the program includes 33 hours of instruction specifically devoted to counterinsurgency warfare. Several segments of the program are of interest to me. We have a 40-hour program on combat injuries and medical, to aid us as officers during combat. This involves both classroom seminars and practical experience in the field.

The school, being Armor, focuses on past battles fought during World War II, in Europe. Most of our fighting today is in the jungles of Southeast Asia, not armor country. Most of us fought as infantry in Vietnam, recently returned, where the shooting was up close and personal. Any enemy with a rifle, within 50 yards, was a danger, and he who shot first and more accurately was usually the survivor.

The "school solution" for winning is accomplished through the "shock" action using the combined forces of armor, artillery, and close air support, followed by infantry to hold the ground. Hours are spent in the classroom where, in small teams of students, we are given an operation order to plan and then execute combat maneuvers. As we move through the scenario, we are provided with new information on the operation (for example, if the enemy has moved, or has been reinforced, or has a weak area, or we have suffered more casualties than expected), all designed to force us to change our tactics to accommodate the changes to win the fight.

In one scenario, we are the commander of a brigade force of armor and infantry, attacking a reinforced enemy position. As we move our armor units forward, we encounter a massive defense of small arms fire with some mortars. The question is what do we do?

My team of students are mostly infantrymen, veterans of Vietnam. Many of the other teams are mostly armor officers. Our solution is based on what we did in combat, in Vietnam. Halt the advance and maneuver around and flank the enemy positions and engage in fire to wipe them out. We are told we are wrong. This is armor; therefore, the school solution is to ignore the small arms fire and continue ahead and move through the enemy. Small arms fire would not harm the tanks, so why stop? The infantry behind the armor would then come along and mop up what remained. Slowly we infantry are comprehending the difference between slogging it out as foot soldiers and combat utilizing the protection of armor.

We infantry types argue that in the real world of combat today (Vietnam), armor is useless, and men on the ground, if they want to live, would not continue recklessly into a barrage of enemy small arms fire.

We believe the Armor School is stuck in the ancient history of the past, ignoring strategies and tactics of combat today.

The Armor School continues to present scenarios and operations which emphasize the combined use of armor, artillery, infantry, and close air support as the answer to combat. We in the infantry believe that the Armor School is short-changing us by teaching us obsolete tactics and strategy. Fortunately for the school an international incident of immense precedence occurs which changes everything.

We Are Now Believers

As I mentioned earlier, many (over a dozen) students were officers from the Middle East: United Arab Republic (Egypt), Syria, Israel, Iraq, Iran, Jordan, and others. On Monday morning, 5 June, when we meet in class, all the Middle Eastern students are missing. We are told that around 1 a.m. (EST, or close to 8 a.m. Israel time), Israel launched a massive air attack against the United Arab Republic (Egypt). Several countries are involved: apparently it is Israel against Egypt, Syria, Jordan, and Iraq. The missing students are staying in their bachelor officers' quarters (BOQ) rooms, anxiously waiting to see if they will have a country to return to.

As the week passes, we receive more information on the war. It becomes obvious that this war is what our school has been preaching to us over the past 14 weeks. The war begins with UAR president Nassar massing hundreds of thousands of troops and hundreds of tanks on the Israel border. Israel feels threatened and retaliates with its Monday morning airstrikes, essentially wiping out the UAR air force, allowing Israel to immediately achieve air superiority.

Simultaneously, Israel initiates armor-led attacks against Syria, Jordan, and Egyptian forces in the Sinai Peninsula. While having fewer troops and weapons the Israelis have superior soldiers and initiate the war by overrunning all enemy positions using shock attacks combining armor with artillery, infantry (both ground and airborne) and close air support. Classic strategic combination of combat forces, exactly as we are being taught, every day.

By the end of the sixth day, Saturday, 10 June, Israel has captured the Sinai Peninsula and Gaza Strip from Egypt, the Golan Heights from Syria, and the West Bank of the Jordan River from Jordan. The country has successfully achieved its military objectives. In several instances, the enemy commanders are panicking and abandoning their positions, fleeing back home. The victory by Israel is further evidenced by these facts: Israel suffered less than 1,000 soldiers killed in action and 4,500 wounded. The enemy losses are not completely known but between 11,000 and 18,000 Egyptian, Syrian, and Jordanian troops were killed or missing. On Sunday, 11 June 1967, a ceasefire is signed by all.

For the rest of our school, World War II battles take a back seat to the Israeli Six-Day War and how the combined use of armor-led assaults with artillery, infantry, and close air support can even win wars today, despite what we experience in Vietnam. This war made the infantrymen classmates believers.

School Is Almost Over

A major segment of our curriculum involves employing nuclear weapons in conventional warfare. Current military combat strategy allows the usage of small nuclear weapons down to the battalion level within a division. For this to be effective, the army must have a cadre of officers trained in the management of a nuclear battlefield, for both offensive and defensive operations. To maintain a group of properly trained officers the army created a Nuclear Weapons Employment (NEW) Course in which graduates would receive the number 5 as a prefix to their duty MOS (Military Occupational Specialty, a four-digit number representing the name of the officer's job). Students selected for this program are the top 10 percent of the students taking the NEW segment in the Armor Career Course. Upon completion of this section, I am in the top 10 percent so my orders are amended to remain at the Armor School three more weeks to attend the secret I Course.

On Tuesday, 11 July, I graduate in the top third of my Armor Career Course class with a grade point average of 89.53, my curriculum grades ranging from an 84.23 (Automotive) to 92.40 (weapons), to begin the Nuclear Weapon Employment Course the next day. On 2 August I complete the Course and receive my prefix 5 to my MOS. My report time to Fort Benning is now 28 August as I have 26 days of leave and travel time.

My original orders to Benning after the Career Course have me assigned to the *Infantry Magazine* staff at the Infantry School. I guess that my liberal arts degree from Dartmouth had something to do with this assignment. I have been a captain for about two years. Promotions to major, due to the Vietnam War, are taking a little over three years. The prime job for an infantry captain is that of company commander. I have no company command time yet, and that could hurt my chances for promotion. Toward the end of my Career Course I send a request, through personnel channels, asking that my Fort Benning orders to the magazine

Suzi (left) and Julie (right) holding trout caught at Tennessee campground en route to Fort Benning, August 1967. Note Jeep and trailer in background.

be amended and I be given a company to command, explaining how I need such an assignment to be competitive for promotion. At Knox, I never receive a response to my request.

When we acquired our mobile home, it was a bargain. We assumed its loan, and now it is already set up in a trailer park. We immediately find an eligible buyer to assume our loan and pay us a couple thousand dollars to boot.

Toward the end of my schooling, I receive a letter describing a fire that did some damage in our kitchen in Columbus. Insurance covered the repair, but the letter also states that the family renting our home is moving on post. The managing agent informs me that he can sell the home quicker than he can lease it. Anita and I say sell, which he does. Therefore, now, we have no home to return to at Benning.

On Thursday, 3 August, our small travel trailer is packed, hitched to the Jeep, which I will drive and Anita the Ford station wagon. We depart early in the morning as we will be spending the next 16 days wandering around the Cherokee National Forest in the Great Smoky Mountains of eastern Tennessee.

Slowly we make our way southeast toward Georgia. On Saturday, 19 August, we arrive at Fort Benning. We have no place to live, I am not sure what my next assignment will be, but we are together, looking forward to our next adventure.

3

Moving into Fort Benning

Monday morning, 21 August 1967, I enter Fort Benning, drive to the Infantry School and go into the personnel office. The night before I had located the Post Duty Officer and signed in from leave, so today I am officially back on duty. To my surprise and wonderment, I am informed that my original orders have been amended and I am reassigned to the U.S. Army Training Center, which is in the area where the 2nd Infantry Division was when I was assigned there from 1963 to 1965. My orders instruct me to report to the Second Training Brigade for further assignment as a company commander, the choice assignment for an infantry captain. I am overjoyed to be able to get the exact assignment I so dearly wanted. I never suspect I will come to hate the job, which will lead to earth-shattering decisions about my military career, my family, and my life.

Fort Benning and Basic Combat Training

Fort Benning began as an army post in 1909, and in 1918 an army committee selected Camp Benning to become the Infantry School. In 1922 it became a permanent army post, then a major training base during World War II, when it also became the home of parachute training. In 1950 the Ranger School was created.

The 2nd Infantry Division, stationed at Benning since 1958, became the 1st Cavalry Division (Airmobile) in July 1965, along with the 11th Air Assault Division (Test), which had been created to evaluate the concept of using helicopters to fight wars. The new airmobile 1st Cav departed Benning during August and September 1965 when it deployed to Vietnam.

So here I am, back at Fort Benning to finally become a company commander, two years after I was last here. The Army Training Center headquarters welcomes me and sends me down to the 2nd Training Brigade located at the Harmony Church area of Fort Benning, which is about seven miles east of Main Post.

Entering the headquarters building, I go to the Personnel (S-1) office and meet the S-1, sitting at his desk. Captain James wears the crossed cannons and missile denoting he is an Artillery officer but is also wearing above his left pocket the CIB (combat infantryman badge) and jump wings. The Ranger tab on his left shoulder and the MACV (Military Advisory Command, Vietnam) on his right sleeve confirm he has served as a combat advisor in Vietnam. I explain why I am here, as he ruffles through a pile of files, pulling out what he is seeking, my Field 201 (personnel) file. Glancing at my papers, he looks at his watch, then peers at a calendar on his desk and says the brigade commander is in his office right now, so I can meet him for a few minutes.

Captain James knocks on the partially opened door and moves in. Sitting at his desk, wearing the short-sleeved khaki summer uniform, Colonel Spears rises to his full height of six feet and five or six inches— probably towering over everyone in his brigade. Tall and lanky, he looks older than his 47 years. His insignia, ribbons, and badges clearly indicate he is an infantryman who wears his CIB above his ribbons which includes the Distinguished Service Cross (second only to the Medal of Honor), personally presented to him by General Patton, the Bronze Star, and a Purple Heart. No doubt about it, the colonel is both a combat vet and a hero. He welcomes me to his brigade stating that James will take me to the battalion I am assigned to. Recognizing I am being dismissed, I turn and follow Captain James out the door. He makes a phone call, stating that if I will follow his car, he will take me to the Eighth Battalion, where I am to become a company commander.

Parking both cars in a gravel parking lot we enter an old, single story World War II building covered in a pale, worn-out yellow color. Inside Captain James introduces me to First Lieutenant Rolph, an Armor officer who has yet to serve in combat. After a few words with the lieutenant, James leaves. Rolph explains that the battalion commander is out in the field all day and won't return until that evening. Checking the colonel's calendar, he sets up an appointment for me for late Friday morning. Then Rolph discusses with me what I need to do to settle in at Benning. When he asks a little about my background and family situation, I indicate that, if possible, I want to live on post. He agrees it is most important is to get me a place to live. Pulling out a map of the Fort Benning Main Post he describes the housing situation at Benning.

My Past at Fort Benning

The Post is divided into four major cantonment areas. There is the Main Post, where all the Infantry School activities are located to include the Army Airborne (parachute) School and Ranger School. On a level area between the Main Post and the Chattahoochee River, on the southwest corner of Main Post, is Lawson Army Airfield, a multi-runway aviation facility, kept busy with its helicopter training, operational school support missions, and air force multi-engine aircraft for actual jump training. About five or six miles northeast of Main Post is Kelley Hill, where the buildings and barracks are post–World War II and more modern.

Just to the west of Kelley Hill is another prominent rise called Houston Hill where Martin Army Hospital is located. My family has a long history with this medical facility. Two daughters were born here, a son died here, Anita almost died here, and I spent a month in the psychiatric ward.

In the summer of 1963, TDY from my job as a rifle platoon leader in the 2nd Infantry Division, I broke my right hip on my third jump in airborne school. The day before, another student did the same thing and had a cast placed on him from just above the knee to almost his chest, the standard procedure then for broken hips at Martin Army Hospital. The orthopedic surgeon who was on duty the night I was injured had been trained in a new procedure of immobilizing the fractured femur using four slim, six inch pins by making a 9 inch incision over the knob at the hip where the femur curves to form the ball which fits into the pelvis socket and screwed in the four Hegge pins, no cast.

I spent a month in the hospital (still drawing jump pay), receiving therapy and beginning to walk, using crutches. A month after the operation, I received 30 days' convalescence leave and returned home (which at that time was a house we rented). Thirty days later I returned to the hospital for extensive therapy to learn to walk again.

In the orthopedic ward were three of us with beds next to each other: me, a lieutenant who had his left arm destroyed in an accident driving to Benning one night to attend the Infantry Officers' Basic Course, and a captain, an army pilot who could fly any aircraft the army had. He was being released from active duty, a victim of a reduction in force (RIF) who had an unknown stomach ailment and somehow ended up in our ward. The lieutenant and I spend our days in therapy while the captain spent his days either on the phone or being tested. If he was in the hospital, he couldn't be released from active duty. But the nights were ours and we would stay up way beyond lights-out playing cards and messing around with each other.

The nursing staff quickly tired of our antics and how our behaviors were impacting the other patients. The solution was to place us in an unused psychiatric ward, next door to our ward, give us the keys and as long as we kept our hospital appointments, the staff really didn't care if we stayed up all night or killed one another roughhousing. So, most of my last month in Martin was spent in the psychiatric ward. I was discharged with a one-year profile (no PT, no running, and no prolonged strain on the right leg) and the lieutenant was medically released from the army. We finally learned what all the captain's phone calls were about. When he learned he was going to be released from active duty, he tried a variety of ways to stay and fly. But he was always turned down and eventually ran out of time. So, he faked a stomach disorder and began a different quest, becoming a warrant officer. When that was approved, he was released from active duty the day he was released from the hospital, the stomach ailment mysteriously resolved, and the next day he was a warrant officer, on active duty as a pilot.

When I was discharged from the hospital in the fall of 1963, Anita was pregnant, due in December. In early December, she began to experience pain and knew she was about to deliver. My mother was visiting to help out with the family and the new baby. She watched our son and daughter while I took Anita to Martin Army Hospital. Anita was admitted but did not deliver. It was a false alarm and she was released the next day, 9 December.

Early the following day, she believed she was about to deliver but because of the embarrassment of the false alarm—she did not want to go to the hospital and be sent home again—she insisted on staying home, until she almost passed out, I raced Anita back to Martin. By now she was listless, white as a sheet, and barely conscious. I was driving very fast and a couple of miles from the hospital came up on a car just dawdling along. I honked the horn and motioned for the car to pull over. I guess the driver thought I was driving too fast so he began to maneuver to block the road so I couldn't pass. Having enough of his nonsense, I pulled alongside his vehicle, my left wheels in the shoulder on the other side of the road, gunned the engine, passing him. What I did must have scared him because he looked at Anita, hanging her head out the window and saw what must have looked like a dead person. He couldn't take his eyes away from her and crashed into the field to his right, off the road. Fearful for Anita, I sped on, not really caring about the other's fate. I pulled up to the ER, and she was whisked away in a gurney while I parked the car. Later that morning, Sunday, 10 December, after our daughter Julie was born, I found Anita on a ward,

A young enlisted female medic was taking her blood pressure but apparently having problems. The medic finally went to bring back a nurse and after a hurried, but quiet discussion, the nurse took Anita's blood pressure, twice, and sent the medic away to get someone else. I had no idea what was happening, but a couple of doctors came to her bed immediately and I was told to leave. One of the doctors and the head nurse held another hushed conversation and the nurse said Anita's blood pressure was low and she was going to be moved and I had to leave, but I could return later.

When I returned later that afternoon, there were two more doctors with her, this time civilians from Columbus. Apparently, she had a negative reaction to her saddle block (lower spine) anesthesia, Nupercaine (an anesthesia that has been in common use since the late 1920s), resulting in hypotension (low blood pressure) and bradycardia (heart beating too slowly). The severity of these postpartum complications suggested that local physicians be consulted. She had her feet elevated, was given atropine to increase her heart rate and another medication to increase her 86/50 blood pressure. All the doctors concluded that she needed to be monitored 24 hours a day. Unfortunately, the army wasn't staffed to provide this care, so the nursing staff volunteered to do this on their own time. She was watched and recovered without further complications. Five days later, I brought Anita and Julie home

In November 1964, we were living in our new home in Columbus, nine miles north of Fort Benning (we bought the home, our first, in February 1964). One night our two-year-old son, Scotty, woke up and went into Suzi's room and told her goodbye, then fell in the hall. Suzi screamed, and Anita and I rushed to our son. He was on medication for a chest cold which did not appear to be getting worse. He was unconscious. Anita called for an ambulance and I began CPR. The ambulance arrived and its emergency medical technician took over the CPR as we rushed to Martin Army Hospital. Upon arrival at the ER, the staff physician on duty was my battalion surgeon, who took over. A few minutes later he came to me to say Scotty never regained consciousness; he died from an undetected viral infection. He is buried at the Army Cemetery at Fort Benning.

In April 1968 our daughter Karen was born at Martin Army Hospital.

The other two areas of Benning are Sand Hill and Harmony Church. Both areas were built as temporary living and training areas for troops during World War II. In the early 1960s both areas were fully utilized by the Second Infantry Division. After the soldiers of the Second and the 11th became the First Cav and departed for Vietnam, these areas became the U.S. Army Basic Training Center.

Rolph explains that most officer housing is scattered around Main Post. In 1963 when I first reported to Fort Benning, due to the countless number of permanent party and army units based at Benning, on-post housing for lieutenants was critical with the waiting period running from several months to over a year. So, we rented a small house and then, later, bought a home.

In 1968 the two army divisions are gone, making the Basic Training Center the major army unit at Benning. While the training center comprised 9,000 to 10,000 soldiers, between 8,000 and 9,000 were recruits, housed in barracks, not eligible for family housing. Thus, the training center had an abundance of lieutenants and captains but few field-grade officers. The same for the Infantry School students, most were at Benning TDY, and not eligible for family housing. The bottom line: family housing, on post, for a captain, would not be a problem.

Foremost is to acquire a place to live, then get the cars registered, find a school for Suzi and kindergarten for Julie. Then process through every place on post where I would have a connection such as a bank, the post office, the officers' club, the moving company where all our household goods and furniture are stored, and all the other assorted offices and agencies on Benning which wants to know I am a permanent resident, where I am assigned, and where I live. Typically, this in-processing when moving to a new duty station takes a week. Since finding a place to live is most important, the Post Housing Office is first on my list.

Finding a New Home

I drive to the Post Housing Office, show them my orders to the Basic Training Center to verify I am eligible for family quarters on the post. There is one place that will be available in a couple of days. It is in a building that contains four sets of quarters in a three-story stucco building with a tiled roof, built in the 1930s for full colonels. It has been upgraded several times, so it has modern appliances, electrical outlets and fixtures and contemporary plumbing. Located on the east side of Main Post, it is on the corner of Stewart Avenue and Running Avenue, at 307A Stewart Avenue. On the south side of the house is French Polo Field and next to that Blue Field, which is like a park. About five short blocks west of the house is the Fort Benning golf course. Behind each building is a small back yard, a paved narrow alley, and a single old wooden building, with a peaked roof, shared and mainly used for storage. In the immediate area, covering about two exceptionally large blocks are 22 identical buildings, housing 88 families. These quarters have already been inspected since the last family left and some minor work is being done to make it ready for its next occupants. I can have it, if I want. I am granted a few hours to make up my mind.

Because we are staying in a trailer park with no phones, I drive there to get Anita and the girls to check out the quarters. It is open with a couple of men doing touch-up painting, so we can go in and look. All four of us quickly agree it is a nice place to live, especially when the girls see plenty of kids their ages playing around the group of quarters. We drive back to Housing, saying we will take the quarters.

The building is divided into two sets of quarters on the ground floor and two on the second floor, with the front door entrances facing the street. The backyard, where the kids play, has one entrance for two quarters on each side. The third floor was originally designed as four separate maid's quarters with a separate set of stairs. Most of the officers use their maid's room as a guest bedroom. Each set of quarters once had on each end of the building a screened sunporch. The army allowed

Worthington's Army quarters at Fort Benning, on right side of building, first floor.

these porches to be enclosed to become an additional room, provided the work done passed inspection. Our porch has been converted into another room.

By Thursday we are moved in but the place is a wreck with packing paper everywhere, boxes all over, many yet to be opened and emptied, nothing on the walls, towels or sheets covering windows until they can be curtained, and the kitchen in turmoil as cooking is being done before all the kitchenware is even unpacked. But we do have clothes out of suitcases, with my uniforms hanging, ready to be worn.

We hastily met some of our neighbors but are too busy unpacking and moving in to spend much time conversing, which they understand. What we do learn, the big news around Fort Benning, is of the making of a major military feature movie.

The Movie: *The Green Berets*

On 7 August Batjac Productions took over a small motel near the main entrance to Benning, on Victory Drive, the main road into Columbus. Batjac is the movie production company for John Wayne, and he is making a film of Robin Moore's 1965 book, *The Green Berets*, about the Army Special Forces in Vietnam. The cast consists of Wayne, David Jansen, Jim Hutton, Aldo Ray, Patrick Wayne, Jack Soo, and several other known actors and actresses. Fort Benning is serving as Vietnam for the movie. Batjac is building a Special Forces outpost which is destroyed during filming when the camp is attacked. Also, a Vietnamese village is constructed, which remains intact to be used for army training. Part of the movie depicts the capture of an NVA general who is living in an old plantation mansion, in North Vietnam. This scene used a house in Columbus which Anita and I were familiar with. It is an old large house across the street and through a small wooded area from the home we used to own in Columbus. We did not realize that until we saw the movie and instantly recognized it. The scene of the entrance to the Special Forces headquarters in Nha Trang is the rear entrance to the Fort Benning Officers' Club Annex, properly sandbagged to resemble a combat unit.

Another scene, where John Wayne (playing an SF colonel) meets with Jack Soo (playing an ARVN colonel) under some trees to discuss how to kidnap the NVA general, is filmed on the golf course just a few blocks from our house. Some of the scenes are filmed away from Benning, with the most glaring error being in the final scene, where John Wayne and a small Vietnamese orphan boy are on the beach (simulating the south China Sea, which is on the east coast of South Vietnam) as the sun is setting. Unfortunately, this scene was filmed on a West Coast beach in California. In Vietnam the sun can rise over the ocean and the beach but must set over the west mountains in Vietnam. So, in the movie, the sun is setting in the east, a major mistake, immediately recognized by anyone who has been in Vietnam.

Much of the movie was accurate and details authentic looking because the uniforms, helicopters, air force aircraft, and extras were all genuine military. One of the actors was an army captain I was acquainted with. Part of the hype surrounding the movie and the actors was the fact that David Janssen had just completed filming the ending of his extremely popular TV show *The Fugitive,* which ran from 1963 to 1967. The ending, the last episode, shown on 29 August 1967, which revealed who killed his wife (whose murder Janssen's character had been accused of before running away in seek of the truth), set an all-time-high viewing record.

John Wayne made the film not to promote the war or present why the United States was involved in the war, but as a tribute to what the Army Special Forces were doing. The movie would premiere at Fort Benning, in June 1968, where it played for about a month. Critics hated the film (1968 was a very low time for the United States in Vietnam) and most reviews were poor. I liked the movie and appreciated the accuracy of the military details. Apparently, despite the wrath of the critics, the movie was a commercial and financial success. Within 90 days the movie box office receipts exceeded $8 million and Wayne claimed he had already covered all his expenses.

For those of us living at Benning, we watch many of the scenes being filmed and see how familiar parts of the post are being magically transformed from an old established southern military post into combat areas of the Vietnam War.

Settling In

Anita takes charge of finishing the quarters, making it our home. She enrolls the girls in their appropriate schools and takes care of the millions of odds and ends of chores necessary, moving into a new home. I have completed my post in-processing and am preparing to meet my new boss the next morning. We are all excited as we move into the next phase of our lives and my career as a company commander.

4

Basic Combat Training Company Commander

Taking Command

I wake Friday morning, early, eager to begin the most sought-after job of infantry captains, that of commanding a company. Looking forward to what should be the best assignment of my career, I cannot foresee that this next year will be the worst of my life and threaten the structure of my marriage.

I drive to the Eighth Battalion headquarters that morning to meet the commander, my new boss. Lieutenant Rolph is waiting for me and, after a few words, takes me to Lieutenant Colonel Watson's office. He stands as I enter, a muscular, stocky man, above average in height, with very short dark hair. He has a large head and a large nose and is wearing fatigues. His left collar sports the infantry's crossed rifles, over his left pocket he has jump wings with a star, signifying he has served in an airborne unit, and above his wings is the CIB. He wears a large ring on a finger, denoting that he is a West Point grad. I later learn he served in the Korean War, where he got his CIB.

He greets me warmly, welcoming me to his battalion. As indicated by the summer khakis I wear with my ribbons and CIB, he is aware I have served a combat tour in Vietnam. He inquires about my background and then my family, asking if we have quarters and are getting settled in.

Colonel Watson explains I will be assigned as the commanding officer for Company B, one of the five companies in his battalion. The other company commanders are a couple of captains and two first lieutenants. Each company begins with between 200 to 220 recruits, but at the end of the eight-week Basic Combat Training (BCT) cycle, only around 180 to 200 graduate. During each cycle a company loses about 10 percent due to a host of reasons from medical, to psychological, to discipline, to unsuitability to become a soldier. He makes it clear that turning civilians into soldiers in eight weeks is not an easy task.

I recall my days in early 1957, as a Marine recruit, going through the Marine's version of BCT. It was more intense, with much more training, especially rifle marksmanship, as Marine basic training was 13 weeks long, not eight. Interestingly, I had two fellow recruits who used to be in the army. One had been a cook and the other an administrative clerk. Both were in Japan in 1950 when the Korean War broke out and within a few days both were in an infantry unit fighting on the front lines. Both were captured and spent the war as POWs. When they were repatriated, both stayed in the army for a few more years, then left as NCOs and enlisted in the marines, as privates. When I asked why, they explained that they enjoyed the military but, in the army, only the infantry trains its soldiers for combat. They learned that the hard way in Korea. In the marines, everyone is trained as a rifleman, even their commissioned officer pilots. So, they decided if they became marines, they would be trained for combat, regardless of their assignments. Additionally, the marines had promised to promote them both to sergeants when they completed their infantry training, after boot camp.

The colonel defines the battalion as sort of a temporary holding organization, with all the real work being done at the company level. The mission of the battalion staff is to monitor the work of the companies, supervise the company cadre, and guide the companies, as an organized unit, to achieve the goal of turning a group of civilians into soldiers, in two very short months. The battalion operates in ten-week cycles, eight weeks of BCT and then two weeks for the companies to complete their own personnel training, prepare for the next training cycle, take leave, and catch up on maintenance of buildings, equipment, or the company grounds. The two weeks between cycles is never a relaxing downtime but a busy period of hard work, catching up and getting ready for the next two months.

Colonel Watson describes the process we are a part of. Draftees would be notified, or volunteers would visit army recruiting offices, located throughout the United States. All would congregate at area induction stations, scattered across our country. Here begins the initial processing into the military. Males arrive for any branch of our military to receive a medical exam, be tested for intelligence and aptitude, seen by a career counselor, and, if qualified, enlisted into a branch of our armed forces. Some are immediately transported to their branch basic training, while others may receive a delay to enter active duty, having to report back at another time.

For us at Fort Benning, buses and trains deliver over 1,200 civilians each week to the Army Training Center (ATC) reception station. This is the time civilians finally become a part of the army. Orientations explain what will happen to them. Hair is lopped off (they become bald), uniforms fitted and issued, more physical exams, and additional aptitude testing. Classification interviews confirm what army assignments are appropriate for each recruit, and continued training is established. Dog tags are made and two handed to each recruit. All of this enters what will become the person's permanent army personnel file. This takes a few days, and when enough recruits have been processed to fill a battalion for basic training, they mount up in trucks and are driven to their new home in a Basic Combat Training company.

Colonel Watson briefly portrays the makeup of his battalion (which is nothing compared to a regular infantry battalion). His staff is minuscule, he has himself, an E-9 sergeant major and First Lieutenant Rolph as his executive officer. He has a couple of other NCOs who monitor company training by keeping statistics, because the army determines the status of its accomplishments via numbers such as body count in combat, or company PT and rifle scores in non-combat environments. Then a few PFCs or spec fours are around to do the grunt work and heavy lifting. But there is no staff such as S-1, 2, 3, or 4. These functions are accomplished at the company and brigade levels. All the battalion headquarters does is watch and count and write it all down on paper (and complain if the numbers are not high enough). I later learn that the effectiveness of lieutenant colonel battalion commanders is heavily based on how high their companies score during their training cycles.

The company has more cadre staff than the battalion does. Each company has the CO, two or three training officers (lieutenants), a first sergeant, a supply sergeant, a mess sergeant (and some cooks), a senior drill sergeant, five drill sergeants, and two spec fours (armorer and company clerk).

After an hour of discussing my immediate future as one of his company commanders, the colonel points out that he expects his officers to be fully committed to the training mission. At this time, I do not perceive what he really is saying, but in time I learn. He tells me to return after lunch and he will take me to the company area and introduce me to my new command.

The company is between training cycles, so that afternoon I can meet most of the men and officers in my command. My first official day as a company commander begins that afternoon, Monday, 28 August 1967.

Introduction to BCT

After introducing me to my company staff, Lieutenant Colonel Watson departs. I begin to learn my new assignment. One of the training officers rides in my Jeep (my own red one, not an army jeep) as our company has no vehicles, to show me around our training areas, all within marching distance. When the company needs transportation, it is set up by the brigade headquarters; we use our own POVs (privately owned vehicles) to get around or by remaining with the recruits, riding on the trucks.

It doesn't take long to understand the training cycle. When the recruits arrive, they are grouped, lectured by our drill sergeants, who explain what they will be doing for the next couple of months, and then assigned barracks. Inside, the drill sergeants demonstrate how beds are made, how to properly set up a footlocker and wall locker. Then a tutorial on how to keep the barracks clean. Fire guard duty is clarified in that the recruits share four-hour night shifts where one roams the barracks while everyone else sleeps, ensuring everything is safe, mainly keeping alert for fires and during the winter months maintaining the coal furnace providing heat.

Recruits are also introduced to KP (kitchen police) or mess duty. During the eight weeks, each recruit will serve several times, but only one day at a time (when I was undergoing boot camp in the marines, the entire platoon would serve one full week and only that one time).

The training cycle begins with drill and ceremony, marching and saluting. Also, PT (physical training). Guard duty and general orders are covered, Saturday morning inspections are held, in the barracks and outside in ranks.

Outdoor training includes hand-to-hand combat and bayonet instruction, followed by a bayonet obstacle course and the infamous pugil stick. Recruits are dressed in a football helmet with a faceguard, heavy gloves, and diapers which are thick groin protectors. Armed with a heavy stick, about five feet long, ends covered with thick padding, recruits practice encountering an enemy, armed only with bayonets (on rifles). Some follow through perfectly on their training in bayonet fighting. Others flail about, knocking their opponent to the ground using the pugil stick more like an axe, a sword, or a mace.

Indoor classes are interspersed with outdoor instruction. Recruits are issued the M-14 rifle, a select-fire automatic .308 caliber shoulder weapon, using a 20-round magazine. While a specific rifle is assigned to every recruit, it physically remains locked in the company arms room until issued to the recruit for use. The M-14 replaced the World

War II .30–06 caliber, semi-automatic, 8-shot, clip-fed M-I Garand in 1961. The M-14 proved difficult in Vietnam as it was long, heavy, and bulky, and humping it through the jungles was a disaster as it would persistently catch on jungle growth. And the wooden stock would swell because of the humidity in Vietnam, affecting accuracy. It was replaced in 1964, but as always, it can take years between when the army officially adapts a new weapon and the time when enough weapons are procured for all the troops. For example, when the M-14 replacement, the M-16, became official in 1964, it wasn't common in Vietnam until 1966, and the M-14 was still the BCT and AIT training firearm until 1970.

By the middle of the cycle, recruits begin shooting on the 25-meter range to develop familiarity with firing their rifle and learn how to zero their weapon. Zeroing means to adjust the rear sight so the rifle will hit the target at a desired spot at a specific range. The next step is moving to the field firing range, shooting at pop-up targets anywhere from 70 to 300 meters away. Electronically controlled, when hit, they fall. The culmination of all the rifle training is firing for record and qualification for a shooting badge. The shooter can qualify as marksman, sharpshooter, or expert, and the awarding of the appropriate badge testifies to one's skill as a rifleman.

Schooling continues with CBN (chemical, biological, and nuclear) classes and a trip to the tear gas building, where inside, having donned one's protective mask, the recruit must remove it in a room full of tear gas and recite name, rank, and service number before being allowed to exit. Throwing hand grenades is scary for many recruits, afraid they will pull the pin and then drop the grenade in the small walled throwing pit. I never saw or heard of that ever happening. Other sessions involve more advanced combat training such as the infiltration course, where recruits crawl under 100 yards of barbed wire and other barriers while real machine gun bullets are piercing the air above their squirming bodies and positioned explosive charges are being detonated around them. Individual day and night tactical training continues.

Toward the end of the cycle one big event is the week-long bivouac. A march of several miles with rifle and full combat gear initiates this exercise. In the field each man carries half of a military pup tent (called a shelter half) so two men join to create a two-man tent. Many of the combat skills learned are now put in practice and living outdoors as soldiers experienced.

The eight weeks terminates with a plethora of testing. The Physical Combat Proficiency Test (PCPT) is five different events, individually scored. Each event is designed to measure a man's physical ability to possess the strength, agility, and stamina to function as a combat infantryman. These include a one-mile run; 40-yard low crawl; run, dodge, and jump; grenade throw; and horizontal ladder. While we have run the recruits through this test, many times, it is done the last time for score. The last big evaluation is the G-3 Proficiency Test. The subjects taught in academic classes, outdoor military training, and drill and ceremony, are all examined by a special team of NCOs asking questions or wanting to see practical demonstrations by the recruits. Individual scores in each area are tallied to arrive at a recruit's overall final score. The cycle terminates with a battalion parade and the presentation of individual awards to both recruits and cadre and company awards for the best company in a variety of areas, from best mess hall to highest company scores in the PCPT, rifle qualification, and G-3 Tests.

All the formal training is conducted by officers and NCOs of the ATC Committee Group. Commanded by a lieutenant colonel, this group operates all the ranges, provides all the classroom instruction and all the outdoor military training. While the committee group instructors introduce all the formal training, it is the responsibility of the drill sergeants to provide supplementary training and to supervise all the hours of practice necessary to develop a degree of proficiency in the basic military arts. Therefore, the company officers and NCOs themselves must be competent in everything the committee group teaches.

Being Decorated

Nine days after I assume command of my company, I am told to report to Colonel Spears' office on Wednesday at 1300 hours (1 p.m.). Arriving at brigade headquarters, I am ushered into the colonel's office and find that Lieutenant Colonel Watson is present along with my training officers and my first sergeant. Motioning me to stand in front of the U.S. and ATC flags, Colonel Spears moves in front of me as his adjutant calls, "Attention to orders." He reads the citations for three decorations I have been recommended for during my first tour in Vietnam.

I receive the Bronze Star with the "V" device for "heroism in ground combat" during a major ARVN combat operation 18–19 October 1966. I also receive two Vietnamese Crosses of Gallantry with Silver Star for valor from the ARVN for two separate operations, one on 17 October 1966 and the other 10 January 1967. Now I can officially wear three combat decorations for valor. This raises my stock with the officers and NCOs in both my company and the battalion.

It doesn't take me long to realize that being a commander of a BCT company in this battalion is no piece of cake. Over time I learn that our

Captain Worthington receiving his first Bronze Star for Valor (U.S. Army).

battalion commander really places an emphasis on the scores of the final company tests. That, by itself, is not a problem. What is, though, is the colonel's insistence that for the next cycle, you must do better. Another is his expectation that his company commanders should work six and a half days each week during the eight-week cycle. I would arrive at work in the company area between six and seven a.m. and usually not get home before seven or eight in the evening. Saturdays I could get home, usually, between five and six. The colonel also expects his commanders to show up for a couple of hours every Sunday at some point during the day.

My Start as an Author

Despite this rigorous and hectic work schedule, I am able to do something quite a bit different. I grew up in rural Connecticut and enjoyed an outdoor life of fishing, shooting, hunting, and camping. I am really attracted to firearms. Like most devoted "gun nuts" of my generation, I began, around 9 years old, with a Daisy "Red Ryder" BB gun. Next came a 20-gauge Winchester model 37 single-shot shotgun, followed a year later by a Remington 514 bolt action single-shot .22 rifle. From there through high school and college, much of my life involved more firearms.

In 1963, after suffering a broken hip in a jump at parachute school, I became a full-time army competitive pistol shooter. My interest in firearms followed me throughout my military career. Part of this activity is fueled by subscribing to and reading several gun magazines, one of which is *GUNS* magazine. In the July 1967 issue (received and read while I was at Fort Knox), one of the magazine's editors, Major George Nonte, had published an article, "Should All GI's Carry a Handgun?" Nonte, a veteran of World War II in Europe, advocated that every soldier fighting in Vietnam should be armed with the .45 service pistol (in addition to his service rifle). I wrote a letter to the editor, explaining how false Nonte's thinking was because jungle close combat is for automatic rifles, not handguns, and then, most GI's are not trained to be competent with the army .45, anyway.

Before I departed Fort Knox, I was asked by an editor to write a rebuttal to Nonte's article. Because of the timely nature of the topic, and me being a combat veteran of the war, I received a contract to be paid $150 on publication. I wrote the article before departing Fort Knox, thinking that this was a real easy way to make more money. It was published in the February 1968 issue.

In the fall of 1967, another gun magazine had an article regarding a laboratory evaluation of Smith and Wesson's new (1965) stainless steel model 60 .38 special revolver. This article was on the same

Christmas 1967. Anita, Suzi, Julie, Bob.

revolver I carried during my first tour in Vietnam. I got another idea for a second gun article. I wrote the editor of the NRA magazine, *The American Rifleman*, citing the lab article on the S&W revolver, asking if they were interested in an actual combat report of the gun. In March 1968, I received a contract for $75 for the article. It was published in the October 1968 issue. This was the beginning of my career as a professional writer. Sadly, though, the demands and requirements of my job and life precluded authoring any additional articles for several more years.

McNamara's Folly

Rumor has it that the colonel wants his eagle. To make full colonel, an infantry lieutenant colonel must command a battalion. The word is the colonel does not want a battalion in Vietnam so arranged to command a BCT battalion. He has come from a staff assignment which did not involve long hours. To make colonel he needs an outstanding record as a battalion commander. As the battalion commander, his work hours are nowhere close to those of his company commanders. For those officers and NCOs in his companies, who just spent a year in combat in Vietnam, his demands seem excessive. For me, at the end of the day I am exhausted, both physically and mentally. What is happening to me is also affecting my family.

In 1968, the war is not going well. In January North Korea captured a U.S. Navy ship, the USS *Pueblo,* an intelligence-gathering vessel, killing one crew member and imprisoning 82. The Tet attacks surprised everyone. General Westmoreland was arguing for more troops in Vietnam, wanting over half a million more. In March President Johnson, trapped in a war not of his making, being opposed by more and more Americans, announced he would not seek election. The next month, Martin Luther King, Jr., was assassinated, inciting riots and protests across America. Two months later, presidential candidate Robert Kennedy was murdered while campaigning in Los Angeles. Nixon was campaigning on his promise to end the war.

In June, General Westmoreland and his very militaristic concept of winning the war by search and destroy strategies are replaced by General Creighton Abrams, who favors a more "hearts and minds" approach emphasizing counterinsurgency and anti-guerrilla warfare while encouraging increasing South Vietnam control of the war. Both Nixon and Abrams are proponents of "Vietnamization," the concept of encouraging more combat roles by Vietnam by expanding the equipping and training of Vietnamese forces, while at the same time reducing the number of U.S. troops in Vietnam.

Youths on campuses all over our nation are protesting the war. At the same time, we are sending more and more troops over there. Even in my small part of this world, I am feeling the results of the slow disintegration of my army.

A major problem everyone in ATC faces is the special program developed by the Secretary of Defense, Robert McNamara, titled Project 100,000. Educated in economics and accounting in the 1930s, McNamara joined the U.S. Army Air Forces in 1943 as a statistician. He left in 1946 and joined the Ford Motor Company, in planning and financial analysis. He rose through the ranks to become president of Ford in 1960. When John Kennedy assumed the presidency in 1961, he asked McNamara to serve in his cabinet and McNamara chose the Department of Defense (DOD).

McNamara, being a numbers cruncher, prefers a systems analysis approach to solving problems and making decisions. One problem he faces is finding enough men to support the war in Vietnam. His solution is a simple one for a numbers cruncher: lower the eligibility requirements for being inducted into the army, and immediately the available supply of men eligible to become soldiers increases. So, he lowers the Armed Forces Qualification Test minimum score from 31 to 10. This increases the pool of eligible American males from 70 percent of the male population to 90 percent. This scheme to get more soldiers, by lowering eligibility qualifications, had also been employed during the Korean War. The problem is, we are now getting recruits who are not capable of becoming successful soldiers. This program is a fool's response to solving a manpower problem.

The program has many names (some very unflattering to both the new pool of inductees and to McNamara) but I know it mostly as McNamara's 100,000. The total number accepted and processed is questioned but probably between 320,000 and 354,000 men. It began in October 1966, ending in December 1971. McNamara defends his program by explaining how the army can train these men, preparing them for a more productive life after their military service. Fifty-four percent of this group was recruited and 46 percent drafted. It is touted by the DOD as allowing more men to join the military, promising training standards would not be compromised.

Here is what McNamara sends me. I receive many Puerto Rican males who cannot speak English, not when they join my company, not when they leave. We have men who are grossly out of shape; many are overweight or so underweight they are physically weak and have no stamina. Many are emotionally or intellectually deficient to the point they are unable to become soldiers; they cannot handle the pressure of the training regime. Essentially 10 percent of my company causes 90 percent of my problems.

Some of these soldiers do very well in BCT; they have been allowed the opportunity to serve in the army and they are motivated to do just that. Some are just able to get through. Neither my company nor the battalion has anything to do with the final comprehensive testing required to pass BCT. This is done by the committee group; all we receive are the final scores. Too many, though, are unable to successfully complete BCT. For some the physical demands of BCT exceed their ability to compete, for others the intellectual requirements are more than they can accomplish. But one of the biggest downfalls is discipline. The rigid environment of the military (strict rules always being enforced and the fact that recruits are always at the bottom of the military food chain) becomes unacceptable for many of these recruits so they rebel by acting out, challenging authority, or just plain leaving by going AWOL (absence without leave).

Later research on this program reveals that these men, as a group, were not successful as soldiers, were killed more often in Vietnam, and after service were not as successful in their vocational or personal lives as their non-veteran peers.

In addition to the exhausting hours demanded by Watson, the top leadership of the army is setting expectations for younger officers and NCOs that cannot be met. I note that several of my NCOs are requesting to be reassigned back to Vietnam rather than endure the continuous ultimatums that become exceedingly difficult to accomplish. From the top military leadership (McNamara) through the generals and colonels who are putting their careers above the welfare of their subordinates, selfish personal desires are destroying the army. For the junior officers and young NCOs, their leaders are creating an environment of distrust and disgust. These leaders' quest for ill-planned short-term outcomes only results in the exit of the young, new leadership, rather than fostering their desire to stay in the military. And this is exactly where I find myself.

For us, having to deal with McNamara's social program causes difficulty in too many ways. The only way we can get this group of men through BCT is for the drill sergeants to spend hours and hours every night and on the weekends providing extra training. Married NCOs are away from home, and single NCOs have no free time. Countless extra hours are spent with very limited results. Young drill sergeants see the future and decide a military career is not inviting. Senior NCOs request transfers, and one way to get transferred, quickly, is to volunteer for Vietnam. In short, this failed program by McNamara is one more reason why the duty assignment of those of us training recruits has become such an undesirable job, resulting in many soldiers rethinking the choice of an army career.

Command Time Not So Good

The unrealistic work hours and demands by upper leaders to consistently achieve better results with every passing cycle are also impacting negatively on families and marriages. Most of us captains are pursuing a military career. But the demands of the BCT work means less time home, and when we are home we are too tired to enjoy much interacting with wife and kids. The family resents the military and by extension the husbands and fathers. Communication between spouses either breaks down or becomes almost nonexistent. Marriages begin to fall apart, and I am not immune to this.

I am not an emotional person. I tend to be stoic, not demonstrative. Maybe it is my upbringing or just the New England reserve. I am not a hugger and keep my feelings to myself. Some call me insensitive. The arduous work, the exceedingly long days, the continual demands heaped upon me by the battalion commander begin to take their toll on me. Most of my life I have envisioned a military career. Now I am internally beginning to question what I am doing, and is it worth it? While my wife senses what is going on, we do not do much discussing of this problem. I find it exceedingly difficult to openly share what is going on and this could lead to more problems in the future.

Another time-consuming problem is the RBI, or Reply by Indorsement. This is a military term referring to a letter, passing through the military chain of command, typically addressing a nasty problem the recipient has and requesting the recipient specify, in writing, what he is going to do to resolve the problem. This formal correspondence dictates to the recipient: "For appropriate action and return." Generally, this dispatch consists of two parts, first a description of the problem and second a statement telling the recipient what to do. Essentially this letter originates from the highest levels of command in the army, and every commander it passes through adds his own comments until it finally arrives at the lowest level in this chain of command, me, the BCT company commander. This missive informs the company commander he screwed up somehow, and the originator demands to know what the company commander is going to do to resolve this problem.

As a BCT commander, I receive several RBIs every training cycle. Here is why. About half the recruits are not here voluntarily, they were drafted. Some were unemployed, needing money to live while others were yanked out of graduate school, or college or had just started a very appealing and lucrative career. They are not happy being privates in the army. Others voluntarily joined the army to escape, attempting to find a better life. Some, even, are willing to risk their lives as a commitment to their country. But in every cycle, there are those who hate the training so much they have a desire to exaggerate the truth and write home fabrications about what they are experiencing. Others, though, want to convince the home folks that they are rough, tough, and mean and their training is making them even more so. Both pen letters, lying about their training.

Little Johnnie writes his girlfriend or brother or mother explaining how tough the training is. He describes having less than four hours' sleep each night; he has lost 20 pounds but now is lean and mean. The drill sergeants make them run 20 to 30 miles every day, and to prepare them for combat we only feed them one meal a day, C Rations, and they learn how to fight in hand-to-hand combat by fighting each other in a pit where only the last man standing wins. The letter goes on to portray other acts of physical mayhem, all of which is whipping Johnnie into a mean, green fighting machine.

On the other hand, there are those recruits who hate BCT, hate their drill sergeants, hate the army, and blame everyone for their miserable existence. So, they write mama depicting the horror and inhumanity of what is being done to them and all the other recruits. These letters illustrate the depraved personalities of all the cadre from the company commander down. If they make the wrong move in formation, a meal is denied them. At night a couple of drill sergeants grab them off their bunks, gag them, and drag them outside where they are beat up. If a drill sergeant doesn't like a recruit, he can be thrown down a flight of stairs, or hit on the head with a rifle butt, while in formation.

Eventually these letters wind up with the parents. Believing the letters to be truthful, mom and dad next contact their U.S. senator or their member of Congress. A staff member then speaks with the parents, makes a few copies of the letter, and then a letter signed by the senator or the representative arrives at the Pentagon. The letter must be read and sent to the appropriate general in command of all the Army Training Centers. Eventually one of these letters lands on the desk of Brigadier General Charles Mount, Jr., the Commanding General of the U.S. Army Training Center at Fort Benning. It will probably be turned over to either his deputy commander or the chief of staff, both full colonels.

Then it will go to the ATC G-1 for appropriate action and return. Next it continues on down through the chain of command to the commander of the Second Brigade, subsequently to Lieutenant Colonel Watson, who adds his comments and passes it down, finally to Captain Worthington, Commander of Company B, who must take appropriate action and Reply by Indorsement. Everyone in this chain from Congress, through all the generals, colonels to a captain, most likely knows that what little Johnnie has described is totally false, but all must play the game, go through the motions, and at the end get little Johnnie to admit, in writing, that what he said was a lie.

Then Captain Worthington's endorsement, with Johnnie's statement attached, goes all the way back through the chain of command until the senator or representative's staff member relates what they have accomplished, and that little Johnnie has tended to stretch the truth a bit, but he is okay and doing very well. Sometimes the parents accept that, knowing their little Johnnie. At other times, they are convinced that everyone in the federal government is promoting a major cover-up and hiding the truth. Regardless, all of this takes a lot of time to resolve, and receiving RBIs for a company commander, no matter what the truth is, can have a negative impact on his officer efficiency report.

Company Training Officers

My training officers are newly commissioned second lieutenants, assigned to the battalion for a few weeks to a few months while awaiting orders elsewhere, such as flight school or Vietnam. These men are mostly 19- to 20-year-old high school graduates, fresh out of Officer Candidate School (OCS). During the Vietnam War, education eligibility requirements are reduced for commissioning.

Unfortunately, too many of these lieutenants are immature, not well educated, and while OCS alumni, not suited to be combat leaders. Lieutenant Calley comes to mind. On the other hand, many OCS graduates have gone on to become distinguished general officers. The officers I am assigned have all finished high school, few have had any college, and many were drafted and think it better to be a lieutenant than a private. A scarce few are married to high school sweethearts. My wife and I would spend hours going over financial management and attempting to convince the married officers why obtaining life insurance for their spouses, prior to going to Vietnam, is a wise thing to do. Because of this large influx of OCS officers, many of the accepted protocols of being an officer are little understood by these new lieutenants who care even less.

My understanding of the role an officer should assume and how one should act became apparent during the time I was an enlisted Marine and then an NCO. Later I had instilled in me the code of the army officer during college ROTC. The code guides officers in their professional and personal lives throughout their careers. It echoes the concept illustrated by General of the Army Douglas MacArthur addressing cadets at his alma mater, the United States Military Academy, in 1962: Duty, Honor, Country. Trying to impart this to my young officers is an unwelcome and foreign notion as they do not see a career in the army in their future. Military traditions, the role of an officer's duty for the welfare of his soldiers, and the professional courtesies expected of officers are of little interest to my lieutenants. Their decision to become officers was the result of it being, to them, a better choice than being enlisted, not a desire to embrace the tradition or responsibilities of being an officer.

All these situations, McNamara's 100,000, RBIs, and the new lieutenants, all stacked on top of the normal day-to-day activities of running a company, are wearing me down. As I encounter what kind of men are entering the army, enlisted and officers, I begin to become disillusioned.

Command Time Becomes Worse

My workday usually begins around five a.m. I get up, shave, shower and get dressed. Sometimes I will grab something to eat but often I would breakfast at my mess hall. The drive to work before six takes about 20 minutes. One does not want to speed on post because the MPs seem to always be around when one is going fast.

Arriving around six, I will first check with the CQ (Charge of Quarters), a company NCO who takes charge of the entire company, essentially representing the commander during the night, to let him know I am in the company area. I inquire how the night went, glance at his logbook, then leave to wander around the company area.

Our real estate consists of several World War II–era two-story wooden barracks, with all the other buildings, all World War II, being single story. These are the orderly room (my office and the administrative center for the company, controlled by the company first sergeant); the mess hall, run by the Mess Steward; the supply building, which is also the company armory where all the M-14s are stored, managed by the Supply Sergeant; and finally the Day Room, a rec room and living room set up with a TV, a small library with books and magazines, cards and board games, and a ping-pong table. This is where the recruits in the evening or on weekends can relax (providing all their work is done and uniforms are squared away). I roam around the buildings, check their condition, and if I find anything amiss, I jot it down in a small notebook, always on me. Later, I mention it to the First Sergeant, who will take care of any slight.

The company, as a unit, runs every morning we can. At the beginning of the cycle, our runs are not long but, as the weeks pass, we increase the duration and distance of our runs. Usually, toward the end of the cycle, we do over a mile, and do not lose many recruits. Occasionally, we will have a cycle that can run, so 1.5- or 2-mile runs are more common. I love running and join the company every time I am able.

The days vary, depending on where we are in the cycle of training. A good deal of my time is spent observing the recruits in their training. Whenever the unit goes into the field for training, I am with them. When the training is repetitive, such as drill and ceremony, PT, or classroom sessions in the area, I remain in the company area, working through the never-ending cascade of paperwork. I interact with all the drill sergeants throughout the day, and the First Sergeant meets with them on a weekly basis. Still, it seems way too much time is wasted dealing with minor problems such as disciplinary difficulties with those few recruits who never seem to stay out of trouble.

Sometimes I might be able to go home for supper, but then return to the company area to do paperwork, meet with recruits who have problems (like that of little Johnnie's letters to Mama). Often, I do not get home until 8 or 9 at night. I arrive home and in fatigues and combat boots, so tired I stretch out on the living room carpet to just relax for a few minutes, only to be woken a couple hours later by Anita, telling me to go to bed.

Additionally, I must deal with the constant pressure from the battalion commander to excel in everything, which I tend to rebel against. Everything with Colonel Watson is a competition. He wants his eagles and that means every company must be best at everything. Within the battalion, all five companies compete against each other, to be the best company. Then the competition continues at the brigade level, where every company of every battalion competes to be the best. Then there is ATC-level competition. It becomes absurd, spending so much time and energy to obtain a score just a fraction of a point higher than anyone else's to get an award. Highest number of rifle experts, highest number of recruits passing the PCPT, the best overall company average score on the end of cycle G-3 Proficiency Test, Best Mess Award, best this or best that. And if the company qualifies 99 percent of recruits on the rifle range, God help you if in the next cycle you only qualify 98 percent.

Over time, the constant insistence by the battalion commander to always be the best, the problems with McNamara's 100,000, the continuing demise in the quality of new OCS lieutenants, and the numbing hours and days at work get to me where I begin to consider what I might do as a civilian. Life at home is not that of a family unit. My job as a company commander (and keeping Watson off my back) interferes with my being a husband and father. There simply is not enough time for both. While I am wrapped up in my job, it seems Anita and the girls exist in their world. And as time goes on, these worlds seem to drift further apart.

Again, my reluctance to share all my feelings with my wife is beginning to create a divide between us. Not overtly, but I tend to keep my growing dislike of my job and my negative perception of the senior leadership in the army inside, not so much shared with Anita.

Promotion Requirements

Getting promoted beyond captain requires an officer to have accomplished many different things. Troop duty is essential; serving as a platoon leader and a company commander are necessary ingredients to make major. Staff duty is also almost a required assignment. For an infantry officer, a combat tour is a basic prerequisite, with earning the combat infantryman badge almost a condition for promotion (unless the infantry officer is a pilot). Education is also very important, first being military schooling such as the basic officer's course and then the career course. Additional skills training such as Ranger or Airborne School count quite a bit, as can any other notable schools such as the Military Assistant Training Advisor, language school, Pathfinder School or any other military training which increases your value to the army. Then there is civilian education. For field grade officers an undergraduate degree is a basic obligation and a graduate degree is icing on the cake. Many officers would take graduate classes from one of several universities which would offer graduate programs at the larger army bases.

Almost all my tickets have been punched, except for company command time, which I am now doing. I understand the importance of having a master's degree, therefore decide to enter a graduate program while at Benning.

The U.S. Army, stressing degrees from civilian schools, fosters this emphasis by allowing several universities and colleges to establish local campuses on military posts. The schools work with the post education center offering associate, undergraduate, and graduate degree programs in a variety of majors. Professors teaching the classes are part-time adjunct faculty who are academically qualified to teach and were recruited from both the local military and civilian populations. The classes are taught at night and on the weekends so working military members can take advantage of furthering their education. Commanders are encouraged to make allowances to ensure soldiers' additional duties will not interfere with their going to school. Most career soldiers could use the G.I. Bill to pay for their classes.

I decide that working toward a graduate degree will only help my selection chances for major. In spite of the hours demanded by my battalion commander, even he has to allow me to attend graduate school.

When I arrived at Fort Benning, I was on track for an army career and I thought I would be up for consideration for selection to be promoted to major. To this end, shortly after I assume command of my company, I pay a visit to the educational offices at Benning. After examining what is available, I apply for admission and enter a graduate degree program in education from American University in Washington, D.C., taking classes in their campus at Benning.

During my year at Benning I am able to complete three graduate courses in education: Methods of Teaching in Secondary School, Statistics, and The Psychology of Education. I enjoy the classes and earn two A's and a B. Math was never my strong suit, so I get the B in statistics. In fact, I like grad school so much, I consider asking the army to send me to graduate school, full-time.

I decide that going to graduate school full-time could be good for me. I contact an Infantry branch officer in the Pentagon and inquire about the army sending me to school to complete a master's degree. The officer gets back to me in a few days indicating the army could send me to graduate school, but only for six months. I reply that I can't get any degree in that little time and ask why only six months. I am told I am too experienced in counter-guerrilla counterinsurgency warfare and the army has invested too much time in my training and experience for me to be away for a year or two. Another idea shot down.

On 11 March 1968, I receive a satisfying notification. The promotion list for captains to major is released. My name is on it. Because of the wartime need for majors, 87.3 percent of eligible captains are promoted, the highest in a very long time. Another factor related to the Vietnam War is that captains are being promoted very quickly. Only six months previously, new majors served as captains for 48 months before being promoted. On this list for promotion, captains are being promoted in 39 months. One good thing about wars, promotions do come faster. The date to be promoted to major is based on when one became a captain. For me, I calculate I will be promoted the end of August or early September.

The FBI

At this time, spring 1968, an announcement comes my way. The FBI needs more special agents. Normally to be an FBI agent one must have a law degree or be an accountant. Due to the demand for more agents, another qualification becomes acceptable. Men who have a college degree and are a combat arms military officers having served a combat tour can apply. I am an officer with a college degree, and I have served two combat tours. Additionally, I was a full-time police officer for over a year with the Hanover, New Hampshire, Police Department while a student at Dartmouth. And more important, I thoroughly enjoyed law enforcement when I was a cop. This seems like a way to get out of a job I hate. I decide to explore this opportunity more.

Unfortunately for me, my decision to investigate this was made before discussing this with Anita. Again, a failure to communicate. Another indication how we seemed to operate in two separate spheres.

The year before, in 1967, two books authored by former FBI agents were published, presenting an incredibly sad exposé of what the FBI was really like. One of the books, *Inside the F.B.I.,* by former agent Norman Ollestad, ravaged the director, uncovering how the Bureau truly operates. The second book was just as savage, giving me serious doubts about the FBI.

The books pictured Director J. Edgar Hoover as a very short, revengeful, dictatorial man who did not allow graduates of the FBI Academy to become agents if, during the graduation ceremony in Hoover's office, the graduates had sweaty palms. It explains the quirky deceptions practiced by agents. For example, each field office has agents who are specialists in exclusive criminal areas. If a crime occurs requiring federal intervention, the first FBI agent on the scene assumes control of the case. If an agent is the bank robbery expert and a bank is robbed, all other agents disappear, go somewhere else or hide, until the first agent to make it to the bank is the FBI bank expert, regardless of how long this may take. Both books paint a very sorry picture of what the FBI is really like.

Not fully convinced I am interested, when I am on leave that spring, visiting my parents in Roxbury, Connecticut, I make an appointment for an interview at the field office in New Haven, a large headquarters with over 50 special agents.

I meet with two mid-level agents, both men older than my 30 years. We discuss my background and my desire to leave the army and why. I also mention my concerns, based on the two books I've read. The agents ask a few more questions and voice two strong opinions. First, most details in each book are true. Second, if I am leaving the army due to leadership concerns, the FBI is a replica of what I want to avoid in the military. We spend another half hour discussing the army and the FBI and they convince me, the FBI is not the answer to my vocational turbulence. I thank them for their honesty and return home in Roxbury.

When we return to Fort Benning, I am disheartened, confused about my future. Add to this the fact that, as before, I keep my feelings bottled up within, not sharing a lot of my internal turmoil with Anita. What I dislike at Benning about my job continues to get worse. Several drill sergeants, fed up with the hours, the continual pressure to always do better, and what now begins to be perceived as focusing on petty small details which the battalion and brigade leaders see as detrimental to military order and efficiency, volunteer for Vietnam. It is during this time when an incident occurs which is the final straw that breaks my back.

Military Leadership?

My company (with me) is in a classroom in a large building in the brigade area, which we have marched to. When marching within our area, the fatigue uniform is also adorned with a helmet liner (a light-weight composite helmet, shaped just like the steel helmet, upon which the steel pot sits), web belt, canteen, and poncho, folded over the back of the web belt. As each platoon stands in company formation, every recruit removes his web belt with canteen and poncho and places it on the ground behind their feet, placing the helmet liner on top, then exits ranks to enter the classroom. One recruit is always assigned to remain outside to guard the web gear (and to get the company commander if a visitor comes by).

About halfway through the class, the guard informs me the brigade commander is getting out of his staff car. I leave the building, stop in front of Colonel Spears, stand at attention, salute, stating "Captain Worthington reporting, sir." Replying "At ease," he asks a few innocuous questions about the company training. Then he nods to the brigade sergeant major, who, in turn, nods to the spec four driver. I stand there wondering what is going on. The specialist runs to the back of the staff car, opens the trunk, and retrieves a large ball of heavy twine, and hurries back to the sergeant major. The sergeant major grabs the end of the string and moves to the beginning of the first row of web gear on the ground. The driver quickly moves to the other end of the row and both move the stretched twine a few inches above the front part of the row of grounded gear. I stand dumbfounded while the colonel moves behind his sergeant major, bending over, eyeing the placement of the gear relative to the stretched string. The string is taut and perfectly straight. The belts, canteens and ponchos not so. They vary an inch or so on either side of the string. The colonel calls me over to look at the straight string and the less straight line of gear. This was repeated for a different row in each platoon section. I then receive a twenty-minute chewing out, a dissertation on the importance of making sure every time the company stops and drops its gear, someone should have a ball of twine to make sure not one belt is out of line.

In disbelief, my mind fast-forwards ten years. Is this to be the culmination of my army career? Making sure I always carry a ball of string to ensure a bunch of gear on the ground is not over a quarter of an inch out of line? I can't believe this. A full colonel just spent over half an hour

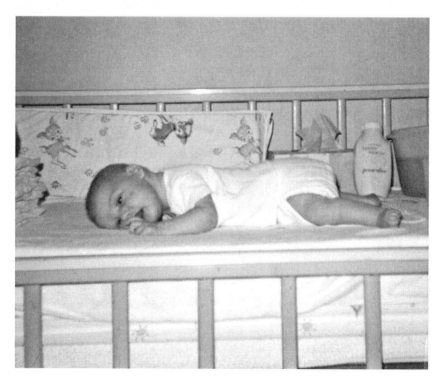

Addition to our family, Karen, April 1968.

agonizing over the placement of some web gear on the ground. If this is to be my future as a colonel, I do not want any part of it. In my mind this is just another petty way to grind down those of us who are working 12–14 hours each day to provide cannon fodder for a war that by 1968 seems unwinnable. The colonel ends his tirade, I salute and all three move back to the staff car. I conclude that if a full colonel has nothing better to do than hassle a captain like this, I want no part of his army.

On 9 April, our third daughter, Karen, is born. The delivery is normal, unlike what Anita endured with Julie. Her two sisters adore her and at times it seems like Karen becomes their favorite doll. With the demands of my job and the addition of a new baby in our household, it becomes very hectic, to say the least.

A Bright Spot in Training

During the summer we encounter a very unusual job. Instead of the typical eight-week cycle of recruits, my company is tasked with participating in a very special Army ROTC program. This program is being offered to graduate students in college who want to join ROTC. We will train them to be soldiers (in a special BCT program designed just for them) and when back in grad school they will complete the senior ROTC classwork and, upon graduating, be commissioned. We will provide a special six-week BCT program, which counts as the first two years in the regular four-year ROTC program. All our students come from schools in Utah, and most are Mormons.

First off, the students are here because they want to be. Second, they are older, more mature and educated than the typical recruits, and very bright. Training them is a piece of cake. They quickly recognize what must be done in both their military training and in maintaining their barracks. There is one slight problem relative to the footlocker display, during inspections: what to do with the Mormons' temple garment.

Adult members of the Church of Jesus Christ of Latter-day Saints participate in an Endowment Ceremony in which they promise to be faithful to their religious beliefs and teachings. Upon completion of the ceremony, both males and females must wear a temple garment, as underwear, day and night. The garment (in 1968) is a white single piece which sort of resembles what a T-shirt and pair of shorts (with the legs reaching almost to the knees) would look like if they were one piece instead of two separate pieces. Since all our cadets are adults most have garments rather than regular underwear. The garments have a deep religious significance to each person so we must decide what should be done.

It seems that each floor of these cadets has a spokesperson who reflects the wishes of the group. I meet with these cadets and we arrive at a uniform way to display their garments that will not disgrace the religious importance of their underwear.

The six weeks with this group are the most relaxed BCT we ever encountered.

What Now?

In a couple months I will be a major and out of this company and out of this battalion. But what next? My wife and I have discussed my increasing dislike of my job and the direction the army is headed. But, as I learn much later, this discussion is more one-sided. A year later Anita admitted she believed she had little say in my desire to leave the army. Adding to this insult was the fact that she enjoyed being an officer's wife, the companionship of being with other wives, and the entire army life. Because she felt my mind was made up, and the fact I was becoming devastated by what was going on in the army, she was reluctant to voice her feelings. Another indication of our growing inability to communicate.

I have a battalion commander who appears to be more focused on wearing eagles than the welfare of his officers and men working hours long beyond what is necessary. He seems to care only about his future and not about those who serve him. I feel the same way about the brigade commander; instead of focusing on the big picture, he seemed to go out of his way to find small, insignificant, picky things to grouse about.

The quality of men entering the army is being diluted; many of the new lieutenants coming out of OCS truly do not belong in leadership positions, most especially in combat. This is not the army I joined in 1961. This is no longer where I belong. For weeks my wife and I debate what I should do. The obvious answer (to me anyway) is to quit the army. But what would I do? My superior skills in running, shooting, and blowing things up are not in high demand in the civilian world. Anita hesitantly agrees with my desire to return to school to get vocational skills to be employable. This seems like a promising idea, but where would we get the money needed for graduate school? At the time I am not cognizant of my bottled-up emotions and how much they are impacting our marriage. I begin a unilateral decision process which excludes much of any input from my wife. Without complaining, she listens to my thoughts about our future and, understanding how I feel and why, goes along with what I voice I want.

We discuss where I should go to school, what program to enter, and what it would take to make this work. We consider many schools, many programs, and settle on the master's degree program in counseling at Northern Arizona University in Flagstaff, Arizona. I apply and am accepted, but now we need money. After careful consideration, I convince Anita the only sure way to get enough money for graduate school is for me to return to Vietnam as a combat advisor again. As an advisor with Vietnamese combat units, I will not be spending much money to exist. Also, the military has created a special savings program for troops in Vietnam. We can save around $5,000, and the interest paid is 10 percent. I figure that during another year in Vietnam, I can save enough for graduate school. I volunteer again, to return as a combat advisor, and my request is immediately accepted. Northern Arizona University approves a delay for a year, so I would matriculate in summer or fall of 1969.

5

Vietnam,
Second Time Around

My last day as company commander is 4 July 1968. This has been the worst job I have ever had. It has been frustrating, taken too much of my time, and exposed me to the inferior direction the army is heading. Throughout the eleven months of my command, I have been extremely unhappy with this assignment, the army leadership directly above me, and the decline of the army as it was when I originally joined. I am ecstatic to leave.

My original orders to Vietnam, issued 22 May 1968, have me assigned to MACV (as I've requested) but not until October. The orders are issued to me as a major (even though I have not been promoted yet) with instructions to go on a temporary duty assignment to attend a two-week Infantry Field Grade Officers Vietnam Orientation Course at the Infantry School in August. I am authorized 30 days' leave prior to leaving for Vietnam. These orders sure do not help my plans to be out of the army and in graduate school by August 1969.

I inquire as to what this Vietnam orientation course is all about. It is a period of instruction for infantry majors, lieutenant colonels, and colonels who have never served in Vietnam. It is a very brief synopsis of part of what I was taught in the Special Warfare School at Fort Bragg, three years ago. The classes cover what the U.S. Army is doing in Vietnam as well as the advisory effort. Customs, culture, religion, geography, economics, politics, and the Vietnamese military are taught. Obviously, this program is not needed by me.

Leave

Since I have received my orders in late May, there is plenty of time to get them changed. But they came from the Department of the Army so that is where the change must be made. I request 30 days' leave and then to be sent directly to Vietnam. Two weeks later my orders are amended for me to arrive in Vietnam no later than 20 August 1968. My leave begins on 7 July.

Towing our travel trailer behind the Ford station wagon, topped with a small aluminum boat and electric motor, we depart at nine in the morning. In four and a half weeks we drive 5,335 miles, visit 14 states and Mexico, going as far west as Arizona, then north through Utah, east to Tennessee, and returning to Fort Benning.

We arrive in Flagstaff on Tuesday 16 July and stay in the Kit Carson Trailer Park. We spend ten days there, sightseeing, visiting a realtor, looking at some homes, spending time just becoming familiar with the city with me visiting various offices at Northern Arizona University. A certificate designating me a graduate student as of 9 July 1968 is obtained. When I wake the morning of 1 August, I realize I am no longer a captain, on this date, I am promoted to major, no ceremony, just me declaring, "I am now a major!"

Arriving back at Benning the afternoon of Wednesday, 7 August, we have a lot of work ahead of us. We have 14 days to move out of our government quarters into our new place and get Anita and the three girls settled before I leave for Vietnam on 22 August.

Family Relocation

My orders to Vietnam very clearly dictate what I must wear en route (summer khaki), the weight of authorized baggage (134 pounds), and what vaccinations are required. At the very bottom of the orders is this statement: "The introduction, purchase, and possession of a privately owned weapon is prohibited in the Republic of Vietnam." Knowing this, I place my Smith and Wesson model 60 stainless steel .38 Special revolver (from my first tour) in a pair of well-used (i.e., smelly) heavy black socks. This malodorous package is then placed in the toe of one of my used jungle boots from my first tour. Both boots are then stuffed with more rank socks and then fastened together such that the socks cannot slip out. Yes, I am fully aware what I am doing is illegal. But in my mind, my personal safety justifies bending the rules, a little.

When I received my amended orders in June, Anita and I discussed where she and the girls should live during my Vietnam tour. Our decision was for the family to remain at Fort Benning. Earlier in the summer we arranged to move them into the Wherry-style housing development known as Battle Park. Located at the very northern tip of the post, close to Columbus, it consisted of two- and three-bedroom single-story red

Bob saying goodbye to Julie and Suzi as he departs for second tour in Vietnam as a combat advisor.

brick homes, two to a unit. We can lease a three-bedroom, one-bath, 920-square-foot place. Even though this development is on base, it is managed by a civilian business and that is who collects the rent. Most residents are married mothers and their children, while the husbands are in Vietnam. Since ours is an end unit, there is room to park my Jeep and the travel trailer.

The two weeks pass quickly and on Thursday, 22 August, we separate at the Columbus Airport. Columbus to Atlanta, change planes and fly to San Francisco, then by bus to Travis Air Force Base. Unlike my first time to Vietnam, where a lack of planes found me and several hundred Vietnam-bound soldiers stranded at Travis for several days, I am processed through very quickly.

Going to War, Again

We board a 60th Military Airlift Wing Lockheed C-141A Starlifter, a 154-passenger (not airline seats) transport jet plane. Its four Pratt and

Whitney turbofan engines whisk us across the Pacific at just under 500 mph. Our first stop is Hickam AFB in Hawaii, where we refuel, stopping next at Wake Island, where we refuel and get a new crew. Then to Clark AFB in the Philippines, where we refuel and swap the crew again for the last leg into Tan Son Nhut in Saigon. The sights, sounds, and smells bring back familiar memories as I disembark and head toward the air force terminal to catch a ride to Koepler Compound in Saigon, the in-processing location for MACV personnel. Saigon is in its rainy season with the temperature at the airport in the low 90s and the humidity around 85 percent. Hot and sticky with a good chance of an afternoon shower. My first day of duty for my second tour in Vietnam begins on Friday, 23 August 1968.

Koepler Compound, a former hotel, is the entrance for MACV advisors. It serves as a temporary place to stay and eat, process in-country, receive one's weapon, field gear and clothes, and attend a variety of seminars and classes to let one know what is going on in Vietnam relevant to U.S. pursuits. Koepler is just under five miles from the airport. It takes about 30 minutes to arrive at the compound, nestled between Le Lai and Vo Than Streets, seven blocks from the center of downtown (Tu Do Street) and around nine blocks from the city docks on the Saigon River. This is to be my home for the next several days.

In Vietnam in early 1966, MACV headquarters was at 137 Pasteur Street, about nine blocks north of Koepler, with various MACV offices scattered all around Saigon. The inefficiency of having a major army command strewn across the city bothered General Westmoreland such that by mid–1966 construction began on a modern 1.14 million-square-foot MACV headquarters a few blocks south of the eastern approach to the runway at Tan Son Nhut Airport. When Westmoreland moved into his new offices in August 1967, he described them as "prefabricated metal buildings." It was a sprawling two-story $28 million complex the press dubbed Pentagon East.

One day a jeep takes me to the MACV personnel offices at the new headquarters. I am surprised to find that a field personnel file on me had been created during my first tour. The clerk hands me my orders for my next assignment: S-3 Advisor at Phuoc Long province, III Corps Tactical Zone, Advisor Team 67. Phuoc Long is a large province 80 miles north of Saigon, on the Cambodian border. As the clerk peruses the papers and orders in my file, he asks me if I ever received my second Bronze Star. I reply that I do not know anything about any second Bronze Star, so he moves a series of papers stapled together across his desk to me and I read them.

Before I departed Vietnam in my first tour, my boss, Major Haines, the senior advisor to the 51st ARVN Infantry Regiment, had recommended me for the Bronze Star for meritorious service as the senior advisor to the 3rd Battalion, of the 51st Regiment. The paperwork was submitted to Colonel Keppler, the province Senior Advisor to Quang Nam province, who approved the recommendation and forwarded it to MACV Headquarters in Saigon. The personnel section at MACV found the paperwork had some errors that had to be corrected so the recommendation was returned to the Quang Nam PSA. All this paper shuffling took several weeks. Major Haines had returned to the States as had Colonel Keppler. The new PSA was not interested in this paperwork, so he sent it back to MACV with a short, terse note that said, "I am too busy to bother with this, either approve it as originally submitted or not," and then he signed the note. The entire package was bundled together and on the front was a typed note that said the recommendation was disapproved due to erroneous submission and then an army regulation was cited as justification for me not receiving a second Bronze Star. As I reread the recommendation and what the "too busy" colonel had written, I am reminded again that the senior leadership in the army is not interested in the welfare of their men, but only in themselves. And this pile of papers proves that to me. The clerk comments on the crappy behavior of the colonel but says he sees this every day. Officers too tied up in their own world to take the time and effort to correct administrative errors that would reward one of their men for doing an excellent job. I return to Koepler with the knowledge of my next assignment but a bitter taste because of what a colonel was too lazy to do.

The classes at Koepler are taught by officers and senior NCOs to orient us regarding the current situation in Vietnam. The orientation begins with an overview of all the U.S. forces currently deployed throughout South Vietnam.

From my point of view there is no clear-cut picture of the Vietnam War. First, the 1968 Tet Offensive changed the face of the war. In June General Westmoreland was replaced by General Creighton W. Abrams. A 1936 graduate of West Point who distinguished himself in World War II as an armor commander and a highly decorated hero. He is often referred to as the best mind in the army, not an intellectual but a man who uses common sense. Abrams was tasked with implementing the various plans for Vietnamization, turning more of the war over to the Vietnamese and supporting the pacification efforts of the Vietnamese. U.S. troop strength was approaching 540,000 men and women with another additional 65,000 troops from South Korea, New Zealand, and Australia, and about 850,000 ARVN soldiers. In May 1968, the Vietnam peace talks began in Paris.

The supreme commander of all U.S. forces in Vietnam is the commander of MACV, now Abrams. U.S. forces include the III Marine Amphibious Force in I Corps (which includes for combat two army divisions and an army brigade). Field Force I has a division and a brigade while Field Force II has three divisions, two brigades, a regiment, and a task force. Add to this mix the U.S. Navy and Air Force units scattered around South Vietnam and just off the coast.

The advisory composition and focus has also changed. Because of the emphasis on pacification by the South Vietnamese, the U.S. contribution was to create, in 1967, a joint military-civil command called Civil Operations and Revolutionary Development Support (CORDS) combining both MACV military and State Department agencies in a single command reporting to MACV. The creation of CORDS changed the roles and placement of the advisory effort. Combat advisors are now still assigned to the various Vietnamese combat units, the same as when I was here in 1966–67. But now all province and district advisors come under CORDS, as do the combat advisors assigned to Mobile Advisor Teams (MAT) and the Phoenix program.

As can be expected, often the goals, tactics, and strategies of these many separate commands are not aligned with each other. A U.S. military organization may be focused on destruction of the enemy while the local South Vietnamese focus may be on rural pacification and security of the local population. Thus, the U.S. is bent on annihilating a local area while the Vietnamese pacification effort tries to rebuild it. It simply is not possible to do both simultaneously. This truth I am to learn the hard way.

Further classes are about CORDS and the Mobile Advisor Teams, the Phoenix program, and then intelligence reports on the intensity of fighting where we will be going and the degree of safety or danger we can expect.

CORDS

The briefer explains a little about how and why CORDS was created and what it means to us as advisors. From the beginning of the desire of North Vietnam to dominate the South, the NVA and VC combat strategy has always been to destroy the rural sanctuary provided by the security forces of South Vietnam. This has been done two ways. One was the construction of a parallel, but subversive, VC government from the hamlet level up. The second was the conducting of small-scale combat operations against the Vietnamese security and military forces.

These attacks consist of raids, indirect fire, political coercion, and terrorism. The action is not just against the protection forces but just as much against civilians to prove that South Vietnam is unable to protect its own citizens.

Despite the massive damage inflicted by the air war in North Vietnam and the major combat engagements by U.S. and ARVN divisions, the war really needs to be won at the hamlet levels, destroying the VC infrastructure and the local VC units. At its basic, South Vietnam must pacify its countryside, and key main force engagements have not done this. In February 1966, President Johnson publicly defined this "other war, pacification," being waged in South Vietnam. This prompted the U.S. to reconsider the advisory efforts in Vietnam. Advisors with Vietnamese combat units would continue unchanged. In late 1966 a new agency, the Office of Civil Operations (OCO), was created to combine military and civil assets to manage U.S. support of the Vietnamese pacification program. This program did not operate as successfully as planned, but supporting the Vietnamese pacification program gained even more emphasis among both American politicians and the military. At the same time, though, America believed that South Vietnam should shoulder more of the burden of protecting itself.

OCO had problems from its beginning; it had the authority to do its job, but not control over all the needed assets, so conflict arose. The creation of CORDS in 1967 created the U.S. support of pacification under the military commander in Vietnam. So General Westmoreland had two deputies, one for military operations and the other for CORDS. Now the U.S. support for pacification has control over both the personnel and the resources. Another change was that the advisory responsibility for Regional and Popular Forces, rural security, and American military advisory teams assigned to local Vietnamese military units, was given to CORDS. A third major change was the development of the Phoenix program (to identify and destroy the local VC infrastructure), which was also placed under CORDS. Finally, the United States had a single coordinated program to support every aspect of the Vietnamese pacification operations.

CORDS itself (for all practical purposes) starts at the Corps Tactical Zone (CTZ) with the country divided into four CTZs. The U.S. CTZ commander (typically the senior U.S. commander in the CTZ) varies. The head of CORDS at the CTZ level is the general's deputy, responsible for all military and civilian advisor activities within the CTZ. The actual field functioning of CORDS begins at the province level, where the province senior advisor reports directly to the CTZ Deputy for CORDS.

Yes, the lines of command in Vietnam in 1968 are certainly

confusing. Within each CTZ there are four separate military organizations, all occupying the same space but often with competing missions. On the Vietnamese side are the regular South Vietnamese military units such as ARVN divisions or separate regiments, operating under the command of the Vietnamese general at the CTZ level. Then there are the Regional and Popular military units belonging to the province and district chiefs, whose missions are to protect the villages and hamlets. On the U.S. side are the American regular military divisions and then the CORDS advisors. During my second tour in Vietnam I operated twice as a district senior advisor and once at the province level as the RF/PF Advisor. Always in the III CTZ and always as a member of CORDS.

But other changes were also needed in the top U.S. leadership in Vietnam. General Westmoreland and Ambassador Henry Cabot Lodge, Jr., were the main managers of fighting the NVA and VC. Leaders who would totally support the pacification efforts were needed, so General Abrams replaced Westmoreland (who was promoted to army Chief of Staff) and Ellsworth Bunker replaced Lodge. Bunker is an Ivy Leaguer who is a career diplomat. He totally embraces the U.S. policies of Vietnamization and supporting pacification, which is why he is the ambassador.

The man in front of us then tells why this knowledge is so important to us. He details that Vietnam has 44 provinces, 250 districts and about 350 Mobile Advisor Teams. Each of these CORDS advisory teams are the tips of the spears in the efforts to destroy the VC infrastructure. Most of the officers in this room will be assigned as advisors to either a province or district or MATs. About 2,400 officers (of the slightly over 6,300 officers who are MACV advisors) are assigned to CORDS. This means that about 38 percent of all MACV advisors in-country are in the front lines of winning the hearts and minds of the Vietnamese people. This is the focal point of the current advisory mission in Vietnam.

He continues to describe what a Mobile Advisor Team is. It is a team of five advisors assigned to either a Regional or Popular Force unit, located within a district or assigned to a province. The team consists of a captain team leader and a lieutenant and three NCOs, either a staff sergeant or a sergeant first class. One is a light weapons advisor and another heavy weapons. The third NCO is a medic. In practice many teams only operate with three or four members. Their role is to serve as teachers of military weapons and combat operations. They live with and accompany their units into battle. Within their local area they may train the unit for six to nine months and then be assigned to another unit and repeat the training process. Most MATs come under the direct supervision of the district senior advisor or the province RF/PF advisor.

The Phoenix Program

Another seminar, another briefer. This one, after introducing himself, proclaims that the Phoenix program may very well be our best friend at the district level. Why? Because what we do as advisors could be dictated by what the Phoenix team discovers about the local VC.

The Phoenix program grew out of a need to identify and demolish the Viet Cong groundwork based on the combination of different intelligence structures. When CORDS was created in 1967, the CIA developed an intelligence gathering unit for CORDS, called Intelligence Coordination and Exploitation Program (ICEX). One mission of ICEX was to create, at the district level, a viable intelligence unit. Thus, the District Intelligence and Operations Coordination Center (DIOCC) was formed.

After the 1968 Tet battles, the South Vietnamese government realized they sorely needed a much improved method of collecting and analyzing intelligence information regarding VC activities. Thus, the Phung Hoang Program was created, named after a mythical bird in Vietnamese culture representing magical powers for virtue, peace, and the dawn of prosperity. The closest American interpretation is the mythical Phoenix, which became the U.S. name of the program. ICEX became Phoenix, which joined the Phung Hoang program to form a joint intelligence gathering operation.

The main administration headquarters of the Phoenix–Phung Hoang program is at the province level. The primary functioning is at the district level in the DIOCC, where the district chief is the DIOCC chief. Accordingly, the CORDS district senior advisor is the district Phoenix coordinator.

I need to comment on my association with the U.S. Phoenix and the Vietnamese Phung Hoang program. It has a reputation as an operation which relies on torture, rape, and killing of suspected VC leaders and members. I never saw any of this happening. I worked very closely with both Vietnamese and American officers and NCOs who ran this program. I served as the DIOCC Coordinator in two districts for the best part of a year. Because of my fluency in Vietnamese I participated in several interrogations of VC suspects or VC. I went on numerous raids to capture VC leaders or attack VC camps. When the VC resisted and shot at us, we fired back, and some were killed. But none of the Vietnamese I worked with used torture or killing as a Phoenix/Phung Hoang procedure.

My Next Move

Between orientation classes we draw our field equipment, weapon, and ammo, and sets of jungle fatigues and jungle boots. During this time, I also learn my orders to join the Phuoc Long province advisory team have been revoked. My duty assignment is changed to be the district senior advisor to Trang Bang district in Hau Nghia province, still in III CTZ, but now with Advisor Team 43.

The day ends with our intelligence briefing on Vietnam and where we are going. I learn that Hau Nghia is a small, impoverished province, recently created to offer better military command and control. It has four, mostly rural, districts, with two, Duc Hue and Trang Bang, being on (or near) the Cambodian border. On the Cambodian side are North Vietnamese Divisions, training in expectation of attacking in Vietnam. While their training can be observed from towers on the border, we are prohibited from crossing the boundary. Cambodia through Hau Nghia province is a main route for transporting weapons and rockets to VC troops outside Saigon. Because of this, combat operations are a daily occurrence and the annual casualty rate of RF and PF units in Trang Bang exceed 50 percent. The province capital is located at Bao Trai, not far from Cu Chi, the home of the U.S. 25th Infantry Division. The intel briefing concludes with the warning that Trang Bang will not be a paradise; currently, it is the most dangerous part of South Vietnam.

I am told a bus will take me to the Air America passenger terminal at Tan Son Nhut airport early tomorrow morning. It is explained that Air America is a passenger and cargo airlines owned by the CIA which provides most of CORDS air support missions. An Air America aircraft will fly me out to the dirt strip at Bao Trai.

6

Combat Flying in Vietnam:
Low and Slow

During my first tour in Vietnam, flying was not among my favorite activities. My thinking went like this: Most of my being in an aircraft would mean flying in combat areas. My concern was that the aircraft I was in, being only a few thousand feet above ground, would be shot down. First, I would have to avoid being shot in the sky. Second, if shot, I would have to survive a crash on the ground. Then lastly, assuming I did not perish being shot while in flight, and assuming I did live through an aircraft crash, then, I would have to fight everyone who shot me down in the first place, now trying to kill me on the ground.

No, I reasoned, it would be best for me to stay on the ground where any fall to earth would be no greater than the five feet and ten inches of my height. This was my thinking during my first tour in Vietnam. But, because of my job, flying was involved. C-123 troop movements of the ARVN battalion I was assigned to, helicopter air assaults into combat zones, aerial recon over enemy positions, and the typical helicopter and fixed wing flights between various higher commands I worked for. Despite my need for aerial transportation of one kind or another, my total flying time in Vietnam the first time probably amounted to no more than 50 to 60 flight hours. Compare this to the typical army helicopter pilot in Vietnam who could easily accumulate over 1,000 hours of flight time in a year.

Standing and waiting for an aircraft to transport me to somewhere near the Cambodian border, I found myself eager for my first flight in Vietnam during my second tour as a combat advisor. For some reason, I found myself, during this tour, seeking out every flight experience possible. I began to look forward to the excitement, the experience of combat flight, and when the tour ended, I had accumulated over twice as many flight hours as I did in 1966–67.

The opportunity to find a flight in Vietnam is not hard. Every U.S.

military unit—air force, navy, marines, and army it seems—possesses helicopters and small light airplanes. Also, the South Vietnamese military has them, but trying to locate one of theirs available for any combat mission is virtually impossible. In two tours, assigned to a variety of South Vietnamese combat units, I never flew in any aircraft belonging to South Vietnam.

Air America

In addition to U.S. and South Vietnamese military aircraft, the Royal Australian Air Force flew often in South Vietnam as well as the CIA. From December 1968 until I left Vietnam in August 1969, almost all my flying was on the CIA airline, Air America. And here I was, waiting for my first flight via Air America.

Air America is a U.S.-registered passenger and cargo airline, originally created in 1950 for the U.S. Central Intelligence Agency as a dummy business to function in Southeast Asia. It became Air America in 1959. Its aircraft ranged from jet Boeing 727s to a variety of World War II and Korean War–era twin-engine cargo planes to smaller single-engine utility airplanes and then helicopters, from huge heavy-lift Sikorsky CH-54 Skycranes to medium-lift Sikorsky H-34s (used for everything from moving troops to gunships to defoliation platforms) to the ubiquitous Bell 204B and 205 helicopters (civilian versions of the military UH-I "Huey" and the UH-1H), down to the Hughes OH-6A Light Observation Helicopter, Cayuse, called by the military the "Loach," a contraction of "light observation helicopter."

Air America operated from bases in South Vietnam, Laos, Cambodia, Thailand, Burma, Taiwan, and Japan. Most of its pilots were former military pilots or military pilots "on loan" to the CIA. They flew for a variety of reasons, mostly being the flying itself, without all the discipline and administrative hassles of the military. Every CIA pilot I flew with was a consummate aviation professional and an expert at the controls of his plane.

From the late '50s to the early '60s, Air America supported a variety of U.S. covert and clandestine operations and missions throughout Southeast Asia. CIA agents and U.S. Special Forces worked in Laos training Laotian military and engaging in counterinsurgency operations to stifle communist infiltration into Laos. In the late 1950s, Operation Ambidextrous evolved into Operation Hotfoot and by the early 1960s became Operation White Star. These and many more secret missions in Southeast Asia were supported by Air America aircraft.

I first learned about "White Star" in late 1964 when I was an infantry battalion assistant operation (S-3) officer at Fort Benning and tasked with creating a counter-guerrilla, counterinsurgency training program for the rifle companies. One of our company commanders, a captain, had earned his Combat Infantryman Badge while serving as a Special Forces officer during White Star. I spent hours with him going over what training was needed and what worked in Laos and what didn't.

When many of the U.S. military secret operations terminated in the early to mid–1960s, Air America had many planes but fewer missions. Even though it continued to support clandestine operations in Southeast Asia, it began flying for other U.S. government organizations to include U.S. State Department agencies in South Vietnam, the U.S. Air Force and Army, and CORDS.

The Air America fleet was big and different. Its aircraft came from a variety of different and unusual sources. Some foreign-made aircraft were manufactured in the U.S., under license, by American manufacturers (an example is the Swiss-designed Pilatus Porter). Often, crashed and destroyed aircraft would be purchased by the CIA and the parts used to build a usable aircraft. An American aircraft destroyed in a crash would be reported to the FAA as such. This aircraft would then be removed from the FAA database. The CIA would purchase the wreck and few months later another aircraft would be added to the Air America list of owned aircraft but having the same serial number as the destroyed aircraft. Because of this rebuilding procedure, it was rumored that many Air America aircraft were not legally certified to fly or operate as U.S. airlines aircraft. But in South Vietnam, who cared about legalities? The only concern would be, Can it fly?

Low and Slow Navigation

Most combat flying in Vietnam is slow and low and done visually. While the navy, marines, and air force use jet aircraft for bombing missions and close air support for ground troops, the bulk of the flying is done by helicopters and smaller fixed-wing airplane recon missions. Because most low-level flights are assisting ground combat operations, the pilots must be able to see the ground and what is happening. Flying by instruments is not possible in support of troops on the land beneath the aircraft.

As a ground-pounder I never really gave much thought to how aircraft, day, or night, could fly to wherever we were in the middle of nowhere during a combat operation. Or how the pilots could take us exactly where we had selected an LZ. Or how a medevac could find a very small clearing in the jungle along the Cambodian border. But they did. I never heard any chopper pilot radio me to ask where I was, saying he couldn't find me. Never. So how did they do this? Magic? No, by using TACAN, terrain navigation, and sometimes radar vectors by air controllers.

TACAN, tactical air navigation, is a military radio navigation system. It uses a ground-based radio transmitter station providing pilots with a compass bearing and a distance in miles to the station. Military aircraft have a TACAN radio receiver and an instrument that presents the compass bearing and the distance from the TACAN station.

Pilots fly with the tactical topographical maps used by the infantry. If the pilot had a mission to fly to a unit on a combat operation, the unit would provide the pilot with the unit's map coordinates. The pilot would find the nearest TACAN station and plot that location on his map. A line would be drawn on the map connecting the TACAN station location to the destination. Orienting the map, the compass bearing from the TACAN to the unit location on the map and the distance is readily determined. The pilot has an outgoing bearing to fly and the distance from the TACAN station to the unit. A piece of cake. TACAN does have its limits. Although the TACAN can provide radio signals up to 449 miles, since it is a line-of-sight navigation device, rising terrain can mask the signal. Flying in the flat, low southern part of the country it works great but in the central and northern mountainous parts of South Vietnam, low-altitude use of TACAN can become impossible.

Military pilots in Vietnam from the 1950s through the 1970s would create, by hand, their own charts and airport (or dirt strip) diagrams (or photographs) with details on the best (and safest) way to approach and land at the airport or dirt strip. These hand-drawn navigation maps were copied and stored at various aviation headquarters and military airports around Vietnam. If a pilot has a mission to fly to an unknown airport, he can request his staff aviation officer radio around and locate a copy of the airport information. These handmade aviation charts almost always also employ data on how an area TACAN can be used to navigate to the desired airport, dirt landing strip or even a frequently used jungle landing zone.

Another navigation instrument on a military aircraft is an automatic direction finder (ADF), a radio which receives a signal from a ground-based military transmitter displayed as a bearing from the aircraft to the station, but not the distance. Pilots can use this equipment in conjunction with the Armed Forces Vietnam Network AM radio stations as another in-flight navigation tool. This is the same radio network where Adrian Cronauer's "Good Morning, Vietnam" radio show was broadcast.

The usable radio frequencies for the ADF also include commercial AM radio stations. Armed Forces Vietnam Network AM radio broadcasting studios are in cities and military bases all along the coast of South Vietnam. While the main studio is in Saigon, other stations are situated in Qui Nhon, Nha Trang, Pleiku, Da Nang, Hue, and Quang Tri. Thus, pilots flying over the mountains or jungles in the western regions of South Vietnam could just put the AM station frequency in their ADF radio and fly the compass heading displayed, leading them to the city.

Pilots also had another source of navigation help, radar. Aviation radar systems were located at all major USAF bases along the coast of South Vietnam. For the low and slow tactical aircraft, radar was seldom used. It was mostly relied on for navigational help in poor weather or dark nights. A pilot could contact the closest USAF base with radar and when identified, receive directions to fly home.

The military pilots in Vietnam were highly trained professionals who would do anything to rescue, save, or assist Americans on the ground.

Vietnam became our helicopter war. This was the first war to rely heavily on the use of helicopters in direct combat. The helicopter allowed commanders to rapidly move assault troops into battle as needed. They could resupply troops in combat quicker than any other form of transportation, and the massive firepower of armed helicopters often made the difference between winning or losing an encounter. In my mind, the young warrant officer helicopter aviators were brave, courageous, daring, and always willing to risk their lives to save the lives of those of us fighting on the ground. I don't believe that any other group of soldiers faced as much risk and danger as those chopper pilots.

Danger

The biggest threat to those fixed wing and rotary wing pilots flying in Vietnam is anti-aircraft weapons. The NVA had thousands of both mobile and fixed placement AA weapons throughout both North and South Vietnam and Laos. Seventy-seven percent of the USAF aircraft losses were by AA fire. Fifty-two percent of the U.S. Navy's aircraft losses were by AA fire. There were almost 12,000 helicopters serving in Vietnam and 47 percent of those were lost, mostly to ground fire from AA weapons. It goes without saying, flying in Vietnam is hazardous to one's health, as I learned one night on the Cambodian border.

The ZPU-4 is a 14.6 mm towed AA weapon with four guns with direct fire into oncoming helicopters. It has an effective engagement range of about 3,300 feet. The ZU-23 is a 23 mm anti-aircraft gun with an effective engagement range varying between 5,000 and 6,600 feet. The ZSU-23 is a 37 mm towed or self-propelled anti-aircraft weapon. It can be fired visually or using radar controls. It has an effective engagement range of about 5,000 feet. These are the weapons most feared by those pilots whose missions require them to fly low and slow.

Air Medal

When I was in-processing in Saigon, at the beginning of my first tour in 1966, I met a captain who was heading back to the States. One evening, he took time to provide some tips on what to do during my tour. As he was preparing his khaki uniform for the flight home, I noticed he had an Air Medal among his rows of ribbons, above his left pocket. I asked how he got that, and he explained how.

The Air Medal was created in 1942 in recognition for a single act of heroism in flight or for meritorious achievement in flight over a period of time. It was designed to reward pilots and flight crews for flying combat missions.

During the Vietnam War a major tactic, air assaults, was the employment of helicopters to swiftly transport troops to a combat location. So now infantry troops would be exposed to the same aerial risks as pilots and air crews. Therefore, if they met the requirements for receiving an Air Medal, they could be awarded the medal. For example, Army Colonel David Hackworth, an infantry commander, who served multiple combat tours in Vietnam, received the Air Medal 34 times (once for valor and 33 times for meritorious achievement in flight).

The requirements for the Army Air Medal are complex. There are two criteria for being awarded the medal. One is the type of mission and the second is the time in flight. The missions are direct combat flying such as in a gunship attack or an air assault, a combat support flight such as a visual recon of an enemy position, or a non–combat service flight such as supply missions or transporting VIPs.

How this worked is 25 hours of flying direct combat missions would be required to be awarded one Air Medal. Fifty hours of combat support missions would get one Air Medal and it would take 100 hours of non-combat support missions to earn one Air Medal. Most Air Medals awarded were for combinations of the different missions.

The captain said I should do this. Carry a small notebook with me and have it marked off by date, type of flight mission, time of flight, location, type of aircraft, pilot's name and signature, and pilot's unit. Thus, an entry into my book might read, "11 November 1966, air assault, 25 minutes, Hoi An to Nong Son, CH-46A, Tom Jones, Captain, USMC, signature, HMM-265, Marble Mt MAF."

When my accumulation of type missions and hours met the combined criteria, I would submit the pages of my flight log through personnel channels requesting the award of the Air Medal. During my first tour I did not fly enough missions or hours to be eligible for the Air Medal, but during my second tour, I did.

For some reason, throughout that second tour, I was fascinated with combat flights. I enjoyed the opportunity to participate in the type of flying so common in Vietnam, low and slow.

7

Flight to Bao Trai

Early the morning of Friday, 30 August 1968, a bus takes me and several other officers and NCOs from Koepler Compound to Tan Son Nhut Air Base. We are dropped at separate locations and I am deposited in front of a nondescript building at the airport. Walking through a door, I realize I am at the passenger area of Air America, the civilian-registered U.S. airline owned by the CIA. After presenting my paperwork, I am told my plane will arrive shortly, as a man points to another door leading outside. Grabbing my gear, I push through the door, slumping my bag on the cement deck, I place my carbine on top of my bag and look out toward a taxiway. Several minutes later a high-wing taildragger, white bottom with a blue upper, signifying the Air America colors, pulls up and stops about 25 yards away.

After shutting down the engine, a tall, young-looking blond man wearing aviator sunglasses steps out from the left side, closes the door, and saunters toward me. Wow! I think. Here is a pilot straight out of the *Terry and the Pirates* comic strip. He looks like a former Flying Tiger fighter pilot, now a Southeast Asia mercenary pilot for hire. Wearing a white scarf and tropical, lightweight flight jacket, he looks like a Hollywood version of a World War II or Korean War combat pilot. But when he is about ten yards away my initial impression of him diminishes quickly. His long blond hair looks greasy and unkempt. The scarf is tattered and dirty, the jacket very worn, colored with sweat stains, and the collar threadbare. His khaki trousers are baggy, worn, and oil-stained, and his scuffed shoes desperately need polish. A glance at his face suggests he is in his late 40s, not 20s, as I first surmised.

He turns toward me, asking if I am his passenger to Hau Nghia province and I nod in the affirmative, responding with a yes. As he approaches the door to the terminal, he says he will be back in a minute and we can board the plane. Shortly later he returns holding some papers, and we begin the walk to the plane.

The plane, while a fixed gear single engine, is certainly not small. It is a Swiss Pilatus Porter PC-6 built under license by Fairchild Hiller in the United States. At 36 feet long with a wingspan of about 50 feet, it carries almost 1,300 pounds of people or cargo. Its turbine engine allows it to perform at peak powers needed to transport people and cargo into the short and rough dirt jungle strips found all over Vietnam, Thailand, Laos, Burma, and Cambodia. During the Vietnam War the CIA owned and operated 23 throughout Southeast Asia.

The plane looks weird to me. The nose is too long. In all single-engine planes I know about, the distance from the front windscreen to the nose is about a quarter the length of the plane. On this Pilatus it is about one-third of the plane, and toward the three-bladed propeller it narrows to a point. The blade is huge with a diameter of about eight and a half feet.

As we approach the plane, the pilot grabs the handle of the rear door on the right side and slides the door back. Inside are six seats made of metal tubing with canvas backs and padded seat cushions. Grabbing my duffel bag, the pilot places it between the rows of seats, mid-plane. Asked if my carbine is unloaded, I remove the magazine (which is full of bullets), and slide the bolt back, showing the chamber is empty. I let the bolt move forward and he reaches for the carbine and the magazine. Slipping the loaded magazine back into the carbine, he places it on the aircraft floor, next to the bag, muzzle pointing toward the rear of the plane.

Leaning forward he swings the right-side crew door open and motions me inside.

Since he has already done a thorough preflight before taxiing to get me, his counterclockwise inspection is quickly accomplished. His hands shake the various tail and wing control surfaces. Tires and engine cowling are visually checked, hands slide over the leading edges of each propeller blade, checking for any nicks picked up when taxiing here. Repeating the process on the left side of the plane, he turns and opens the left door, hops in, checks my door and fastens both our seat belts.

Most of the cockpit is like any other single-engine plane, except the Pilatus has a shelf running across the bottom of the instrument panel. On the floor in front of each seat is a control stick for maneuvering the plane, except my column has been removed. Rudder pedals and brakes for both seats are on the floor, forward of the control column. On the left panel, are the primary flight instruments and other gauges providing information on the health of the engine. To the right are engine control levers and behind them, on the panel, are more engine gauges. Further right are all the radios and navigation instrument controls. The shelf is cluttered with a variety of loose papers, maps, aviation charts, and checklists.

The pilot asks if I am ready and I nod in the affirmative. He reaches in front of his control column, removing the locking pin. Slipping on his headset, he grabs his checklist from the shelf, placing it in his lap. His right hand rotates the control stick, ensuring freedom of movement. He begins the process to start the plane, first checking to confirm no one is nearby and the taxi area is clear.

His left hand reaches forward to select an igniter starter, then moves to grip the control column as his right hand extends to the center of the instrument panel to push the start switch. The prop slowly rotates, speeds up as the turbine engine spools to life in a few seconds.

My original thoughts as the pilot first walked closer to me after parking his plane were, here is a real loser, unkempt, dirty, and much older than me. My confidence in his piloting skills was pretty low, based on how he looked. But as I watch his hands flutter around the cockpit, turning switches for radios and navigation equipment, eyes moving constantly, checking gauges, I can see he is a professional.

Adjusting power, radio frequencies and navigation instruments set, the pilot releases the parking brake as power is added to move the plane forward. We begin to taxi, but then the pilot moves the plane aside and stops. I wonder why but remain closemouthed.

Fully stopped, the pilot glances around again, reaches into a shirt pocket to retrieve a pair of clear glasses. Removing his sunglasses, he drops them into the shirt pocket as he dons the eyeglasses. The airport diagram for Tan Son Nhut with its radio frequencies is consulted, checked against the radios, and the pilot calls ground control. He receives taxi instructions to the active runway, adjusts the altimeter to the current barometric pressure and moves again. Because the plane's tail is on a wheel on the ground the nose is too high to look over. So, the pilot must make a series of S-turns to be able to see the taxiway in front of the plane.

Stopping short of the runway, he calls the tower, signifying he is ready for departure. The tower releases him, providing the initial heading to fly. Looking over to the approach end of the runway to ensure no plane is landing, the pilot moves into position, and reaches overhead to crank the proper adjustment to the flaps as the left hand reaches down to adjust the rudder trim. Lined up with the center of the runway, he changes the idle control and pushes the power lever full forward for takeoff. Feet dancing on the rudder pedals to counteract any engine torque or crosswind, he eases the control column forward to lift the tail. As the tail rises and the aircraft speed approaches 70 mph, the plane gently rises above the tarmac as it passes from ground-based movement into flight. The control column pulled back, we ascend at 900 feet per minute, the hot humid air, rising from the black runway, bumps and tosses the Pilatus along its climbing path.

The pilot turns westbound, toward Bao Trai, and holds the stick back until easing it forward at 5,500 feet. Its power controls reset, the plane purrs along at 130 mph, above any rough air burbles, smooth and cool. Glancing at the gauges the pilot makes sure all are in the green, indicating that for this flight the engine is functioning perfectly. The sunglasses are back on his face.

In this plane is an array of various navigation equipment and radios with different frequency ranges. This allows the pilot to talk on the civil aviation band (with other aircraft, and on all the various controlling frequencies) or talk to combat units on the ground or different military aircraft.

Apparently, flying into the Bao Trai strip is a common occurrence for the CIA as the pilot seems to know exactly where he is going. Flying westbound, he intercepts the Tan Son Nhut TACAN outbound heading for 287 degrees, which is the compass heading to fly to the Boa Trai airstrip. When the needle centers, the pilot makes a gentle turn northwesterly and flies, keeping the needle right in the center of the dial. Looking at his DME he notes that he still has a few more miles to go to reach Bao Trai. The airstrip is exactly 17.25 miles from the Ton Son Nhut TACAN station. In a couple of minutes, we will be over the Bao Trai airstrip.

The pilot calls on a frequency and talks to the driver of the Hau Nghia province advisor team jeep, waiting to pick me up when we land. The airstrip comes into view, in front of us, off the pilot's side.

Bao Trai airfield is a very crude dirt strip oriented almost due east and west (80 degrees and 260 degrees). It is not completely dirt as it has 1,500 feet of pierced steel plank (PSP) with 300 feet of dirt overruns on each end. The runway is 83 feet wide with ditches running along both sides. PSP are interlocking pressed and perforated steel mats (later made of aluminum), each 10 feet long, 15 inches wide, weighing 66 pounds, created during World War II for use as portable materials to quickly make aircraft runways. They are found throughout Vietnam, used not only for runways but also for bunkers and other reinforced emplacements such as ceilings and roofs, where sandbags can be stacked.

This airstrip does not have a wind sock but pilots use the Vietnamese flag, flying above the province compound just northeast of the airstrip, to get the direction of the wind, as aircraft always land into the wind (and therefore runways are built oriented in the direction of the normal flow of wind). This combat strip is on the north side of a main road and parallel to it. At the midpoint is a dirt parking area, about 100 feet by 150 feet, where the jeep is waiting for me.

While daylight flights into the Bao Trai airstrip are classified as mostly secure, pilots are urged to use caution. This means the pilot would approach the landing strip flying above the main road. Since the runway is only 30 feet above sea level, landing aircraft must drop a mile very quickly, as a slow approach such as into a normal airport is not wise. The aircraft must make a combat approach almost over the runway. This can be exciting, seeming just like a rapid roller coaster ride.

A few miles out from the airport the pilot begins to set up the PC-6 for a combat landing. The Vietnamese flag (on the nearby Vietnamese compound) suggests that a landing to the west is okay, and the plane is already flying in that direction. He glances at the panel, eyes and hands moving around, sets the throttle to full idle, slows to about 120 mph, adjusts his trim, and descends in a hurry. Hands, arms, eyes, and head movements are hurried but measured as he seems to be all over the cockpit in front of him. He switches on the auxiliary fuel pump, retards the power control lever, stretches up to crank in flaps and drops the plane on the end of the runway. Control column forward, as the speed decreases the column is gently eased rearward, and as the tail slowly touches the ground, the plane is braked to stop. Somewhere along the rough taxiing, the sunglasses were removed and replaced with the spectacles. Wow! What a ride. It seems like just seconds ago we were a mile in the air, and the next I know we are on the ground. Just a subtle reminder that I have re-entered another hostile and dangerous segment of my life.

At the dirt end of the runway, he turns the plane around, switches back to his sunglasses, taxies to the parking area and stops. At idle, he removes his headset and explains to me how to get out, slide open the rear door, retrieve my gear and weapon, and cautions me to not move forward at any time but always move toward the rear of the plane to avoid the propeller.

A specialist fourth class, the driver, approaches the plane and has the back open when I alight from the cockpit. Handing me my M-1 carbine, he grabs my duffel bag and removes it. I move to the back, away from the plane as he shuts the door and moves toward the jeep. Stowing my bag in the back seat, he flashes a thumbs-up to the pilot, who waves and taxies to the east end of the strip. We watch as the pilot reaches the end and twists around. Spooling up the engine, the plane is braked so at full power it doesn't move. Engine roaring, brakes released, the plane rockets down the PSP but does not take off. This is to gain speed on the ground so when he does lift off, he has power to zoom rapidly, make a left turn over the road and quickly climb above small arms range. He swiftly disappears into the eastern sky. My flight from Saigon took less than 30 minutes.

I introduce myself to the driver, who tells me his name, explaining we are now going to the province advisor team compound, where I will meet Lieutenant Colonel Bernard, the province senior advisor. Both of us climb in the jeep and the driver shifts into gear, letting the clutch out as we move onto the main road, heading toward the advisor compound.

8

District Senior Advisor
at Trang Bang

The Battle at Trang Bang

Pulling into a dusty parking area next to an older stucco-like building, the driver stops. During the jeep ride from the airstrip the driver said that during the night there was a big battle in Trang Bang; it was attacked by an NVA unit. Early in the morning a relief force from the province departed Boa Trai to join the fight. Apparently the NVA were fought off and a province convoy is preparing to leave shortly. Colonel Bernard is going to take me in the convoy to Trang Bang. The driver tells me to leave my gear and carbine in the jeep and he will watch it because soon we will join the convoy. I am to go inside and meet the colonel.

Entering the building, I am confronted by a group of men. The man I move toward is a lieutenant colonel, in his early 40s, thin, lanky, darkish hair but beginning to become bald, average height, wearing glasses. He looks more like a history or English college professor than a highly decorated combat infantry officer (he was awarded the Distinguished Service Cross for valor as a lieutenant in Korea). He is an expert in counter-guerrilla warfare (Ranger School, Special Forces, and curriculum development at the Army Special Warfare School) and a proponent of low-level combat. Next to him are other officers, a major and a couple of captains. I introduce myself, handing him my orders. He says he has been expecting me, but the normal tour of the province advisory team will have to wait because both of us are leaving for Trang Bang in a few minutes.

He explains what happened during the night. Two nights ago, 28 August, a battalion of the 101st NVA Regiment was ambushed by two battalions from the U.S. 101st Airborne Division, just north of Trang Bang, and destroyed. Bernard says that August has been a tough month as the NVA and VC were staging many mini-Tet assaults throughout

HAU NGHIA
PROVINCE ADVISOR TEAM

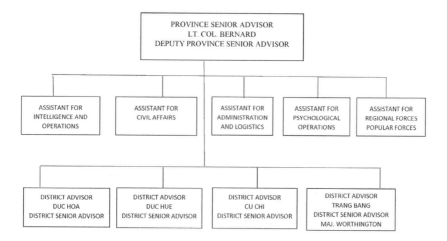

Hau Nghia province. During last night, another NVA unit attacked the town of Trang Bang and the district compound. The district soldiers defended the compound viciously.

Province was alerted of the attack and the province chief, ARVN Lieutenant Colonel Ma Sanh Nhon, led an ARVN Ranger battalion to Trang Bang in the early morning hours, joining the fight, driving the NVA away. Few South Vietnamese were killed or wounded while over two dozen NVA soldiers were killed. The area was secured at daybreak. The American advisors were ecstatic, because the Trang Bang garrison force held off a superior NVA force and the province relief force chased them away.

Bernard gives some last-minute instructions to his staff officers, then, grabbing me by the elbow, he escorts me out the door, motioning me to get in the back seat of the jeep, next to my gear. He motions his hand for his driver to join the Vietnamese convoy. As we move out, I grasp my carbine, slide the magazine out, making sure it is loaded with bullets, pull the bolt back, glance at the chamber to confirm it is empty, let the bolt slide forward and re-insert the magazine. Laying the weapon across my knees, I pull a second loaded magazine from my duffel and drop it into the pocket on the leg of my jungle fatigue pants.

The issued World War II M-1 carbine is a .30 caliber semi-automatic shoulder weapon. It is lightweight and the bullets are small. Its accuracy is good to 100 yards, printing three- to five-inch groups. It is issued with 15-round magazines, but 30-round magazines are available, and many soldiers would tape two magazines together so with a quick magazine reversal the shooter had double the rounds available for combat.

The carbine was developed early during World War II as a replacement for the .45 service pistol for rear area support troops. While it lacked the power of the World War II M-1 Garand service rifle, it was a much better defensive weapon than either the pistol or submachine guns, and its size made it a vastly easier gun to carry and use than the much heavier and larger service rifle. It was also a better fit for Vietnamese soldiers than the M-1 rifle. Because the Vietnamese I advise are issued carbines, so am I.

At this time, the fully automatic M-16 rifle is now issued to all U.S. military and ARVN units. Its implementation has not reached down to the RF/PF forces yet but is only a few months away. The M-1 carbine is about twice as powerful as the .45 service pistol but no match to either the M-16 or the enemy's AK-47.

On the way to Trang Bang Colonel Bernard describes my new assignment and my new role. He says I will not be the district senior advisor as that role is already filled by a civilian CORDS advisor, Tony Lorenzo. Tony is a Foreign Service Reserve officer in his late 20s. He is a former Special Forces sergeant who served in Vietnam in the early to mid–1960s. He is fluent in Vietnamese almost like a native. He is extremely good with civic affairs and the local officials, but he really needs help with the local military militia and the military members of his team.

Bernard says he had requested a major, an experienced combat advisor who spoke Vietnamese, explaining why my orders were changed. I learn Tony is excellent with the district and village officials handling the non-military aspects of pacification. But he either is not able or not interested in the military discipline of the U.S. soldiers assigned to the advisor team. Colonel Bernard continues by explaining that the military side of the district team is in disarray with low morale. It needs a leader to take charge and their current leader, an army captain, is not doing that. Additionally, the military aspect of pacification needs an experienced senior military advisor to work with the RF/PF units. The district chief is a Vietnamese Marine major and he and Tony don't always see eye to eye. The Trang Bang advisors desperately need a military leader with combat experience to work with the district chief.

Obviously, I am disappointed. I am not the district senior advisor but now second in command. Quite a letdown, but the manner Colonel Bernard uses to describe my job and its importance, being the deputy, in this instance is not that bad. I am left with the impression that my importance is greater than that of the DSA. Well, I guess that time will tell.

As the convoy pulls into the Trang Bang district compound, our jeep stops in front of a single-story stucco building with a silver aluminum sloped roof. Approaching our jeep is a tall, muscular man, about my size, with longish black hair, dressed in jungle fatigues with the black CIB and black jump wings sewn above his left pocket, with both Ranger and Airborne tabs on his left shoulder. He wears no name tape or any rank. He stops in front of the colonel, grabs his hand and welcomes him. Colonel Bernard introduces me to Tony, inquiring about the fight. He then turns me over to Tony, excusing himself, saying he needs to join his counterpart, Lieutenant Colonel Ma Sanh Nhon, as he walks away.

Tony asks the driver to put my gear inside the advisor building while Tony takes me around to where the fighting just took place. He says the district compound and the downtown area were hit during the middle of the night by an unknown NVA force. But the district officials had a warning that something was up so the district soldiers in the compound and area guard posts were on full alert and not surprised by the attack. Then during the latter stage of the attacks, the province chief arrived with his Rangers and the fight was over.

As Tony is explaining this to me, we begin to leave the compound and move around the exterior perimeter, along the outside walls. He says that they found 31 dead bodies around the battle area, just outside the compound. He explains that the January Tet battles, then followed by the mini-Tet attacks by the NVA and VC in the spring and summer, left the enemy decimated, with few seasoned combat troops. As a result, many recent small skirmishes have found the enemy composed of young, untrained, ill-equipped boys. It is apparent that the enemy is hurting for combat soldiers.

Walking around the outside of the compound, I see well over a dozen dead soldiers. In the latter months of my first tour, I encountered NVA soldiers in battle. At that time, they were outfitted in a tan khaki uniform with a tan pith helmet. By 1967 the NVA had switched to the uniforms being a light green. But the dead soldiers I was looking at were not in green but in the older khaki uniforms. I examined the bodies lying on their backs or sides and became astonished at what I was looking at. These dead soldiers were not men, but boys 14, 15, 16 years old. Also, their weapons were not real rifles but wooden replicas of rifles. Many of the attacking soldiers were just kids, not even armed with real guns. I could only wonder, why? Moving around the perimeter, most of the dead bodies I saw were those of unarmed boys.

This is my introduction to the war I will fight over the next three and a half months in Trang Bang, near the Cambodian border. As we return to the compound, Tony says he wants to introduce me to his counterpart, the district chief.

In the center of the compound parking area stand Colonel Bernard and two Vietnamese officers; one, dressed in a dark green and black camouflage utility uniform, has his back toward us. As we approach, all three turn toward us and I can't believe my eyes. I recognize one officer, a Vietnamese Marine major. The other Vietnamese officer is a lieutenant colonel, medium height with a muscular build, his long black hair askew on top of a round face. He is wearing typical army fatigues, adorned with both U.S. and Vietnamese paratrooper wings and the Army Ranger tab; these insignias testify to his warrior training.

He moves toward me, exclaiming in perfect English he is Ma Sanh Nhon, the Hau Nghia province chief, as we shake hands. I learn later his precise command of English is due to his having spent four years in the United States attending military schools and training. He looks the part of a combat warrior (in fact, he is later awarded the U.S. Silver Star for gallantry in action while serving with U.S. forces).

The other Vietnamese officer turns toward me, and I say, "It's nice to meet you again, Major Ai." I mention to the others that in the spring

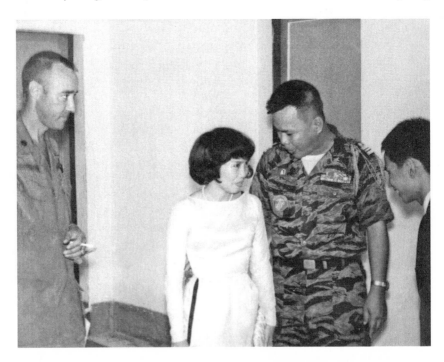

Major Ai (Trang Bang district chief) and his wife.

of 1966 Prime Minister Nguyen Cao Ky sent his marines to take control of the City of Da Nang when the Buddhists violently protested for the ouster of Ky. At that time, I was the Senior Tactical Advisor to the ARVN troops responsible for the security of the city. One morning in April I went to my office in the Da Nang garrison only to find all the ARVN guards replaced by Vietnamese marines. In my office was then Marine captain Tran Trung Ai, telling me in perfect English my services as an advisor were not needed, suggesting I leave, immediately, which I did.

He acknowledged recalling me, identified himself as the Trang Bang district chief, commenting how he looked forward to us working together, this time. Other than his rank, he has not changed at all, is even wearing the same uniform he had 28 months ago. About five feet eight inches tall, he is stocky, with his same Marine haircut, almost shaved on the sides with a half-inch of black hair bristling on top. His demeanor is unchanged, all military, reflecting the no-nonsense bearing of a confident combat officer.

Wow, I am thinking, what a coincidence. I hope this time around our relationship is better.

The two Vietnamese officers excuse themselves and move away. The convoy is preparing for its return to Bao Trai, so Colonel Bernard bids us goodbye. Over the next few days, Tony takes me under his wing to orient me on the province, the district, the district government and its troops, the combat situation, and the district advisor team.

Trang Bang District Advisors

The district advisors live in a big single-story house with several rooms inside. Sleeping quarters for the team members, a radio room, a small office for our tactical operations center, and a kitchen; we eat in a poorly screened back porch. It is very sparsely furnished. The cooking, housecleaning and clothes-washing are done by local Vietnamese women. These quarters are actually pretty bad. Messy, not clean, and very disorganized. I quickly learn that Tony spends little time in these quarters except to sleep at night, so apparently the conditions are of little importance to him. His interaction with his military advisors is limited so he leaves them alone, providing little leadership over them or how they live.

Our building is located within the Trang Bang district military garrison or the district headquarters, which is on the northeast side of town. One side of the compound is adjacent to the town and a main

TRANG BANG DISTRICT

ADVISOR TEAM

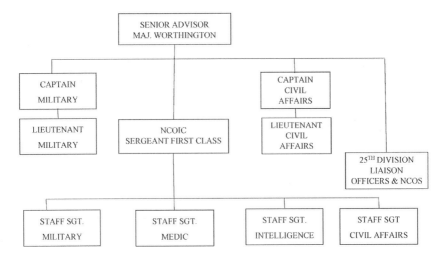

street. The other side of the compound, which has a concrete wall around it, faces open rice fields with heavily forested, jungle-like trees surrounding a small group of rural homes a few hundred yards away, across the rice fields. Right outside the compound walls is a helicopter pad, easily accessible from our advisor building. Within the small compound are several other buildings, mostly working offices for the district officials, the Vietnamese military and sleeping areas for the military and quarters for the district chief and his wife. The compound is guarded day and night by both roving guards and stationary sentries in the corners.

The advisor team consists of several different men, both civilian and military. The DSA is Tony, a U.S. State Department employee, and his deputy is me, an infantry major. There are two captains; one is the RF/PF advisor and the other focuses on civil affairs, working with the district officials regarding schools, medical facilities, roads, villages, and hamlets. The RF/PF advisor captain is the officer in charge and the team operations officer. There are two lieutenants; one works with the civil affairs captain and the other is an army intelligence officer who advises the District Intelligence and Operations Coordination Center and the Phoenix program. We also have a Filipino agriculture advisor. Several other nations provide civilian experts to help in Vietnam in areas of agriculture, health and medicine, education, and various civic action construction projects. These individuals are often placed in district or province advisor teams.

The team also has several enlisted advisors. One sergeant first class (E-7) is our intelligence and operations NCO and the team NCOIC (non-commissioned officer in charge of all the enlisted men), the senior NCO in the team. The second sergeant first class is the infantry advisor, who works primarily with the RF/PF captain advisor. We have a staff sergeant (E-6) medic, who enjoys a favorable reputation with the physicians in the 25th Division Medical Battalion because of his expertise in treating difficult combat wounds and understanding the exotic diseases common to rural Vietnamese folk but unknown by the 25th doctors. Our youngest team member is a specialist fourth class radio operator.

Our medic works at both the small district hospitals in the district (only one has a doctor) and goes to the villages when the Vietnamese medical people host medical clinics. At times 25th Division doctors accompany our medic to learn more about medical care in the field. We also have officers and NCOs from the U.S. 25th Division. Most are civil affairs people from division G-5, assigned as liaison between the 25th military operations in Trang Bang and the Vietnamese pacification efforts. Also, some captains are assigned as liaisons when we conduct joint Vietnamese and American combat operations. Mostly these captains will only be with us a week or two as they are short-timers, waiting to leave Vietnam.

The mission of the team is twofold, the first being military and security. We advise the local Vietnamese military on intelligence gathering, locating VC infrastructure targets, and destroying them (hopefully by capture, but sometimes, when they resist, they are killed). Also, small military operations are constantly conducted to secure a village or hamlet (usually after a firefight with the VC). At that time the military and police enter to verify the identities of the people, VC suspects detained, and often some security forces will remain. Advice and support are provided by the team for these military operations.

The second part of our mission is to advise and support the Vietnamese pacification efforts. While the military eliminates the VC influence on a rural hamlet, the Vietnamese government civilians then evaluate what the hamlet needs to improve the lives of its inhabitants. The condition of sanitation and health care, homes, roads, schools, crops, whatever in their lives the Government of Vietnam (GVN) can better is examined to determine what can be done.

It quickly becomes obvious what Colonel Bernard was talking about regarding the morale of the team. The captain in charge of the team is a constant whiner, always complaining. His behavior permeates down through the team. In less than three weeks I fire him and send him back to province. Working with the rest of the team members, we produce a list of what needs to be accomplished to improve our living conditions as well as our safety.

The Enemy

It is said that the day belongs to the South Vietnamese government while the nights belong to the VC. One man knows how to challenge this. John Paul Vann, a very controversial deputy for CORDS for the III Corps Tactical Zone, a retired army lieutenant colonel, now a U.S. State Department employee. His position is like the military equivalent of a brigadier general. He is the undisputed boss of every American advisor, military and civilian, in the corps area. He was a former PSA to Hau Nghia province and before that, when in the army, a combat advisor. His thoughts on the Vietnamese are kind. Yet it is his belief that if they are not pushed, they have less incentive to move. They need guidance and Vann expects his advisors to advise by doing. Therefore, it was up to his advisors to do the pushing. If the VC owns the night, then they must be stopped. And the best way to do this is by conducting night combat operations. To ensure these night ambushes, patrols, or raids were conducted, American advisors would accompany them. Bottom line, Vann's advisors would spend two to three nights a week on nocturnal operations with the Vietnamese. As a major I would find I went on more small unit combat operations than I ever did as a captain.

John Paul Vann is almost a myth. Up to now, I have only known of him by his reputation, of which he has several. But, now in Trang Bang, he does visit us a few times or we attend briefings by him at province headquarters. The rumor is that you can know where he spent the night by the where he kept .30 caliber carbine magazines, taped together, on a table next to a bed. On the other hand, he is known for his fearless manner and the respect he has earned from both civilian and military leaders in this war in Vietnam. Vann is a walking encyclopedia on all things Vietnam. He knows the districts in III Corps, the roads, the villages and the hamlets, and the enemy. Ironically the one thing he does not know is the Vietnamese language. Being tone-deaf, he was unable to become fluent in this tonal language. For example, a word could be spelled one way but pronounced five separate ways, each inflection having a totally different meaning.

His knowledge of the country and its people and their enemy allowed him, contradictory to his military and civilian leaders, by late 1967 to realize that something major, throughout Vietnam, was coming. And it did, in January 1968. Tet. Vann often harbors a different view about the war than his contemporaries. He is an expert in unconventional warfare and insisted that the large-scale warfare promoted by General Westmoreland would never win the war. He passionately believes in the pacification program, convinced that counterinsurgency and counter-guerrilla tactics are the way to go. He fully comprehends that the NVA and VC use political warfare more than conventional warfare. The way to win is to be better than the enemy at waging unconventional warfare. This he preaches and this he expects all his advisors to follow.

Hau Nghia Province

Tony takes time to brief me by describing Hau Nghia province. It borders Gia Dinh province on the southeast (where Saigon is) and Cambodia on the west. The distance from Saigon to Bao Trai is around 20 miles, with the distance to Cambodia another 10 to 15 miles. The province is very irregular in shape and roughly 27 miles north to south and 31 miles across. Through it runs Vietnamese Route 1, the main highway between Saigon and Cambodia's capital, Phnom Penh. The province is mostly flat farmland but forested and jungle-like in the northeast and becoming wetter with more swamp in the southwest extremities as the land approaches the Mekong Delta. In between it is a very verdant, rich, and fertile agriculture area. The land is almost totally covered with vegetation (except for the rice fields), ranging from scattered brush and trees to dense jungles. Beginning in the much higher elevations far inside Cambodia, the Vam Co Dong River (fast flowing and about 200 yards wide) flows through the western side of Trang Bang and through Duc Hue district.

Within the province are three more main roads, province Routes 8, 9, and 10. These are typically main roads between districts, all hard surface, and they utilize several bridges to cross rivers, which are habitually destroyed by the VC and rebuilt. None of the roads are safe and none should be traveled by any lone vehicle.

The province population is almost 183,000 people, mostly Buddhists and rural farmers. The province is new, created in October 1963 as a military expedient to better control the area. It has four districts (Trang Bang, Cu Chi, Duc Hue, and Duc Hoa), with 24 villages and 155 hamlets. When Hau Nghia was created, the VC National Liberation Front (NLF) refused to accept the GVN changes and the VC infrastructure continued under the political-geographical structure of old (in fact in February 1976, the communists would officially obliterate the

Hau Nghia Province

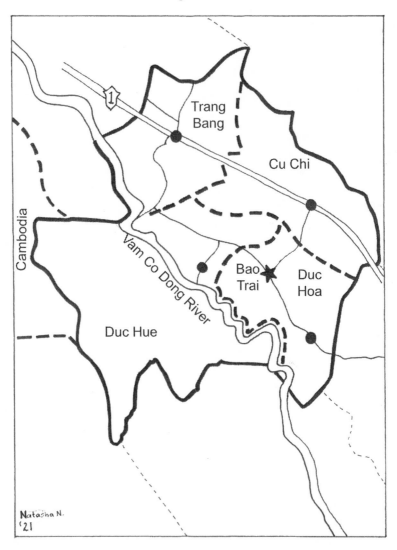

political boundaries in the province, returning it to the way it was before October 1963).

This area for decades has been viewed as the land of "haves" and "have-nots." Prior to World War II the area was part of the French colony and it was a thriving agriculture industry region. Here, a short drive from downtown Saigon, the French controlled the large estates that grew sugarcane, pineapples, and peanuts, while in the north were rubber plantations as well as the large sugar mill in Duc Hue (once the largest sugar mill in Vietnam). Most of these endeavors ceased to function during World War II, and after the war the French and the Viet Minh fought, with looting, violence, and killing becoming a way of life in this area. In 1954 the French departed Vietnam, replaced by the corrupt and disorganized government of South Vietnam.

Through the mid–1960s the GVN was losing the loyalty of the local people. The National Liberation Front, or NLF (the covert civilian communist component from North Vietnam active in South Vietnam) harps on the fact that 44 percent of the people working the land are not owners. Fifty-five percent of the land is owned by only 10 percent of the people. The NLF promises land distribution, pointing out that most of the rural people are toiling only for the benefits of absentee landowners. To emphasize this fact even more, it is pointed out that most of the GVN officials in Hua Nghia are from elite urban areas near Saigon while the NLF leaders are mostly local people, born and raised in Hau Nghia.

The NLF accentuates family and a very conservative lifestyle. When the U.S. 25th Division moved into Cu Chi, the prevalence of alcohol, drugs, prostitution, and sex became more common and another point for the NLF to advocate against. First it was the French who controlled Vietnam and now the decadent Americans are doing the same and even worse, supporting the corrupt Saigon government.

Add to this already virulent mix the truth that Hau Nghia is a hotly contested part of the war. Duc Hue district lies on the Cambodian border, with its northwest corner defining the bottom portion of the area referred to as the Angel's Wing (because of the shape outlined by the border). The middle of Duc Hue's border with Cambodia is the tip of the area called the Parrot's Beak, due to how the border resembles the beak of a parrot. Within eyesight from towers on the Vietnam side are thousands of NVA soldiers and units inside Cambodia, training for their cross-border raids, safe in their Cambodian sanctuaries from any U.S. or South Vietnamese attacks.

The western border of Trang Bang district is established by the Vam Co Dong River, with about three miles of Tay Ninh province separating Trang Bang from Cambodia at the Angel's Wing. This narrow piece of land is a haunt of the Viet Cong and the North Vietnamese Army, essentially no-man's-land. During the hours of darkness, anything moving here is fair game for being bombed or shot. Trang Bang troops often conduct combat operations in this area.

Hau Nghia has become a major infiltration route for weapons and troops to attack Saigon and fight in South Vietnam. This province, during 1968, has become one of the most dangerous areas in the country. By mid–1968, pacification efforts have virtually stopped here due to the heavy fighting against VC and NVA units.

For province security forces (police and military under control of the province and district chiefs) there are 589 National Policemen

Trang Bang District

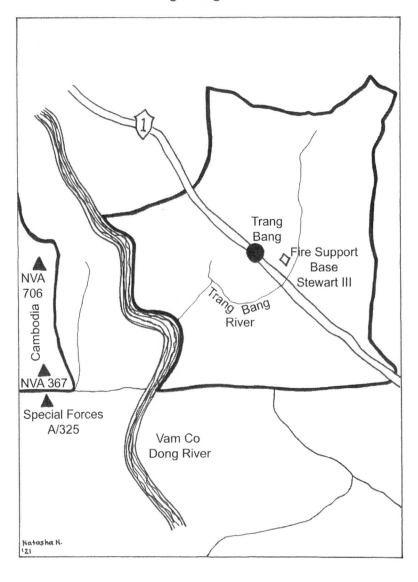

assigned to the province and districts and just under 30 Regional Force companies along with 49 Popular Force platoons. Tony mentions that the RF companies, starting in November, will trade their M-1 rifles and M-1 carbines for the M-16 rifle.

Also within the province are both the U.S. and the ARVN 25th Divisions.

About one-third of the province is west of the Vam Co Dong River and under control of the VC. The province has four districts which are home to 155 hamlets. Of the 183,000 people living in Hau Nghia, 57,600 live in secure hamlets, 71,200 in contested hamlets, with 53,700 people under total VC control. Looking at this another way, only 32 percent of the province population live under GVN safety, and only one-quarter of the hamlets are safe.

Trang Bang District

Within Trang Bang district, which is probably more affluent than its neighbors, live about 28,000 people. The military forces consist of 59 National Police, and about 500 RF and PF soldiers manning outposts. Because the RF units tend to fight where the action is, many are located at the province headquarters, available as a reaction force or for combat operations anywhere within the province. We also have two U.S. 25th Division fire support bases, a 25th mechanized infantry battalion, and elements of an armored cavalry squadron from the U.S. 11th Armored Cavalry.

On the other side we have a hard-core main force VC battalion located south of town, elements of the Viet Cong 83rd Services Group, a major logistical supply unit, and to the southeast, toward Cu Chi is the Viet Cong C3 all-female guerrilla company. Within the district is the Quyet Thang (267th) Viet Cong Regiment and the Viet Cong F100 Special Forces Group. Additionally, at various times we also have different regular NVA units, stationed across the border in Cambodia, either transiting through our district or on combat operations in the district.

This is the situation I have volunteered for, just so I can afford to attend graduate school. Maybe not such a wise choice.

Tony and I work out what each of us will do. He will focus on the civic affairs of the district and I will focus on the military and security side. While together, we would plan what each week would bring, and which members of the team will work with each of us. But the admin control of all the military men assigned to the team will be my responsibility. I will work with Major Ai and his operations staff, the DIOCC and

Phoenix program, and I will advise the RF and PF units in the district, and the members of the two mobile advisory teams in the district will report to me. Additionally, I make the organizing of our quarters a priority along with the enhancement of our safety.

What District Advisors Do

Tony has the civil affairs captain and the 25th civil affairs team work directly with him, as does our Filipino ag advisor. They advise the district civilian officials as well as the village and hamlet chiefs. They work as liaison with the largesse of the U.S. Agency for International Development (USAID), which provides supplies and equipment for village and hamlet repairs to medical clinics, schools, roads, government offices and vehicles. USAID also provides materials to build refugee resettlement housing and rice and other food products as well as cash to pay for local supplies or local hires to work on district projects. This requires quite a bit of work because the U.S. does not provide an open faucet to fund everything and anything.

Every project begins with a budget at the highest U.S. levels in Saigon. These monies are portioned out to various needed areas such as public safety, public administration, public works, education, public health, new life development, self-help projects, refugee support, and revolutionary development.

The supply of funding comes down through the CORDS channels from Saigon to the Corps Tactical Zones to the provinces and finally to the districts. The Vietnamese have to work with the American advisors to get the funding, materials, food, equipment, et cetera. Together the district chief and the DSA begin before the funding year to consider project requests from the hamlets and villages.

Three major considerations can determine who gets what. First is who benefits? How can a project benefit the most people? Second, how secure will the project be? Is the project located in a "safe" area or a "contested" area? Once built or funded, how secure will it remain? Third, does the village or hamlet have the human resources (enough talented, skilled, young, strong people) to ensure the project can be brought to completion. Then costs must be attached to every project, completion dates determined, and the requests passed forward from the district advisor up the chain of CORDS command.

During my first tour in Vietnam as a combat advisor, winning battles and defeating the VC were our priorities. On this tour, though, it seems that reports and record keeping tend to compete with trying to win the war. It appears that every aspect of this war is being reduced to statistics as required by everyone up the chain of command.

This is what the DSA and the PSA do as a big part of their advisory tasks. The projects accepted become funded, workers are obtained, schedules established, and the money and resources passed down to the district. It is not hard to envision how easy it is for Vietnamese officials (and some U.S. advisors) to line their pockets or to use the clout of doling out money or commodities to attain power. Graft, illegal transactions, skimming of funding are common. To many Americans (especially John Paul Vann), corruption is not to be tolerated. This becomes another major concern under CORDS. How much should an advisor tolerate before complaining, and who do they complain to? Often the Vietnamese officials see partaking of a slice of the funding or commodities as simply a way of doing business or receiving compensation for the risk of VC endangerment to their families. This is a constant challenge at one level or another for the American advisors.

And these are just some of the issues and concerns district advisors must attend to. Working with his counterpart, the district chief, must establish costs and then supervise and monitor tens or even hundreds of thousands of dollars in a vast variety of projects.

While creating and managing the advisory efforts within the district, Trang Bang advisors have an additional concern of even greater importance: security. The NVA and VC have most of the territory either under their control or are hotly contesting the GVN regarding who can do what. This is where I come in.

Hau Nghia is the only barrier between the NVA troops in Cambodia and the Saigon-Cholon area. And Trang Bang happens to be the front edge of that barrier. Combat operations are normal, both day and night. Advisors are required by Vann to accompany as many operations as possible. This accomplishes several things. We show we don't advise only from the rear; we share the dangers with our counterparts. American advisors have access to American combat resources such as artillery, close air support, reinforcement U.S. troops, and medical evacuations. Going on operations with our local Vietnamese soldiers also allows us to evaluate their condition and ability and their effectiveness in battle.

Most operations begin with gathered and verified information. The National Police, government Rural Development cadre working in villages and hamlets, intelligence agents, and other GVN officials all provide information to the intelligence officers and NCOs manning the DIOCC and the Phoenix program. As info comes in telling us about VC activity or about new VC leaders, or movements of VC members, it is catalogued, compared to other similar information, analyzed, and verified, then shared with the district military operations people. Our advisors are involved in each step and provide suggestions on what to do. Combat operations are planned, needed resources identified and committed, operation orders prepared and issued, and another mission executed.

Day operations are consistent. Typically, the process begins in the darkness of early morning. The designated troops are moved (by truck or on foot, sometimes by U.S. helicopters) to the vicinity of a small village or hamlet and surround it. The mission is to locate hidden weapons or supplies or capture suspected VC leaders or members which intelligence suggests will be there. Sometimes the VC resist the advancing soldiers and shooting ensues. Other times the troops safely secure the area, and the intel people, police, and government officials take charge of locating or capturing whatever is being sought. Sometimes the enemy has moved, or if the intel is false, nothing happens, and the soldiers return home. Often, an American advisor accompanies the maneuvering unit, and if a firefight begins, the advisor is in as much danger as the Vietnamese.

Daytime combat operations come in one of three flavors. Most common are district-instigated missions, as described above, usually involving RF or PF platoons or less. Generally this is a one-day event, but sometimes the GVN troops remain in place overnight while various district or province officials promote the government using entertainers to capture the attention of the herded-together residents.

At times district assets will participate in province-initiated operations, usually multi-company operations where the target is a VC or NVA unit. Occasionally district and province military units will conduct joint operations with various U.S. units, normally the U.S. 25th Division. This operation may last several days.

The third type of operation is a hastily assembled unconventional warfare raid, created to attack an objective discovered in a narrow window of opportunity. A target is identified, and the forces needed quickly gathered and the mission begun. Often this type of mission is over in a few hours.

Night missions, historically patrols or ambushes, are different. The Vietnamese are not big on night patrols. First, they can be extremely dangerous, and second, they are usually nonproductive. More acceptable, with fewer losses and greater success, are night ambushes. An area known to be habituated by the VC is identified for an ambush. As soon as it is dark, a small unit (a squad or less) moves into position (usually a small stream crossing, an intersection on a lesser used trail, or an entrance trail into a hamlet). Booby traps and claymores are set up.

Hunkered down, the unit waits for any movement as only enemy combatants move during darkness. If motion is detected—either people moving or a booby trap set off—the ambush commences. It is short, noisy, and very violent. The ambushers usually win. Bodies counted and if possible identified, documents and weapons collected, and then the soldiers quit the ambush site and high tail it home.

Most operations—daytime, raids, or night—begin in the Vietnamese DIOCC and tactical operations center. Intelligence indicates that the enemy is or will be at a certain location at some point in time. The district chief, his officers and the American advisors must verify the accuracy of this information and create a way to eliminate the enemy. This procedure goes on 24 hours every day. It never stops and is the nucleus for how we fight in Trang Bang district.

Tony is an impressive and enthusiastic man. With his excellent fluency in Vietnamese and his energizing personality, he is readily accepted by all Vietnamese. He works hard for their benefit, and it shows. Mostly he wears loose sport shirts and slacks. He travels everywhere on his mid-sized Japanese motorcycle, typically solo without any armed guards. But it is not the VC who get to him; it is hepatitis. During my first three weeks in Trang Bang, some days he suffers, bedridden with fever and abdominal pain, progressively worsening. Finally, on 20 September, he is medevaced to a hospital in Saigon for prolonged treatment, never to return. By default, I become DSA.

9

Combat Operations
in Trang Bang

With Tony gone, I inherit the most distasteful aspect of being the district senior advisor: the job of preparing the never-ending stream of reports mandated by CORDS. Reports are required on the safety of every hamlet in the district. Then reports on monies spent, civic action projects initiated, status of ongoing projects, projects completed. Reports on the RF and PF strengths, losses, weapons, combat operations, morale, and the list goes on and on. There are District Intelligence and Operations Coordination Center reports, intel reports, advisor accompanied operations reports. Accounts on everything from what the police activities have been to how the farmers' crops are doing need to be tabulated. Almost everything we advisors do (except what we eat, it seems) must be condensed, analyzed, and reduced to some type of statistical measurement as a means of determining who is winning the war.

As the DSA, I am responsible for overseeing all things from combat operations to rural development to security to civic action projects and compiling reports on each. Typically, each day involves combat operations or monitoring projects or interacting with various district, village, or hamlet officials. Some nights are spent on night patrols or ambushes, or meetings with officials in the district. Because of all these activities and the never-ending requirements for reports, I often find myself bent over a desk at 1 or 2 a.m., filling out forms and writing narratives on what we did or did not accomplish. I was never trained in the administrative aspects of what to do or how to do it. This is the self-trained, do-it-yourself method of learning how to be a DSA. This is killing me, as I am exhausted most of the time.

The days seem to blend. Each night, instead of looking at a list of accomplishments or achievements, we have just too many deficits. Instead of tasks completed it seems like we end our days with a list of new tasks that take priority over what we thought we should be doing.

On the plus side, though, is the remodeling of where we live. As a team, we have generated what needed to be done, and everyone had assigned tasks to complete. We added more bricks to the interior walls. Constructed heavy beams to safely hold sheets of PSP and a couple of layers of sandbags. All of this is to protect us from shrapnel from the occasional evening barrage from enemy mortars. Order and organization are restored to our home and it becomes a better place to live and eat. We divide our building into four bedrooms (all under the sandbagged PSP), the smallest for me, one for the other officers and one for the enlisted men. The kitchen is redone, and the back porch enclosed with screening and half walls to eat in. The morale of the team members improves considerably.

I do learn something different. The roof of our quarters is thin aluminum. Whenever we experienced a mortar attack, shrapnel would pierce the roof, leaving several small gashes in the metal. One day, after an attack, one of the NCOs showed me how to fix it. He took an empty tin coffee can and dropped into it ripped up scraps from Styrofoam cups. He then got another small metal container of gasoline. Telling me to follow him, we both climbed up on our roof. Sitting next to our newest holes, he poured some gas into the metal tin with the pieces of Styrofoam and stirred it with a thin stick.

The bits of Styrofoam immediately turned into a light orange semi-liquid, which the sergeant quickly poured over the holes. As soon as the gummy fluid flowed into the holes, it began to congeal, forming a solid closed seal over the them. It solidified so quickly it did not drip completely through the rupture, just enough to become a plug-like patch, creating a watertight cap over the shrapnel damage. When it rained, we kept dry.

As DSA, if I am not accompanying a combat operation, I spend time in the Vietnamese tactical operations center to monitor its progress and be available to provide American assistance if needed, via medevacs or initiate artillery or gunship fire support. This task also allows me to envision how the war is being waged from a higher level. I quickly realize that too often the missions of the U.S. 25th Division clash with those of the Vietnamese. The 25th is mostly engaged in Trang Bang with combat operations in areas which conflict with Vietnamese rural development projects.

While the Vietnamese are attempting to provide security and aid to rural hamlets, often the VC will sneak into an area of huts, alongside main roads where farmers and their families live. From this cover, the VC attack American convoys with machine guns and rockets, then very quickly withdraw. In retaliation, the Americans attack where the fire came from, destroying homes, with the local civilians often becoming casualties. My disgust with the leadership at the higher levels of the army does not fade in Vietnam. As an advisor my job is to improve the lives of the Vietnamese I work with. On the other hand, too often the 25th destroys all the Vietnamese have accomplished. Sometimes it seemed that the best friends of the VC are American soldiers.

Arc Light Missions

One night, shortly after I arrive, actually early in the morning, around dawn, I am awakened by soft, but loud, explosions. But what gets to me is the shock or concussion waves of such force that they lift the heavy PSP planks, layered with sandbags, several inches off the heavy wooded timber framework that supports our ceiling.

Oh my god, I think, are we under attack? Apparently, others were woken by the noise and the movement of the PSP. Someone explains to me, this is just the aftershocks of the B-52 strikes. Confused, I ask what is going on. Are we being attacked by our own air force? The carpet-bombing strategy, called Operation Arc Light, is then explained to me.

USAF B-52s stationed at Andersen Air Force Base on Guam depart in the middle of the night to conduct bombing missions over South Vietnam. The flight to Vietnam takes about 6 hours with in-flight refueling just west of the Philippines. The strategy is to drop the bombs around dawn. The flight usually consists of three planes. The bombs are dropped into target areas of a box about 1,000 feet by 3,000 feet. Each plane can carry between 27 and 84 bombs, depending on the mixture of 500- and 750-pound bombs. Some bombs are airbursts, some are high-explosive ground explosives, and others time delay to penetrate the surface and explode underground to destroy enemy bunkers and tunnels. The underground bursts can penetrate down 10 to 20 feet. The target areas are between us and the Cambodian border. The minimum safe distance between target areas and friendly forces is 3,300 yards or about 1.9 miles. In times of need the strikes can be closer, but that never happened while I was in Trang Bang.

I never witnessed any B-52 strikes, but I have been on operations just a few hours after a strike. The burst causes a crater about 20 to 25 feet across and about 3–4 feet deep. In our area, these craters typically fill with groundwater in a few hours. On operations where there are older craters, they resemble natural ponds or water holes. The nitrogen-rich soil surrounding the crater encourages the growth of vegetation, adding to the natural look of a pond.

The effectiveness of the B-52 strikes has been documented as worthwhile. In our area it is used to hit known enemy locations or staging areas or well-used trails from Cambodia into South Vietnam. One day on a combat operation we find two young NVA privates, both in their late teens. I spend some time talking to them (in Vietnamese, of course).

They were drafted in North Vietnam, trained, and then sent down the Ho Chi Minh Trail into Cambodia. These two never reached the terminus of their journey. Instead they came under attack by the B-52s near Trang Bang. The B-52s fly so high they can't be seen or heard, so there is no warning of a strike, until the explosions. The explosions wiped out most of their unit; these two boys are shell-shocked, dazed, famished, and totally scared. They were so terrified of the bombs that they ran away, and we find them wandering around, scared and confused. They surrender peacefully, only wanting to get away from any more airstrikes. This convinces me of the value of the B-52 Arc Light missions.

We should be focusing on rural development of the hamlets and villages, but our daily emphasis seems to be concentrated on combat operations. After all, it doesn't make sense to spend the day repairing roads or bridges in a hamlet if the VC can destroy them during the night. Yes, we can identify, locate, and eliminate various aspects of the local VC infrastructure in a remote hamlet. Then, the men we have taken down are only replaced by more men, often from the safe havens right across the border in Cambodia. It seems like for every step forward we make we are pushed back two steps. It is very frustrating.

Meeting a U.S. General

My days are split between leading my small advisor team, accompanying combat operations, promoting hamlet and village development efforts, and trying to work with and keep peace with the American 25th Division. Each week I probably personally go on a couple of combat operations and occasionally a night ambush mission. Infrequently some days are spent in the Vietnamese TOC. Because of my fluency in Vietnamese I handle requests from district RF or PF forces in contact which need U.S. support. I easily work on both the Vietnamese and the U.S. military radio nets, coordinating various military combat operations.

On the Vietnamese net I receive the request for help. Moving to the U.S. net, I try to obtain the required support such as artillery fire or medevacs and occasionally additional U.S. troops to successfully complete the mission.

One such day, shortly after I become the DSA, I am working two Vietnamese combat missions simultaneously. The Vietnamese TOC is in a building which has a doorway, down a short hall, out through the wall of our district compound. While we have guards at the doorway into the TOC, a vehicle can pull up to the wall and door, and in a few steps, move down the hall and be inside the TOC.

As is typical, I am in a green T-shirt with no rank apparent, as the TOC is hot with no air-conditioning. Working the radios, fully focused on getting help, I am arranging for a medevac for one op and artillery support for the other.

A hand taps me on the shoulder. Turning, I see an American with the bronze leaf of a major and crossed rifles of an infantry officer from the 25th Division standing next to me. He asks for the senior advisor. I raise one finger as the American net begins to provide me with the coordination information (radio frequencies, call signs, estimated arrival time of the medevac helicopter). I quickly write down the details as the major begins to grow impatient. He demands to know who I am, and I reply with my rank and name but explain I can't talk now as I am working a medevac. I move back to the Vietnamese net to relay the info to the commander. The major stalks out of the room and I immediately forget about him. I am about to help save the life of a district soldier.

Next an American full colonel enters the TOC, demanding my attention. The room becomes quiet as the colonel steps in front of me and tells me to stand at attention. Then the U.S. radio announces that my request for fire support has been authorized and who I need to contact to initiate a fire mission. It becomes apparent that an immediate reply is needed. Ignoring the colonel (who obviously is not used to being ignored by a major), I reply, writing down the fire mission coordination details. I continue to work both radio nets as the colonel fumes. Then a Vietnamese NCO grabs my arm, pointing to the door. I see a helmeted head swing into view, instantly recognizing the single star on the helmet. I then realize the head must belong to one of the two 25th Division assistant commanders.

He very quickly sizes up what is going on, the single American advisor, fluent in two languages, coordinating a medevac and supporting artillery, does not have time to talk to anyone, even a general. The general acknowledges the urgency of the missions, apologizes for the intrusion, and informs his colonel that he will return at a more opportune time. As quickly as they appeared, they depart. I never see the general or the colonel again.

My First District Unconventional Warfare Raid

The Vietnamese TOC is the heart of everything that happens in Trang Bang. It is a large room, with no windows, walls lined with maps and banks of radios. It is the seat of Major Ai's power and staffed with both Vietnamese officers and NCOs as well as various American advisors.

One morning Major Ai calls me into the TOC. Inside with him are two 25th Division MPs, an American NCO and Ai's police commander and a couple of his intel NCOs. The American NCO explains that at a Vietnamese and U.S. security checkpoint, two young Vietnamese women tried to get by with phony IDs. The Vietnamese at the checkpoint spoke to the two girls, confirming where they lived. It was a small VC infested hamlet, just beyond the perimeter of a 25th Division unit. But more important is that the hamlet had been identified as the home of a VC mortar, used to attack the U.S. unit at night. The Vietnamese at the checkpoint convinced the Americans to turn the girls over to the district chief, which they are now doing. Major Ai has accepted the girls and invites me to sit in on their interrogation. The Americans leave and we move into another room with a table and a few chairs. The two girls, about 17 years old, are very frightened and worried. Major Ai takes over. He introduces himself to the girls, explaining who else is in the room. He asks a few questions, at the same time trying to convince the girls they have done nothing wrong and they will be taken back home.

Ai's tone and posture invite compassion. He is not threatening but trying to reassure them he will not harm them. Next one of the intel NCOs begins to talk. His soothing, fatherly voice soon has the girls freely talking about their hamlet. Yes, the hamlet is home of the VC mortar. The VC, after midnight, would set up the mortar, and quickly fire a few rounds into the nearby U.S. unit. Before counter-mortar detection could locate the mortar, it was disassembled and hidden. The girls explain that the local VC have a deep hole in the hamlet, in the middle of intersecting paths, where the mortar is buried. Being in the middle of an oft-used footpath, the covering dirt was constantly pounded and twisted by the feet of all the hamlet residents, hiding its location.

Leaving the girls in the room with guards, the major moves the small group back into the TOC. He plots the location of the girls' hamlet and the 25th Division unit. The hamlet is less than a mile from the unit, with there being some jungle growth and some clear rice fields between them. The hamlet is surrounded by a thick hedgerow of thorns and vines. The Vietnamese begin to discuss the veracity of the girls' story and the possibility of finding the mortar. We agree the girls are telling the truth and we could use them as guides to locate the buried mortar. We need to quickly assemble a force to secure the area and dig up the mortar.

Major Ai and I deduce that since we have the girls as guides, we can locate the mortar, but we need help getting into the hamlet. Because the mortar is being used to shoot Americans, the 25th Division has a reason to support our mission.

Ai and I create a small Vietnamese combat force of two National Police officers and one district intelligence NCO. If I could get a small American security squad, we could use helicopters to fly over the village and the girls could show us where the mortar is buried. We could land in a clearing just outside the hamlet, quickly move in, secure the intersection, uncover the mortar, and leave. It was a perfect operation, a speedy raid, in and out, but it had to be done now. I contact the operations officer of the brigade to which the division unit on the ground belong. Brigade agrees and says it will provide two Hueys and some Rangers for security. They will land at our district helipad in 30 minutes. Major Ai goes to assemble his team while I go to put on my combat gear. The two girls agree to return by helicopter and point out, in the air, where the mortar is buried.

The two helicopters arrive, and one has five Army Rangers. We place the National Police on the helicopter with the Rangers while the two girls, the intel NCO, Major Ai and I board the other. I describe to the pilot in the right seat what the operation is, where the village is, and where he can land. I explain how we needed to first hover over the hamlet so the girls could tell us where the mortar is buried. All is good and off we go.

It isn't long before we are over the girls' hamlet. One of the intel NCOs is talking to the girls, asking questions, pointing down, then telling me where the pilot should circle. The NCO becomes aggravated and much more animated with the girls. With open doors, the wind, and the noise of the helicopter I am unable to hear what they are saying but I begin to get a feeling this op is going sideways. The NCO leans into my ear and explains the girls are totally confused; they do not recognize anything from the air.

I think about that. Why? Then I realize that the girls' view of the world is most likely limited from the ground to about five feet above it. What they identify with is what is in front of them, their people, doorways, windows, fences, furniture. They have never seen the world from 1,000 feet so what they see is unfamiliar to them. The visual impact from above means nothing to them, they cannot comprehend what they see below.

Well, we knew we would have to land to dig up the mortar; now, we will just have to walk around the hamlet until the girls can recognize its burial location. Discussing this with the pilot, we look for the clearing, in the open, between the hamlet and the 25th unit, where the two helicopters can sit for a brief time while we locate and dig up the mortar. The pilots quickly land to wait. Taking the girls, the Rangers, the policemen, the intel NCOs (with a couple of short-handled shovels), Major Ai and I cautiously move into the hamlet.

I guess when the helicopters landed the local folks took off as we entered the hamlet; we see no one. The girls acknowledge where we are and move down a path between grass-covered huts toward the center of the hamlet. For some reason it is bisected by a massive thorny, thick, impenetrable hedgerow, right through the center of the hamlet. The hamlet seems to be divided in half and there is no passage through this shrubbery; one has to move around it. The girls agree that at a junction of two paths, this side of the hedgerow, is where the mortar is buried. More conversations with the girls convince us they are telling the truth, so the digging begins.

The Rangers take up defensive positions around us, covering the footpaths leading in and out of the hamlet and around the hedgerow. As the hole becomes deeper, we hear movement and voices on the other side of the hedgerow. The voices knew a couple of helicopters landed in the clearing but did not know who were in them. We are not sure who the voices belong to but assume they are the hamlet VC who own the mortar.

The voices discuss what they should do. The deciding voices argue for getting weapons and moving around the hedgerow to confront us. Neither side knows how many are on the opposite side. It now seems like this op is no longer slipping sideways but now tipping totally upside down. I explain to the Rangers what is happening on the other side of the hedgerow. Digging faster, the NCOs are going deeper. One of the Rangers has a PRC-25 radio for communicating with the helicopters. The AN/PRC-25 is a 920 channel FM tactical radio, weighing just under 20 pounds. With the standard field antenna, it has a range of three to seven miles. The squad leader motions to me, shaking the radio handset.

Grabbing the handset, I answer to hear the senior aircraft commander with the helicopters say they are leaving. I can't believe this. He replies his commander radioed them for a priority mission and they are leaving. As we talk, I can hear the engines start up. I plead with them to stay, to no avail. Our little op has a very low priority and they are needed to support a 25th Division unit in contact. The pilot explains that the

Rangers know how to get back to the 25th unit less than a mile away. The pilot signs off and as I look toward the engine noise in the clearing, I can see our two helicopters rise and leave us in the VC village. I explain what is happening to Major Ai and the intel NCO.

By this point in time, the voices on the other side have decided to arm themselves and engage us. The digging has stopped, and the Vietnamese acknowledge two things. This was a fresh hole, large enough to bury a mortar, but it is empty; the mortar is not there.

Knowing that in less than a minute or two, an unknown number of armed VC will be coming at us from around the hedgerow. We decide to pack it up and move out. The Ranger squad leader knows how to move to the perimeter of the nearby American unit, so we tell the girls goodbye and exit the hamlet across the clearing where our steeds left us.

I pull out my map, we cross the open area and enter an expanse of heavy growth of trees, on the far side of the clearing. The squad leader and I decide where we are and where the American unit is. About a quarter a mile through this jungle and we arrive at another vast clear area, in front of the American unit.

We doubt if the VC will follow us across the clearing, since they have no idea of the size of our force. We can stay in the jungle-like area between the VC hamlet and the American unit, but somehow, we must contact them so they will not shoot us down crossing the clearing in front of them. The Rangers do not know who they are, so we have no radio call signs or frequencies. I do not know who they are so I can't contact them. Then one of the Rangers points toward the hamlet.

The VC now have more men than we do, and they have decided to move around the clearing and flank us. This op went from slipping sideways to flipping over to now possibly a total disaster. I talk to the intel NCO and explain we need to contact a nearby RF or PF unit which can contact the 25th Division. We must get into the jungle growth but can't exit into the clearing in front of the American unit, so we have to remain hidden in this growth of trees and heavy vegetation. We move into the center of the jungle and the intel sergeant begins using the PRC-25 radio to try and contact a Vietnamese radio.

Eventually the sergeant has a frequency for the 25th Division, which I call. I describe where we are, providing map coordinates requesting the American unit be notified and how to contact me so we can pass through their lines. I convey the urgency of this request, explaining that we are being stalked by a VC unit, bigger than us.

I have a couple Rangers just back inside of the jungle area we are in, watching the approaching VC. While about a hundred yards away, the VC seem reluctant to enter the jungle area in which we are hiding.

Quickly I receive a call from the American unit we hoped to contact and enter safely. Passwords are exchanged and the entry point identified as we move out of the heavy growth into the clearing in front of the American unit I was talking to.

Despite everything that went wrong with this operation, we get through without firing a shot. But no mortar. We decide that when the American MPs took the two young girls away, the hamlet VC dug up the mortar and moved it. Because we had entered the hamlet and knew where to dig, the VC must have felt unsafe firing the mortar from that hamlet any more as the Americans reported no more mortar attacks after our misguided op.

This was a typical operation. Information comes into the district intelligence staff, be it about a VC meeting, weapons, enemy troop movements, or an operation, and the district creates a mission to eliminate the threat.

Most operations begin before daylight, sometimes using a platoon of PF or as large as an RF company. Moving into position to surround a hamlet, we secure the area to seek out the VC. Quite often, when the hamlet is surrounded, moving into it to secure the area leads to gunfights as the VC are reluctant to just give up or go away.

These operations are dirty and dangerous. Most hamlets are located inside thickets of growth for security, weather protection, and being slightly higher than the surrounding rice fields, which are often in water. Daily rituals of the local inhabitants involve waking and moving out of their huts to the berms between the hamlet and the fields. Here is where the residents do their morning business (urinate and defecate) on the outer edges of the berms. The soldiers (and their advisors) cross these fields before daylight, and hunker down on the outside of these berms, before the hamlet wakes up. As I said, this is a very dirty business. If shooting ensues, the soldiers (and their advisors) hunker down into the ground as low and close as possible, so hands, arms, knees, and faces are mushed into the berm and also whatever may lie on top of the ground.

I have been in Trang Bang about a month when I note I am losing weight. I go to the 25th Division Medical Battalion to get looked at. The physician asks how long I have been in-country and I reply a month. He says that my body isn't used to the restricted diet we advisors follow. I explain that this is not my first tour as a combat advisor, and I believe losing 15 pounds in less than four weeks is excessive. He proclaims I am healthy and soon the weight loss will cease. He thinks I have a stomach virus, so pills are prescribed. I am not convinced but he insists that nothing is wrong.

Rome Plow Operations

One of the major reasons Hau Nghia province was created was to manage military activities on Vietnamese Route 1, the main, all-weather surfaced road between Saigon and the capital of Cambodia. This highway runs through Cu Chi and Trang Bang into Tay Ninh province. While of essential commercial and strategic value to Vietnam, it is full of ruts, potholes, suffering from neglected maintenance and subjected to ever increasing civilian and military traffic. In rural areas it is also prime for command detonated mines and explosives used to destroy and disrupt military convoys. The onus of security and protection for this highway falls on its primary user, the 25th U.S. Division, as this road is its main supply route. Every day, 25th Engineer units sweep the road between Cu Chi and Tay Ninh to clear it of mines and explosive devices. To assist in keeping the road safe, the 25th determined that a swath of nothing but bare ground on each side of the road would go a long way in eliminating any cover for the enemy to hide or use to sneak up on the road to mine it. And the easiest way to clear the jungle on the sides is to employ Rome Plows.

The Rome Plow is one of the most unique tools of war. Named after the company where it is made in Rome, Georgia, it is a massive blade, typically mounted on a Caterpillar D7E bulldozer. Weighing 4,600 pounds it is about 5 feet tall and around 12 feet wide. The blade is straight across the front, but curved top to bottom. The D-7 "Cat" has a special protective cab for the operator. In use, the knife-sharp blade glides about six inches above ground, capable of cutting down trees up to three feet thick. An expert dozer operator can cut through trees six feet in diameter by ramming the tree, over and over, with the sharp blade and by maneuvering the blade crossways, like a saw.

These Rome Plows came to Vietnam in 1967 to clear jungle growth beside roads and to clear enemy positions and tunnels in areas of very heavy foliage. They became so effective that the engineers created land-clearing companies with 30 plows used primarily in the flatter geographic areas of South Vietnam. Hau Nghia province was premier Rome Plow country. The 25th Division used these plows to maintain a clear zone reaching out about 100 yards on either side of Route 1.

In the early days of the 25th using Route 1 as their main supply route, the armor cavalry units would run the road to secure the area. When the convoys followed on the highway, they were protected by the armored cavalry armored personnel carriers and M-48 tanks. Heavy brush and sides of the jungle lay all along the highway, concealing VC ambushes which would attack the 25th, and by the time a reaction force responded, the VC would vanish into the jungle. Eventually much of the jungle growth alongside the road was demolished in areas where no people lived.

Rural Pacification, Rural Development

During my time of direct participation in working as an advisor with the Vietnamese, one thing I noted was how many programs were created by people who were not directly involved in what they wanted accomplished. One big example was how to deal with rural people who were victims of VC cruelty.

In 1962 a "new" program called the Strategic Hamlet Program was created. The idea was to take farmers and their families from contested hamlets and relocate them into new, safer locations. This created more problems. First, the rural folks did not want to leave their ancestral homes yet were forced to move. Second was the fact that even though moved to a different (more secure?) place, the GVN did not have enough troops to provide adequate security for the residents. The failed program terminated in 1964, only to be replaced by another brainstorm of someone far removed from where the problem existed. Thus, the New Life Hamlet Program was developed.

This new concept was not to relocate the farmers but to recruit a cadre of local men for security, arm them and train them. The plan was to allow the farmers to remain in their family homes but to provide sufficient security to protect them. This program also failed as the inadequate training and lack of weapons did not provide the safe refuge the program envisioned.

When CORDS was created in 1967 the "next" method of protecting rural people was now part of the overall Rural Development Program. This time relocation of rural peasants was re-initiated but now they were to be relocated in areas already deemed as safe. "Safe" areas were closer to populated areas or along protected lines of transportation. Unfortunately, this program was created at the top levels of both Vietnamese and American leadership but left to be implemented at the district levels.

This meant that district chiefs (and their advisors) had pretty much free rein of what to do and how to do it. Therefore, this program had built-in problems even before it began. From the top on down, there was no single plan, no organization, and no communication on how to integrate the program at all levels.

This was visibly present when the Trang Bang district decided that creating new hamlets was best done alongside the U.S. 25th Division main supply route. Was the 25th involved in this plan? I doubt it. Thus, again, what senior leaders do, or do not do, creates more problems. As a participant in this boondoggle, I am frustrated, angry, and disheartened because of the divergence between the pacification missions of the Vietnamese and the combat missions of the 25th.

From late summer of 1968 into the fall, the increase in combat operations removes Vietnamese resources and workers involved in pacification and rural development to focus on security. In Trang Bang, instead of devoting limited resources attempting to protect and rehab rural hamlets, it was decided to relocate rural people to resettle in safer areas, already under a degree of GVN security. People have been moved out of unsecure rural areas into newly created, but safer, hamlets built alongside Route 1. With constant commercial and military traffic on this major road, daytime is mostly secure, so it is a good place to relocate farmers and the degree of security aside the road encourages farmers to plant and raise crops.

We have within Trang Bang a couple of successful pacification hamlets; one on Route 1 just west of the town of Trang Bang and another area, mostly Catholic, northwest of Trang Bang. Our most unsuccessful pacification efforts are found east of Trang Bang, along Route 1 between the town of Trang Bang and Cu Chi. This is primarily due to the conflicts between the 25th Division need for security on their main supply route and the proliferation of Vietnamese moving into hamlets along the highway.

The VC begin to sneak into these refugee hamlets at night, holding the elders and hamlet officials hostage, threatening to kill their families if they try anything to stop the VC from mining the highway in front of the hamlet.

Command detonated mines, accompanied with automatic weapons' fire from concealed locations in the hamlet would maim the 25th convoys. The 25th would be reluctant to open fire and destroy the hamlets but being forced to react, a group of huts would be destroyed. The 25th is now very angry about the attacks while the Vietnamese are grieving over destroyed homes and the death of innocent people.

Finally, the 25th said enough is enough and they got the Engineers to use Land Clearing units with their Rome Plows to ravish the earth and clear a wide 100-yard bare area beside the road, destroying the hamlets and thus denying any roadside concealment to the VC. This then, essentially negates the GVN rural pacification efforts. My job is to try and convince the 25th that indiscriminate use of the Rome Plow creates real problems for the Vietnamese.

The 25th has three U.S. Army generals and dozens of colonels and lieutenant colonels who all outrank the Trang Bang DSA, who happens to be a U.S. Army major. The expected outcome is that when the generals or colonels bark, the advisor major jumps, only asking, "how high?" The problem facing the 25th senior officers is that this army major believes his loyalty belongs to the Vietnamese he is advising, not the 25th. Second, this major is no longer a career officer but one who is leaving active duty in less than a year. Therefore, any threat to destroy this major's career becomes meaningless. Third, I entered Vietnam for a second time with a large chip on my soldier regarding senior army leaders. And this attitude most likely influences what I do.

The Vietnamese are very reluctant to remove the resettled refugees (primarily because there is no other place to put them, nor do they have the resources to relocate) so the continued destruction of roadside hamlets by the Rome Plows slows down until CORDS can decide what to do. During this time, though, the relationship between me and the 25th continues to erode.

It is a mess of gigantic proportions. Both sides are right, but everyone loses (except the VC). The 25th wants all refugee hamlets moved away from Route 1. The province and district chiefs claim they do not have anyplace to relocate the refugees. They have no personnel, money, resources or means to move the families. Besides, this is where their livelihood is; their crops and livestock are located adjacent to their homes. If they are moved, how will they live? The Vietnamese come back to the 25th with promises of increased security in the roadside hamlets. They suggest the 25th also help with allowing combat squads to also live in the hamlets with the local PF soldiers.

The 25th counters that hamlet security is not a part of their mission. It is to seek out and destroy the enemy. The division does not have spare soldiers for hamlet security. As the DSA I am visited by various division lieutenant colonels and full colonels to get me on board and convince the Vietnamese to move everyone away from Route 1. Implied threats are used to convince me that not agreeing with what the 25th wants is not a wise career move.

They do not sign my officers efficiency report, so I side with the Vietnamese and explain to the division that it is impossible to move the families living along the road, wholesale, into other secure places that don't exist. An unhealthy situation exists. One neither side is happy with, a condition that only leads to more trouble and the loss of more innocent people.

And herein lies my major conflict with the 25th Division.

The Fighting Intensifies

In August, the NVA and VC begin to conduct their heaviest attacks from Cambodia to Saigon since the January Tet. On 22 August, a major rocket attack against Saigon results in 18 killed and 59 wounded. Three weeks later over 1,500 NVA and VC troops pour out of Cambodia and assault the town of Tay Ninh. The influx of combat units from Cambodia in the fall overwhelms the RF and PF units in Hau Nghia. As the fighting intensifies, the border districts are hard-pressed to stop the enemy from entering Vietnam. As the NVA troop buildup increases so do combat operations with the U.S. 25th Division.

In the U.S. thousands of college students across the country demonstrate and protest the Americans in Vietnam. The presidential race is plagued with problems. Current president Johnson refuses to run. Democratic front-runner Robert Kennedy is assassinated, and the Republican candidate, Richard Nixon, is running on a Vietnam campaign of "peace with honor."

The war is not going well; more American troops are needed so the army and the Marine Corps announce that some 2400 men will be sent to Vietnam for involuntary second tours. The American solution to win this war is more money, more soldiers, more weapons, and more large-scale battles. U.S. and North Vietnamese peace talks in Paris continue.

Against this background of trouble, indecision, and disagreement on how to fight this war, more and more NVA combat soldiers cross the Cambodian border to fight in Hau Nghia. As more U.S. 25th units engage in combat, the demand for combat supplies increases. As more convoys laden with needed food, weapons, fuel, ammunition, and medical supplies move along Route 1 to support the fighting, the enemy escalates the employment of mines and explosives on the MSR.

The fighting continues as does my weight loss. I believe that the constant demand of fighting and rural pacification and the sleepless nights drafting reports are the cause of my weight loss. Our Filipino agriculture advisor has a close friend who is a medical doctor serving as an advisor to a province hospital. The ag advisor says his friend has much more experience dealing with health issues in Asia than the 25th doctors. So, one day we both go to Bao Trai to see his friend. After a thorough exam, the doctor admits he is puzzled. The doc says I am overall in good physical condition but my symptoms of weight loss, rapid pulse, swelling of the lower joints, and fatigue are all signs of a heart disorder, but my age and condition suggest it is not a heart problem.

He explains he doesn't have access to run the usual lab tests so suggests I return to the 25th and ask for more blood tests, especially to examine me being anemic. He says something isn't right, and it definitely is not my diet. I note I will do just that and get back to the 25th medics.

By late September, my weight is down by 20 pounds. I again visit a medical clinic at the 25th Division. Again, the doctor finds nothing wrong with me. Blood tests are not necessary, he maintains. He is convinced my recent return to Vietnam as an advisor, my diet and the demands of the job are the reasons I am losing weight. He also insists that everyone who is assigned to Vietnam loses weight upon arrival, so I am no different. I am not sure I agree with him, but who am I to assert he is wrong.

Command Responsibility

As the commander of our small army advisory group, discipline is one of my responsibilities. We have a sergeant first class, a veteran of the Korean conflict who was awarded the Silver Star for valor in combat in Korea. One of his jobs is to liaise with the U.S. 25th Division engineers' early morning security sweeps of Route 1.

During his work with the engineer units he has been subjected to command detonated bombs alongside the road and the occasional ambushes of the engineers. The bombing and ambushes are a constant happening, and usually some 25th Division men are hurt or killed. Eventually this became a problem for our sergeant.

At night he stayed by himself, and as time passed, he interacted less and less with the other advisors. We discovered he was drinking himself into a stupor every night. The noncommissioned officer in charge talked to him and I talked to him. He said the only way he could escape the fear he felt every day was to drink into oblivion every night. Unfortunately, this behavior is a liability for our team.

A drunk soldier is incapable of fighting during an attack. Additionally, his intoxication requires another soldier to then care for him, lessening our defending force by two men. I discuss this with Colonel Bernard and tell him I need to get rid of this sergeant. The colonel agrees that it is a bad situation but advises me if I send the sergeant to the province advisor headquarters, we will not get a replacement. I discuss this with our NCOIC and we both agree that being without him and without a replacement would still be better than having an inebriated advisor to deal with during an attack. The sergeant is transferred out of our team. No one replaces him.

While I do not believe I was conscientiously aware of it, my letters home to Anita appear to say the same thing, repeatedly. Oh, they do include specific details on where I live, who my team members are, the long hours, and the demanding work in the civic affairs area. But I purposely neglect to mention anything about the combat missions and the dangers of just being in Trang Bang. While I want to spare her of bad thoughts for my safety, my behavior seems to follow what happened before at Benning. I am again not sharing all with Anita, and she senses this by the identical theme of all my letters. My letters to my parents do cover more details of what I am doing and the associated dangers. I ask them not to share with Anita what I write them. Down the road, my being truthful with others, yet excluding Anita, returns to bite me in the butt, big-time.

Helicopter Warfare

One day we have a joint U.S. and Vietnamese combat operation. The 25th Division is in contact and needs additional forces for blocking. Province is working with the 25th so a PF platoon from Trang Bang is

Bob, a 25th Division officer, and Major Ai.

selected to accompany a rifle company from the 25th. We are to be airlifted into a small LZ (landing zone) and set up blocking positions. The 25th company will be choppered in first, then the PF platoon. I am to fly into the LZ with the 25th but remain on the helicopter. I will then brief the PF commander on the landing and where to set up.

After depositing the American troops, the assault helicopters rise to get the PF troops. As my helicopter turns back toward Trang Bang, the 25th company commander, on the ground, calls the aircraft commander of the helicopter I am in. He explains he is drawing quite a bit of machine gun fire but can't see where the gun is. He asks the pilot if he can fly low, over the LZ, and spot the machine gun. The pilot says roger and does just that. He banks the chopper around and at ten feet above the ground, flies swiftly across the small LZ. I cannot believe what is happening. Before he exits the LZ clearing, the helicopter shutters as over a dozen bullets punch holes in the aluminum side of the aircraft. The ground commander radios he sees the muzzle flashes as the pilot confirms the machine gun location.

I question my sanity for wanting to fly in Vietnam. But we return to Trang Bang, I brief the PF commander and I again ride into the LZ to drop off the PF troops.

On Saturday, 19 October, we receive a surprise. I am assigned another infantry captain to serve as the assistant district advisor. Wonders never cease.

Back in our compound another evening, a Vietnamese runner comes to me, asking me to meet Major Ai, which I do. The intel people have information on a VC infiltration in a hamlet early the next morning, would I like to go on the operation? I say yes.

An RF platoon leader oversees the operation. Before dawn, we depart the compound in a few trucks, drive within a mile of the hamlet and dismount. The platoon surrounds the hamlet and a firefight ensues. My role is to avoid getting shot (which is usually done by lying flat on the outside edge of a berm separating the hamlet from their rice fields) and providing advice to the unit commander on everything from fire and maneuver to asking for help from U.S. assets. After fighting the resisting VC, part of the unit establishes a perimeter defense while the command group (the RF lieutenant, some intel NCOs and a couple National Policemen and myself) go to the hut where the VC is, capture him and recover a couple weapons. No friendly troops are injured.

Another typical small combat operation.

10

Overnight Operations in Trang Bang

A common operation employed by the province and district officials is one designed to demonstrate to the rural hamlet residents how much the government cares for its people. It involves RF or PF troops surrounding the hamlet and then district or province officials moving into the hamlet. What happens next almost resembles what we Americans might view as a county fair. National police and intelligence soldiers begin to check the IDs of all people in the hamlet. A medical clinic may be set up, district social service representatives provide clothing or food as other district political agents create a small stage, set up generators, assemble sound systems, and erect lights for the evening entertainment. Because of the education level of the rural population, the GVN has published comic books (without words) extolling how much the government does for its people.

This type of operation is a two-day affair with the soldiers and district officials remaining overnight. Because this is typically done in contested hamlets, staying the night presents its own dangers. An operation like this may require twice as many soldiers as one being completed during daylight hours. In addition to the extra RF or PF soldiers, if the district or province chief is present, then their bodyguards and personal security forces are also present.

Often the chiefs do not accompany the initial movements surrounding the hamlet and securing it. After the hamlet is determined "secure" the chiefs arrive via vehicles (in armed convoys) or sometimes by helicopter. The plan is to show the local farmers that the top leaders are not afraid of the VC, and this is reinforced by the chiefs staying all night.

During the evening entertainment the province and/or the district chief would address the audience. Often, he would be joined by the village chief and, of course, the hamlet chief. The province chief is akin to the governor of an American state while the district chief is like the elected head of an American county. The village and hamlet chiefs are like one of our mayors. Province and district chiefs are appointed by GVN, and the lessor chiefs may be appointed or the only person willing to serve or the person who posses the most power or influence among the residents.

The evening program involves professional musicians, singers, actors, and other show people who perform late into the night providing entertainment that readily retains the attention and amusement of the residents. I also enjoy this county fair operation and especially the evening's production. The singers and actors are incredibly good. Their songs reflect current Vietnamese popular tunes as well as old folk songs and ballads. The actors (and actresses) do skits reflecting old fables or modern soap operas. At times magicians or comedians carry out their brand of entertainment. The rural folks normally go to bed early as they arise early. Yet I am astounded because I have attended some of these events where the shows continue way beyond midnight, and throughout, they enthrall their audience and no one, it seems, wants to leave.

One day we initiate a district county fair operation in which the province chief, Lieutenant Colonel Ma Sanh Nhon, will be staying with us, overnight. The selected hamlet has been hotly contested by the VC. It is another collection of rural families where the GVN controls the day while the VC rules the nights. Often, after the county fair terminates, district soldiers remain in the hamlet to attempt to extend GVN control through the nights.

The primary purpose of this exercise is to show the hamlet residents that GVN supports the people, can fight the VC and protect them. When the district or province chief spends the night in the hamlet, this goes a long way convincing the locals that their leaders do care about them.

This county fair goes as expected. I accompany the RF leader from the beginning. The troops surround the hamlet, and after a brisk firefight, secure the hamlet. The district officials do their work in setting up the medical clinic and putting the stage together. The day progresses without trouble and as darkness envelops the hamlet its residents mass together to enjoy the evening's show. Because of how the entertainment works, the outdoor area where the families congregate is not like any theater or auditorium. In order to see the show, people are crowded together, some sitting, some crouching and others standing, the common denominator being that everyone presses against their neighbor as the people are packed in a small area.

About a quarter of the way through the show, someone on the other side of the crowd from me tosses a hand grenade into the people. When it explodes some twenty people are injured with a couple being killed. It is chaos, adults screaming in pain, children crying, dust and shrapnel everywhere. Soldiers take immediate charge and the province bodyguards surround their chief. Soldiers cordon the crowd and begin searching for the thrower. Medics rush into the crowd, locating the most badly hurt, and begin treating the victims.

The joyous audience very quickly turns into a very scared group of innocent farmers, wives and mothers, and children, unable to grasp why this violence has happened. The person who threw the grenade is never found. I do not believe anyone slept that night. I know I didn't. I spent the night as another sentinel, frustrated by what happened and worrying if it could happen again. At daylight we departed back to our district compound. This was another hamlet where the VC proved they still controlled the night and there was nothing we could do about that.

What gets to me is the fact that this war between the north and the south, between two governments, hurts most the people of Vietnam. These people do not want war. They want a peaceful existence, the ability to raise families, without being harmed, but that is not happening. By the very fact that they live in Trang Bang, one of the deadliest areas in South Vietnam, they have no alternative but to do their best to survive. And as we saw, because of someone willing to sacrifice innocent men, women, and children, the people are the real victims in this obscene war.

VC Propaganda

On another overnight county fair operation with Major Ai, he relays to me a story I find hard to believe. We are in a hamlet that is listed as being contested, another where GVN rules during the day but the VC during night. The hamlet chief told Major Ai what had happened one night recently when the VC gathered the residents together to try to turn them against the Vietnamese government and the Americans in South Vietnam.

The National Liberation Front and Viet Cong expend quite a bit of time and energy convincing rural families how bad the GVN and Americans are. They spend hours presenting political talks in front of their "captured" audience. I say captured because they are forced at gunpoint to congregate and listen to the VC spiel about their corrupt government and the evil American aggressors.

The VC correctly point out how unfair it is that these rural farmers must work hard raising crops and livestock while forced to pay part of their labor to the rich landowners living in luxury in Bao Trai or Saigon. The VC continue, describing what the French colonists did in claiming the best land and coercing the parents of the crowd before them to work hard for the benefit of the French.

Now the Americans are attempting to take over South Vietnam, the same as the French. Look at Cu Chi, the VC exclaim. The American troops wallow in greed, whiskey, and drugs, while turning daughters and sisters into sex slaves. The Americans are vile and evil and must be defeated and driven out of our country.

The speeches continue for hours, over and over presenting claims of GVN corruption and the depravity of the Americans. It is not difficult to for the VC to get their audience to agree with them. After all, corruption by government officials at the province and district levels is a major problem CORDS is dealing with. The off-duty episodes of the 25th Division soldiers at Cu Chi are known by everyone. Additionally, the division Rome Plow destruction of New Life Hamlets and their adjacent farmlands only reinforces belief in the malevolence of the Americans.

And here is where the Viet Cong go one step further to convince the poor people in front of them how horrible the Americans are. Major Ai then describes to me what the hamlet chief said the VC did next.

The rural families lack much of any formal education. While unschooled and illiterate, they are not dumb. If shown "A" and "B," they can intuitively and readily arrive at "C."

Presented with enough facts, they can connect the dots and generate logical conclusions. I cannot verify the credibility of this event, but it does make sense to me.

The VC produced a box of various cans and bottles. They said they would present proof on how evil and despicable the Americans are. Reaching in the box, they extracted several cans with labels. While the Vietnamese are unable to read English, they are familiar with American products, could recognize English writing and knew that most containers of American products usually had a picture of what was inside the container.

The VC would produce an American can of vegetables or fruit, known to the audience. The picture on the label would be emphasized so the group in front would realize that inside would be exactly what was pictured on the label. Cans were opened and of course, the can contained what was shown on the outside. Several cans were shown, then opened to demonstrate that whatever was on the label, was inside the can. Throughout this demonstration, the VC would describe in detail, how nasty the Americans are. How mean they are. They are so bad they even eat their own children. Now this was a statement the peasants found hard to believe.

Then a jar of Gerber's baby food is presented. On the label is a picture of a baby. Now the crowd has already been shown that whatever is on the label is inside the container. The jar is opened and shown to the people. Inside the jar is a green pureed substance (which doesn't smell good) that convinces many that Americans do, indeed, eat their own.

The propaganda machine of the VC is dynamic and convincing. It is just another weapon we must engage. And often that is almost impossible to counter what with the GVN creating New Life Hamlets that American Rome Plows destroy.

Attempting to win the hearts and minds of the rural people of Trang Bang is a never-ending battle which we always seem to lose.

11

Dying in the Morgue

Another early morning raid on another hamlet sort of went according to the plan. The village is surrounded, and the command group enters without a shot being fired. We locate the hut where a suspected VC is supposed to be in a meeting, but it is empty. Either the intel was totally false, or the get-together has been postponed. At any rate, the op is over by midmorning, so we all return to the compound, in time for lunch.

Lunch is usually something light like a sandwich or salad or soup. All advisors in the compound eat at a large table on the screened porch, off the kitchen area. All our meals are prepared by a Vietnamese cook.

Today there are several advisors present for lunch, including one of my captains and Sergeant Chesterfield, our medic. I am on one side of the table when the cook sets a plate of food in front of me. I sit there in a catatonic state, attempting to move some food onto my fork, I can't. I feel totally wasted, bone-tired, and my vision begins to blur. My fingers don't work and the fork drops. I glance at Sergeant Chesterfield and move my mouth, but no words come out, only some nonsense utterance.

The medic looks at me as a complete feeling of helplessness overcomes me. I am unable to move or talk. I sit, alive, yet realize something is very much wrong and it is awfully bad. I feel my life slowly slipping away, I am present, I am here, but I have no control over me anymore. I am very scared.

The medic stares at me and comprehends that I am extremely sick. My other table companions begin to recognize that their major is bad off. My skin is pallid, my eyes glazed, and my breathing rapid and shallow. The medic jumps out of his chair and grabs my wrist; he cannot detect any pulse. He shouts to the captain to call Dustoff (the medical evacuation helicopter), the old man is dying. Chesterfield takes charge, telling a sergeant to bring a jeep to the door to take me to the chopper pad. He instructs two more advisors to grab the litter leaning against the wall, place me on it and move me to the jeep.

The captain reports a 25th Division Dustoff is on the way. I lie on the stretcher, inert, almost like a corpse. The jeep rushes to the helipad at the same time the medevac from the 25th hovers over the pad, touching down. Several arms move my stretcher to the floor of the Huey, as Sergeant Chesterfield tells the Dustoff medic to take me to the 25th Medical Battalion.

As the medevac lifts off and heads toward Cu Chi, I realize I am dying. I can see, but not clearly; I can move my head, slowly, side to side, I am able to hear and understand, but I cannot talk. Otherwise my body is unresponsive. I am scared as this is not how I thought I would die. I feel very much alone, terrified and try to cry. But I cannot even do that.

In a few minutes we are over the 25th Division as the pilot drops down in front of the 25th Med tent. As is the practice, a senior medic or a nurse or a doctor, accompanied by two young medics carrying a stretcher, meets the helicopter. As the patient, lying on a stretcher is removed from the helicopter, an empty stretcher is placed inside the medevac, to replace the one the patient is on.

The senior man bends over me before the two medics can remove me on my stretcher out of the helicopter. He checks my pulse, opens my eyelids more, touches my carotid artery on my neck, then tells the Dustoff medic to take me to the 12th Evacuation Hospital a short distance away, just down the street. He tells the medic I am too far gone for them to help me. Motioning his two medics aside, he steps away as the helicopter lifts off to move a short distance away to stop in front of a rambling U-shaped composite of wood buildings, Quonset huts, and canvas tents.

Another team repeats what just happened at the 25th, except this time I am traded for an empty stretcher and moved into a field combat hospital emergency room where clothes are removed and medics push, pull, probe, pinch, and jab me, all collecting samples of this or that. Different people come in, examine me, looking puzzled, and move on. I just lie there, able to comprehend some of what is happening, but mostly inanimate and unresponsive.

After some time, a sheet is pulled over me and I am removed from the ER into what resembles a tent with a wooden floor, sort of like a storeroom, but has sawhorses scattered across the middle of the floor. My stretcher is placed on a couple of sawhorses off to one side and my carriers leave.

My vision becomes even more blurred. I can move my head partially from one side to the other, but nothing else. Shortly a couple more men enter carrying another stretcher with an all-gray person on it. He is garbed in gray jungle fatigues; his hair is gray, and his skin is gray. A third person enters with a clipboard, asking what happened. One of the men reports the man was on an operation along a river when they were ambushed. This man, who is Black, was shot several times and fell into the river. He was pulled out, bandaged, and placed on a medevac and flown to the 12th. He has bled out and died. His loss of blood turned his dark skin to gray and his soggy clothing looked gray when wet. The man with the clipboard took some notes and a sheet was pulled over the man on a stretcher, on the floor, by my feet.

A few minutes later another stretcher is placed on two sawhorses next to me. The stretcher bearers depart, and a couple of nurses and a doctor come in. The nurses ask what happened and the doctor tells them he was a pilot in an L-19 (like a Piper Cub) observation plane dropping down to land inside the 25th Division headquarters. Before he touched down, just outside the division perimeter, he was shot up. He crashed in the barbed wire entanglement on the perimeter and his plane started to burn. Perimeter guards rushed to his plane, but his hands were stuck somehow in the cockpit wreckage. Because of the fire and possible explosion, the guards just cut his hands off at the knuckles to extract him as quickly as possible.

I turn my head enough to see his body. The doctor reaches for his wrists, pulling them up, showing the nurses his hands, minus all his fingers. The doctor then moves in front of the top of the man's head and turns his head aside. The doc points to his head where it was punched in with a hole the size of half of a grapefruit, exclaiming, this is what killed the pilot, hitting his head when he crashed. The doc pulls a sheet over the pilot's head and they walk out of the room, leaving me alone again, this time with two dead bodies.

It is then I realize I am in the hospital morgue; I am dying, soon to be just like my two roommates. I then pass out.

The 12th Evacuation Hospital is a semi-mobile hospital with enough wards to accommodate up to 317 patients as well as preparing patients for further evacuation and treatment elsewhere. It is located within the 25th Division, arriving in Vietnam in September 1966. It is staffed with 312 personnel, to include 30 physicians and 60 female nurses. It has two intensive care units, one for medical-surgical patients and one for burn patients.

The main units of the hospital are in metal Quonset huts, which look like huge corrugated steel drainpipes cut in half lengthwise. The huts are half a circle from one side to the other with flat ends. The doors are on each end with windows cut in the curved sides. Outside, sandbags are piled about four to five feet high all along the curved sides to prevent shrapnel from punching through the metal, injuring or killing patients lying on cots inside.

Inside the huts used as patient wards, it is very austere. The patient beds are standard army metal folding cots with thin mattresses. Meals are served via trucks from a main mess hall elsewhere.

Medical personnel live in wooden buildings, surrounded by sandbags. The emergency and operating rooms are housed in sandbagged Quonset huts. The facilities have modern equipment, but it seems like medical supplies and essential equipment are always short. All in all, though, the staff is very competent and the care the best possible, considering the combat conditions.

I slowly begin to become conscious, feeling dazed, drugged, and very confused. I am in a small bed, a cot, in a very sparse room, with other cots and other men in them. I am able to move, looking around I notice a young, blonde, female, in clean jungle fatigues, holding a clipboard moving from cot to cot. I watch as she moves silently, wordlessly around the quiet room. The bright sunlight, crowding a small window near her, makes me think of an angel watching over me. Noticing me move, she walks toward me.

It Wasn't Your Time

Bending over, next to my head, smiling, she asks how I feel, explaining I have been out over 24 hours. Feeling weak, stiff, exhausted, and not understanding what occurred or where I am, I very groggily strain to ask, what happened?

She is a ward nurse, a first lieutenant, and explains that when I entered the ER all kinds of bodily fluids and samples were taken and brought to the lab. When I passed out, the lab was told to look for some form of parasite and the lab discovered hookworm eggs in my stool sample. I was medicated, which was also strong enough to keep me asleep for so long.

She says I should go back to sleep, but I have one more question. If the lab did not find the eggs, would I have died?

Moving away from my bed, she turns toward me, and with a bright smile says, "Maybe, but it wasn't your time, soldier." She leaves and I fall back asleep.

Hookworm is a parasite which inhabits the small intestines of humans and certain animals. Its larvae enter the body via skin after developing in human feces on the ground. Hookworm is most prevalent in the moist tropic regions of the globe.

After entering the body, it travels through the blood into the lungs, where coughing assists its movement into the esophagus, thence into the small intestines where it lays eggs, moving out of the body via feces, starting the cycle over again.

The worms exist on protein and blood building materials in the body creating anemia. The symptoms are exactly what I had, which mimic a heart condition. If left untreated, in severe cases it can lead to heart failure and death.

How I got hookworm is no surprise. Crawling around in combat causes cuts and scratches on hands and arms. Crawling around berms where hookworm-infected feces are prevalent allows the worms to enter my body. Lying flat on the berms to avoid getting shot presents another risk.

The treatment is rather simple, using different anthelmintic drugs to treat infections caused by the worm. In Vietnam in 1968, the treatment I receive is a single massive dose of the toxic drug tetrachloroethylene (a chemical used for dry-cleaning clothes), which eliminates 90 percent of the worms in the body. Two more doses over a brief period should completely rid my body of all worms.

After a few days I take a second dose of the drug, which puts me out again for over 24 hours. During my stay at the 12th Evac, I am allowed one five-minute MARS call home.

MARS

Inside the 25th Division is a MARS station (Military Affiliate Radio System), a unique means of talking to family back in the States. I say unique because of how it operates. It is a combination of using both regular telephones and ham radios to talk. Essentially this system is a collection of amateur radio operators (who use professional equipment and are licensed) that can connect and talk across continents and oceans. The term "ham" means amateur, which came about when Morse code was used and operators who were not totally professional were called ham-fisted for clumsy finger taps. The term stuck, so today the amateur radio operators are still called hams.

The way the system works is that a person in the system (in this case either soldiers stationed at the 25th Division or hospital patients) use the telephone to contact a ham radio operator (based in Cu Chi at the 25th Division). The ham operator is given a telephone number of someone in a city or town in the U.S. that the soldier or patient wants to call. The ham operator in Cu Chi then radios a MARS member who has a ham radio in the same area where the local phone is. A phone, though, is a two-way instrument in that one can talk (transmit) and listen (receive) at the same time. Ham radios cannot do both simultaneously so one either listens or talks.

A switch on the radio can be depressed to allow either talking or listening (transmit or receive). So, the people talking on the phone must tell the ham operator when they are through speaking so the other party can talk. This is done simply by saying, when you are done speaking, "over." When the MARS operators connect with the home party, the procedure is explained, and for most civilians, not used to using transmitters and receivers, it becomes a verbal circus.

Thus, a soldier in Vietnam, using MARS to call home would say, "hello mom, this is your son George, I am in Saigon talking to you over a MARS radio, over." This tells mom to talk and, in most cases, she is so excited she babbles on and wonders why George never says anything. But it does work with the help of the patient MARS operators and allows patients to call home for free.

I call Anita but do not tell her why I am able to call. The 25th MARS operator is able to connect with another radio operator in New Jersey who places a long-distance call to Anita at Fort Benning. I do not want her to worry. I say I am at the USO in Saigon, on a break, using MARS to call her (I have done that before, from the Saigon USO, during my first tour, so she knows about MARS). She wants to know what is going on and I reply I am a district advisor as I had explained in my letters home. But I avoid mentioning the dangers of my current assignment.

In eight days, I am released from the hospital with one last dose of the medicine. I am to take it a few days after I return to Trang Bang. Sergeant Chesterfield explains to the team that when I take my last dose, I will be out for 24 to 30 hours, and that does happen. But I am completely cleansed of the parasite. I did not die!

12

More Combat
Around Trang Bang

Joint U.S.–Vietnamese Operation

As we move deeper into fall, the border crossings increase. More NVA units and weapons are moving through Trang Bang and Hau Nghia toward Saigon and the coastal cities. Often as the units move during the night, local Popular Force outposts or rural people sympathetic to the government of South Vietnam will pass along what they see or hear. Our police or intel specialists (Phoenix agents) follow up and attempt to get more realistic details. The enemy moves when its dark, making distance traveled not far because they have to hide during the day. Sometimes we gather enough information to be able to set up an operation and ambush them at night or attack them during the day.

One night the Vietnamese tactical operation center receives information on a large movement of troops heading southeast along the Tay Ninh and Trang Bang border. Information such as this is usually passed on to province for a couple of reasons. First the size of the unit, not a squad or platoon but a company or larger. Second, it appears the unit is only moving through our district, heading elsewhere. Often a province would share this info with the 25th Division, which they did. And this does not happen often, but the province chief and a brigade commander at the 25th decide to mount up a joint U.S. and Vietnamese operation to intercept this enemy force.

A plan is quickly formulated where two Vietnamese Regional Force companies will form a blocking force (the anvil) while a 25th battalion will become the hammer, driving the NVA into the RF anvil, a classic counter-guerrilla strategy. One RF company would come from Trang Bang (with me as the senior advisor), with the other RF company coming from province with the province chief, Lieutenant Colonel Ma Sanh Nhon, the overall commander of the Vietnamese forces.

A second RF company will remain on call at province headquarters as our reserve.

The RF companies will be moved by trucks, well ahead of the enemy, and establish the blocking force. The 25th battalion will be moved by helicopters in the rear of the enemy and the three American rifle companies will then begin to drive the NVA into our blocking positions. The American commander is the battalion commander, a lieutenant colonel. The overall task force commander is the 25th brigade commander, a full colonel.

While the NVA unit hunkers down for the day, the task force units move into position and the operation begins. As the 25th battalion begins their push they encounter some resistance, and by the middle of the night, all of us realize the enemy is larger than originally estimated. The heavily wooded and wet ground hinders observation and clear fields of fire. To remain an effective pushing force the U.S. battalion must stay close together, therefore, not able to stretch out to cover all the terrain surrounding the NVA. The American battalion commander explains his situation, requesting from the American colonel another unit to secure the flank of the NVA, forcing them into our blocking force. The colonel makes the request to division and there just happens to be an American airborne rifle company, on a short R&R, between combat missions, which can join our operation.

U.S. combat units may be in the field on combat operations for days or weeks before being pulled out for a few days' rest. They then shower and get clean clothes, eat regular meals, relax, sleep, or watch movies and are often allowed a couple of beers. For this airborne company of close to 100 men, it came out of the field late in the day, cleaned up, got new clothes, ate a big meal, had their beers and most were so exhausted they just went to sleep. About four hours later the company was rousted up, equipped for combat and choppered into a flanking/blocking position to prevent the NVA from escaping out the side.

Unfortunately, this unit is not a fresh, wide-awake combat force but a hastily organized group of very tired, sleepy, soldiers moving at night into unknown positions, facing an enemy they have no knowledge of. It is a disaster waiting to happen.

The 25th battalion is behind the NVA, in contact, but now that the enemy's open flank is covered, the battalion continues to press the enemy.

The NVA sends small patrols out. To its rear is a U.S. battalion. On its right flank is a large fast river, making it virtually impossible to safely move a large body of soldiers across. On their left flank is a new, unknown force, just deploying. Their patrols, ahead in front of the NVA main force, encounter our outposts and quickly realize that it will take a lot of fighting to move through us. So, the NVA begins to probe the front lines of the U.S. airborne unit, on their left flank.

Establishing a blocking position, at night, in an unknown location defending against an unknown enemy force is a poor situation for a

Joint U.S.–VN Operation

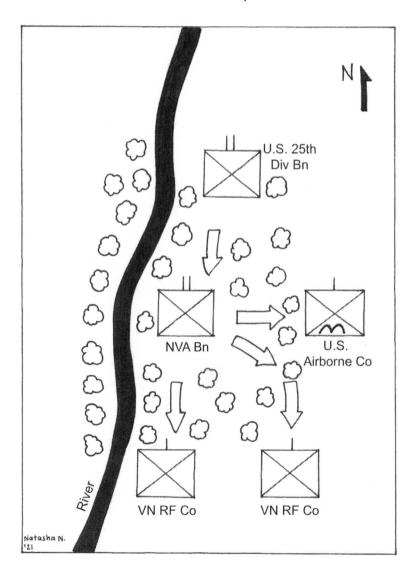

company commander to be in. Add to this insane situation the fact that most of the airborne soldiers are bone-tired, and are feeling the effects of their beer; therefore staying awake is next to impossible. The NVA quickly discover this.

The NVA pull back away from our blocking force. They disengage from the 25th battalion behind them and they avoid contact with the airborne company. The night becomes quiet and everyone thinks the enemy is hunkering down to fight another day. But it is not.

When the airborne unit joined the fray, we got their internal company radio frequencies. A common behavior is for us to monitor the company command nets of those units in the same operation as we are. This way if anything happens, we will know it as soon as they do. The airborne unit is a few hundred yards, but through the dense jungle, away from our positions, so we have no hands-on contact with them; we just know about where they are. About two hours before dawn we hear a muffled cry on the airborne net. Next some whispered voices we can't understand. Then screams on the radio saying they are all around us. Automatic weapons begin and we can faintly hear shouting, grenades, then Claymores exploding. Putting together what we believe we are hearing over the airborne radios, we figure the unit is being overrun by the NVA.

At night, in the dark, being so far away, there is nothing we can do but listen and cringe. The firefights in the airborne positions became intense, mortar flares, followed by artillery flares and then artillery bombardments, tear the night apart and illuminate the jungle surrounding us.

Apparently the NVA learned the airborne soldiers were slumbering in their positions so one NVA unit decided to exploit this and began to creep between sleeping soldiers to move away from the Americans. The movement awakened a soldier who was quickly knifed by an NVA, but the American was able to scream. Other airborne soldiers recovered, and hand-to-hand combat ensued, with hand grenades being thrown and Claymores going off and M-16s mixing it up with enemy AK-47s.

The airborne company is badly mauled with several NCOs and officers killed, many soldiers slain where they slept. But they did hold their own, dislodged the NVA, and held their flank. At first light they are pulled out and replaced with a fresh and combat ready 25th rifle company.

The day is marked with numerous clashes and firefights between the NVA and the American units. By the end of the second day, another 25th rifle company joins its sibling on the flank. By night we have three rifle companies continuing to push at the back of the NVA with two more U.S. rifle companies holding the NVA's left flank. By night, the

NVA begins to focus on us, the blocking force. The distance between the RF blocking companies (the anvil) and the attacking 25th Division (the hammer) is slightly over a half mile, with the NVA between us.

Small probing patrols become intense combat attacks, directly at us. Exploring our defenses, the NVA are attempting to locate weak areas to exploit and attack during darkness. Well after midnight, the attacks become more intense and we need help defending our positions. Each unit in this task force is given an American artillery radio frequency for defensive fire support. Each unit in this task force has an artillery piece or two, dedicated to them for this operation. I am told all we have to do is ask.

Because of the enhanced attacks, the RF commander and I decide we need artillery to force the attackers to back off. Because there are a few isolated civilians living in the contested area where the NVA are hiding, all artillery fire must be at pre-designated positions to avoid hitting noncombatants or their houses. These pre-designated targets were plotted during daylight when we set up our blocking positions. Each target already has a letter designation and because we know why we would need artillery (enemy soldiers under dense trees, overhead cover) the type round and fuse has already been discussed. The radioed fire mission ends with the comment "danger close," meaning that friendly troops are within 650 yards of the target.

Because our RF company is taking most of the incoming enemy fire, Lieutenant Colonel Nhon is also with my RF company commander. He agrees with our need for artillery support, so I call in a fire mission. To my surprise, a fire direction center operator does not respond. It is some artillery headquarters clerk. I explain what we need and the man on the other end tells me that only his colonel can authorize any fire missions and he is asleep and can't be disturbed. I explain we are under attack and need the artillery so get his damn colonel up and start shooting. The clerk refuses.

I cannot believe this. Here I am being shot at, attacked, and an American colonel does not want his beauty sleep disturbed, so this just reminds me why I want out of this army. Colonel Nhon, places a hand on my shoulder, and with his other hand makes a waiting motion, palm out, nodding okay. He turns to a tall Vietnamese soldier standing next to him, holding another radio. Nhon turns, speaks to his soldier, who twists a dial, changing the radio to another frequency, and the colonel takes the handset and speaks softly into it, in English.

I cannot hear what he is saying but he then asks the RF company commander a couple of questions, speaks again in English, and then hands the handset back to his soldier. I wonder what has happened but Nhon remains silent. About 90 seconds later some artillery rounds come crashing down, several hundred yards to our front. The intense automatic weapons fire to our front lessens and our returning fire increases. The artillery barrage makes the difference.

Colonel Nhon gives me a thumbs-up and silently moves away into the darkness.

The next morning the 25th companies sweeps across the battlefield and complete the fighting. Several NVA escape but even more are killed. Few live prisoners are captured but quite a bit of weapons, ammo, and military supplies are found scattered around the battlefield.

The operation is a success from the point of destroying the NVA and capturing much of their equipment. From the standpoint of our losses, the airborne unit suffered too many killed and wounded. That unit never should have been selected for this combat mission. Another extremely poor leadership decision that was totally wrong.

The 25th Division Captain

Back home in our compound, I am discussing our recent combat mission with a liaison captain from the 25th. He is about ten days from leaving Vietnam to return home. He is going through a bundle of mail that finally caught up with him from his old unit in Cu Chi. He opens the ubiquitous vanilla-colored military-style message envelope tied with a short red string, and finds a set of orders along with a 4" by 9" hinged dark blue case embossed with gold edges and gold lettering on the case.

He studies the orders and opens the box. I see inside a Purple Heart medal. Closing the case, he goes back to studying the orders. I asked what he has, and he shows me his orders. He is being awarded his second Purple Heart for being wounded in combat. He explains he received his first Purple Heart as a company commander. I ask how he got his second medal. Glancing at his orders again, he says he was back at Cu Chi, after an operation and he was watching a movie. I inquire if it was a mortar or sniper and he replies no. I look dumb so ask what he was doing to get wounded? He said nothing. I ask what does he mean?

He clarifies that according to the orders when he was shot, his unit had been pulled out of the field and was resting for a few days. He said when he was supposed to be wounded again, he was watching a movie and he was never shot or wounded a second time. Someone made a mistake and somehow, he was erroneously awarded a second Purple Heart. It was all a mistake.

When I asked him what he was going to do about this mistake he replied, "I'll wear it."

U.S. Special Forces CIDG Camp

The district of Duc Hue is the westernmost district in Hau Nghia, and the largest. Most of the district is west of the Vam Co Dong River and most of its northern and western borders are with Cambodia. In the northern part of the district, along the Cambodia border, is A team 325 of the 5th Special Forces Group (airborne). This camp has about a dozen U.S. Army A detachment members and around 350 indigenous soldiers of Vietnamese-Cambodian-Chinese-Montagnard heritage. The mission of the camp is border surveillance operations and border-crossing interdictions.

Often the U.S. Special Forces cadre work with Vietnamese SF troopers. The local soldiers are divided into various combat units such as recon, mortar, recoilless rifle, and psy-ops (psychological operations). On a couple of occasions, I visit this A-team in its camp to observe a sight that is hard to believe.

The camp has a tall tower that is high enough to be able to see across the border into Cambodia. Just over a mile away are elements of the NVA Base Area 706. It has wooden buildings, dirt streets and roads and supply depots. With the powerful binoculars the SF have, I watch NVA soldiers training and preparing for various border crossing raids and weapons transportation.

It blows the mind to be able to watch the enemy, unfettered and undisturbed, preparing for their next sojourn into South Vietnam to hurt, kill, and destroy as much as they possible can. And to make matters even worse, there is nothing we can do but watch and endure the pain of helplessness for not being able to do anything but react when they next attack, across the border, in Vietnam. Isn't this a very weird way to fight a war?

Ironically, in early spring, 1970, when I am a civilian graduate student, President Nixon does authorize American units to cross this exact border and attack these NVA soldiers. Some of my fellow grad students protest it as one more U.S. invasion into another foreign country for no reason at all. How little they know about what is really going on.

Fire Support Base Stuart III

Scattered around Trang Bang district are various American units. Some are only temporarily encamped for a short duration while others occupy semi-permanent positions, such as two 25th fire support bases. The more permanent positions I would visit often to talk to more Americans and of course to exchange useful information.

One such 25th Division position is Fire Support Base (FSB) Stuart III, located on the north side of Route 1 and nine-tenths of a mile east from the center of the town of Trang Bang. Fire support bases are semi-permanent military camps containing various artillery units to support combat troops in the field on operations. Security for the FSB is usually an infantry unit and possibly armor units (depending on the terrain around the FSB).

This FSB is about 150 yards west of the Trang Bang River, a stream 30 to 40 feet wide, with steep banks, overgrown with brush, on both sides of the water. The FSB itself is about 300 feet wide in a circle, but the bulldozed flat earth around the outside of the berms provides another clear area of red and tan dirt that extends at least another hundred feet.

FSB Stuart III is a miserable place to live. During the monsoon season it is a quagmire of thick, heavy mud with the consistency of rubber cement glue. It is evil smelling, damp, cold, and even the most heavily oiled ferrous metal will turn red with rust overnight. During the dry season it is hot, muggy, dusty, with the only shade pieces of canvas or cloth tied to poles over worn-out, falling-apart sandbagged bunkers. The space is shared with all kinds of crawling and flying insects and creepy-crawly animals that can be very poisonous to humans.

FSB Stuart III is populated with a reinforced rifle company, which is about the largest size infantry unit the FSB can accommodate. It also has a battery of M110 203 mm self-propelled (SP) howitzers from 3rd Battalion, 13th Artillery of the 25th Division.

These guns are massive, 36 feet long, weighing around 30 tons; they fire an 8" projectile weighing about 200 pounds. Self-propelled, the entire gun is an M115 howitzer installed on a special built chassis with an eight-cylinder, 405 hp turbocharged diesel engine. The unit consists of the SP gun with another armored personnel carrier (APC) carrying most of the crew and its two rounds. It takes five men to fire the weapon but eight more to move it and set it up. This is the largest army artillery weapon and it hurls its rounds 10.5 to 15.5 miles with pinpoint accuracy. It is a general support artillery weapon.

Quite often elements of the 25th Division reconnaissance unit, the 3rd Squadron of the 4th Armor Cavalry Regiment, spend time at FSB Stuart III. The unit has M-48 tanks and APCs and is tasked with both route and convoy security for the 25th Division main supply route, Route 1, between Cu Chi and Tay Ninh. They provide security for division convoys or clear the road before the convoys move.

At the point where the river crosses under Route 1 is a many times damaged, yet sturdy, single-vehicle wood bridge. The bridge is secured by district PF soldiers, who man twin bunkers on both ends of the bridge, on the south side. On each side of the bridge are dirt parking areas. The PF soldiers control the traffic crossing the bridge, because only one lane can cross at a time, resulting in a long line of vehicles parking, waiting their turn to cross. Throughout the day, one side or the other quickly fills with all manner of civilian trucks and cars, motorcycles, motorized bikes, and scooters, as well as public conveyances such as buses and vans.

As the vehicles wait on one side or the other, the passengers and drivers dismount and move to the side of the parking area to relieve themselves; obviously urinating or defecating in public is not a concern. Over time, especially during the dry season, the edge of the parking area becomes very messy and smells. Additionally, while waiting, many Vietnamese eat a meal from boxes or hampers they have. The refuse from the consumed meal, bottles, cans, containers, paper products, and uneaten food ends up on the ground. Often the parking areas at the end of the day more closely resemble a garbage dump than a vehicle pull-off. And the PF soldiers envision their job as bridge security and traffic control, not custodians to maintain a sanitary parking area.

I visit the FSB often. I enjoy the camaraderie of the rifle company commander and we always exchange information on what we know about the local VC and what they are up to. The rifle company spends a lot of time on night patrols. Essentially, a squad or a platoon will move out at dusk into an ambush position, a distance away from the FSB, and spend the night watching and hoping to encounter a VC group, moving. In Trang Bang, no one moves during darkness except the enemy. Therefore, any movement has to be VC or NVA and thus a legitimate target. Often, the unit returns at daybreak, dog-tired, without firing a shot. Food consumed, weapons cleaned, and then the soldiers try to sleep. Rest is almost impossible. The heat, the bugs, the muggy weather make it difficult to treasure worthwhile sleep, but they try, and eventually, exhausted, seem to pass out, despite everything that prohibits rest.

During combat, the VC try to identify the American advisors and kill them. Doing this could cripple communications and isolate the Vietnamese unit from obtaining U.S. combat support. Therefore, I almost never wear any rank or military insignia on my jungle fatigues. This suggests to anyone observing me, I am a private, a soldier of no importance, which is fine for me. Because I meet with province advisors or attend formal Vietnamese functions, I do also have jungle fatigues with proper rank and insignias.

One day I am visiting the FSB commander. It is a hot, muggy day. Many of his soldiers are attempting to sleep, having spent the night on various ambush sites. The FSB is quiet, civilian traffic on Route 1 is very heavy, with overloaded parking spaces jammed with all sorts of transportation waiting their turn to cross the bridge.

Most of the American living spaces and company admin offices are in heavily sandbagged shelters halfway below ground level, topped with PSP roofs covered with more layers of sandbags. The weather and climate have worn out many sandbags that are leaking sand if brushed against. In the past the commander has requisitioned more bags but is only resupplied with a few, never enough to replace all the crumbling, worn-out bags. His clerks spend hours filling out requisition forms for all kinds of needed supplies to make the FSB safer or more habitable, only to be told that they are on back order. So, the soldiers are forced to make do with what they have.

On this day, a Huey circles the FSB to come in for a landing. It is obviously a U.S. Army helicopter, but whose is unknown. The captain turns away as the helicopter settles down, its blades sending sand cyclones in every direction, blowing down the more wretched sandbags. The engine winds down and the blades slow as a man steps out. As he exits the rear of the chopper, he hands a pilot's helmet to a man inside and places a baseball style cap on his head. I am amazed: he wears starched jungle fatigues, the toes of his jungle boots spit-shined, a camouflaged scarf on his neck, his gait full of confidence and authority as he strides toward the captain. I see the single black star on the front of his cap. On his left shoulder is the subdued black and olive colored 25th Division patch. This is one of the 25th assistant division commanders, a brigadier general. The captain moves toward the man.

Stopping short and smartly saluting, the captain reports to the general as the commander of the occupying rifle company. The general returns the salute, sort of halfway between a salute and a wave. I am standing next to an open bunker where two NCOs are. I ask them what is going on. They do not know.

The general is not happy. First he orders the captain to attention, then he points toward the bridge over the Trang Bang River and begins to berate the captain for the unholy garbage mess on both sides of the bridge. Now, the bridge is about 150 to 180 yards away from the closest point of the FSB and it belongs to the Vietnamese, not the Americans. The general makes it noticeably clear that he expects his soldiers to police up that mess and not let it happen again. While the captain tries to explain he has no authority to do anything about the bridge, the general isn't interested.

The general looks around and spots the advisor jeep parked next to one of the falling-down sandbagged bunkers. He focuses on my jeep, appearing to look like he does not quite understand what he is looking at.

The U.S. Army in 1959 replaced the M38A1 round-fendered jeep (the military version of the civilian CJ-5) with the Ford M151 quarter ton 4x4 utility truck (which was prone to rollovers when cornering at high speeds). This was the type of jeep used by U.S. military during the Vietnam War. For American advisors (and their Vietnamese counterparts), though, the M151 is not their military jeep. Instead the Vietnamese and advisors use a military version (M-606) of the civilian CJ-3B. This is probably why the general looks puzzled. He is seeing a military jeep that obviously is not a U.S. Army jeep. These are flat-fendered utility vehicles provided to Vietnam as part of the Mutual Defense Assistance Program (MDAP). The ones we have are old, battered, worn, dirty and dusty. This is what we advisors drive.

MDAP was created by passing of the U.S. Mutual Defense Assistance Act in the late 1940s to provide military assistance and support to countries who would not support communism. It was sort of a loan program (with the regulations altered several times to meet changing world conditions) in which the United States would provide military equipment to foreign countries to help them defeat communism in their country. Vietnam was one MDAP-supported country and often the jeeps would have a shield on the side with clasped hands on the top of the shield identifying the vehicle as a MDAP vehicle

The general continues to look around, sees the sleeping soldiers and demands to know why they are sacked out and not performing soldierly duties? The captain tries to explain they were up all night on patrols or ambushes, but again, the general isn't interested. He decrees that when he returns, he doesn't want to see so many soldiers sleeping. He asks where the command bunker is, and the captain escorts him there. Standing next to the doorway, the general looks at the sandbags and begins to lecture the captain again about the overall condition of this FSB and the deplorable condition of his sandbags. The captain explains his numerous unfilled requisitions for more sandbags, and again the general is not interested in excuses; he only wants results. For another five minutes the general just chews out the captain, finally stating he will return and the captain had better clean up his act or else. The general pivots away and, as the captain salutes, stomps off to his chariot, awaiting him.

The captain moves to me, visibly embarrassed over what has happened. I tell him that is one reason I am leaving the army—idiots like his general. Instead of asking how he could help the captain, he just bawled him out with no justification at all. To me this is just another demonstration of leadership at the top levels of the army. I want out.

I ask the captain what he is going to do, and he explains, ask for more sandbags, which he knows he will never get. I wonder aloud what he will do about the debris around the bridge; he says he has no clue. I say I can talk to the PF commander at district but explain that while most Americans fight in Vietnam for only 12 months, the Vietnamese are here forever. Picking up trash on a piece of land they have no ties to is of no interest when just staying alive takes so much time and energy. I doubt if the Vietnamese will show any interest in policing the bridge parking areas.

At a later visit the general returns and again chews out the captain for the messy bridge and he is especially incensed at the captain's sandbags. The captain has whittled some twigs into large toothpicks and pinned dozens of pink carbon copies of his original sandbag requisitions on the rotting sandbags around his command bunker. The general does not appreciate the captain's humor and humiliates him again.

Night Operations

As previously mentioned, John Paul Vann dictated that his CORDS advisors would spend time on combat operations, especially night ops. So, all my combat advisors go on some night missions. According to Vann's thinking, a Vietnamese combat leader is not going to go out at night with his unit, find a safe place to hide and then go to sleep if an American advisor is along. Hence, off we go.

I am not an admirer of night patrols because the danger outweighs the results. Wandering around in the dark is an effortless way to get shot. My reasoning is it's best to select a place to hide and wait, then shoot the other guys wandering around in the dark. So, most of our night operations involve setting up ambush sites, waiting for the enemy to walk by. During my time in Trang Bang I never went on a night ambush that ever resulted in anything but lost sleep. Indirectly, though, we do get some kills due to our night ambush ops.

The soldiers I go with sometimes would carry a long bamboo pole with a GVN flag attached at the top. Others carry some string or trip wire and a tin can. Most often our ambush site is at a junction of footpaths on the backside of a VC hamlet, next to open areas. We select a location where we can defend the path with gunfire and have plenty of cover from gunfire ourselves. As we are setting up our ambush site, after it becomes dark, two soldiers would take the flagpole, the string, can, a small entrenching tool and a grenade and crawl into the middle of an open area. One would scrape out a hole and bury the bottom of the flagpole, tightly secured in the ground. A second small hole would be dug, and the can placed in the hole and secured by tamping the soil tightly around the can. The string would be tied stoutly to a grenade, which would be armed by pulling the safety pin. The grenade would slowly be inserted into the can, snug so the grenade handle could not pop off, igniting the grenade. The can, grenade and the hole would be covered with debris, hiding it. Then the string from the grenade is tied to the flagpole, again using debris to hide everything. The two soldiers would crawl back to our ambush position.

The next morning, if a VC saw the GVN flag, he or she would want to take it down, its presence signifying that during the night GVN soldiers defied the VC and planted the flag, showing the VC that the GVN also owns the night. Then a VC would venture, carefully, out into the field and grab the flagpole, pulling it out of the ground. Along with the pole would come the grenade, out of the can, with the handle flying off, allowing the VC four to six more seconds to live.

This stunt could only be used rarely. If it became a common occurrence, the VC would quickly learn and then tie a long cord or rope to the flagpole, get under cover and yank the rope, dislodging the flag, igniting the grenade to explode harmlessly with no one around.

MEDCAPs

One of our team medic's responsibilities is to coordinate the Medical Civic Action Programs. Sergeant Chesterfield enjoys a reputation for being an expert in this endeavor. As a combat medic, he is without any peers, he is so good. He works with the local Vietnamese medical personnel, province medical people and physicians from both the 25th Division and various army medical units in Saigon. Both the U.S. military and the senior CORDS officials advocate this practice.

Essentially a district RF or PF unit surrounds and secures a rural village or hamlet. Next province or district officials announce that a medical clinic will be set up in the hamlet and anyone can be seen by doctors, be inoculated, have wounds and injuries treated, and babies and children examined. Medicines would be available. This draws the people's attention and always the clinic fills quickly with women and children.

Trucks laden with medical practitioners, supplies, and security enter the hamlet, set up shop, and begin seeing patients. The American physicians who participate volunteer because they want to help, and they get to practice a brand of care never seen by them. One trait I noted in the American military physicians who favor MEDCAPs is a fascinating scientific curiosity about everything new and different to them.

During my first tour as a combat advisor, I met a U.S. Navy

physician who enjoyed treating rural Vietnamese patients. Because I frequently went on MEDCAPs (often to help with interpretations), I came to know this doctor and discovered he had a very unusual scientific hobby, which he could not enjoy in the U.S. He collected sea snakes. Until I met him, I never even knew sea snakes existed. One day I visited him at his office, and he took me to a back room filled with shelves. The shelves were covered with all sizes of closed jars. Each jar was filled with formaldehyde and coiled inside were various snakes.

Sea snakes are unusual snakes, in that they do not have gills, must breath like regular snakes, but live in the warm tropical seas and oceans. Most cannot survive on land. Mature snakes are about four to five feet long, but some can grow to ten feet. Many have a very potent, poisonous venom. The doctor spent a lot of time at China Beach, collecting his sea snakes (this was before the beach, outside the city of Da Nang, became a military in-country R&R center).

During our MEDCAPs in Trang Bang, I meet another army doctor who assists in Vietnamese medical clinics in both Saigon and our rural district. He tells me of a scientific study he is conducting and collects data every time he comes out with Sergeant Chesterfield. He works in clinics in both the countryside and the city. He has noted a difference in the physical development of young female teens, the difference being prominent between city teens and their country sisters. He formulated the opinion that the breasts of the city teens were larger than those of the country girls. He questioned why and began to research the subject. He evaluated various reasons but settled on their diets. He took detailed notes on what each of the teens ate, their foods, portions, variety, and nutrients in the foods each group consumed. The physician was professional, scientific, and very comprehensive in the data he collected. He had interviewed dozens of young girls and had a wealth of data, which to his mind, was conclusive. The physical development of Vietnamese female teens is distinctly different depending on where they are raised. His research determined that the different diets of the girls made a distinct difference in their development. I do not know if his study was ever published, just as I never knew how the navy doctor ever got his collection of hundreds of sea snakes back to the United States. But each pursued their own scientific studies, which most likely helped them pass their year in Vietnam.

13

Firefly Missions

In October we have a new captain from the 25th Infantry Division assigned to us as a liaison officer. His job is to assist in coordinating with the 25th when the Vietnamese are planning any combat operations to avoid territorial conflicts and to help us with obtaining 25th Division assets such as medical evacuation support or artillery gunfire.

Part of my briefing with this captain is to provide information on our missions of interdicting weapon and resupply transportation runs across the Cambodian border when the North Vietnamese Army would supply local Viet Cong. Even though we can watch the NVA units in Cambodia preparing equipment to move into South Vietnam, our rules of engagement prevent us from doing anything until the transportation units are physically in Vietnam.

I explain how difficult this is because most border-crossing movement is done during the darkness of night. Additionally, there are no regular travel routes used so there are no reliable places to set up an ambush. We must know where the border crossing is to take place in advance to be able to get our troops in position to set up an ambush before the NVA get there. Because of the difficulty of getting advance info on NVA border crossings in time to get there first and set up an ambush, usually the best we can do is to position night ambushes around possible crossing locations and hope we will be lucky enough to spot enemy movement and eliminate the threat. Essentially this is a hit-and-miss proposition which usually results in no contact, especially due to the darkness of night and the reduced visibility.

The captain asks if I am aware of the U.S. Army's Firefly helicopters and their night assault capability. I reply I am not, so he explains. He says that the 25th Division has been using the Firefly helicopter teams with phenomenal success mostly along the Saigon, Thi Tinh, and Song Be Rivers on the Cambodian border, north and east of Trang Bang. The use of these helicopters at night has denied the NVA the safety of using the waterways as a main infiltration route to transport rockets into

South Vietnam to attack Saigon. This information also explains why we are encountering more border crossings, on the ground, in our area. He says that the unit with the Firefly helicopters is the 334th Aerial Weapons Company, stationed at Long Binh.

The 334th is assigned to the 12th Aviation Group, which was created at Fort Benning, Georgia, in June 1965. That August, the 12th Army Aviation Group departed Fort Benning to deploy to Tan Son Nhut airport in Saigon to provide tactical aviation support to both II and III Corps Tactical Zones. In June 1966, the unit moved to Sanfield Army Airfield at Long Binh. Long Binh is 15 miles northeast of Saigon and just east of the Dong Nai River. It is the largest U.S. Army base in South Vietnam, home of the headquarters of the U.S. Army Vietnam (USARV) and several other major army support commands.

The Firefly is a UH-1C Bell helicopter that has, in the right doorway

The lights on the helicopter (light ship) of a Firefly team (U.S. Army).

behind the seat of the aircraft commander, a circle of seven C-130 landing lights bolted together. This circle of lights is mounted on a metal pedestal fixed to the helicopter floor. These lights can move up, down or sideways, casting a powerful beam anywhere on the ground. This device was originally created by the 197th Air Mobile Light Aviation Company in 1965 as a unit assigned to the 145th Aviation Battalion at Tan Son Nhut Airport. It moved to Long Binh in June 1966 with the 12th Aviation Group and its assets were transferred to the 334th.

The best way to interdict night movement is with a Firefly team of three UH-1C helicopters. There is the command and control (C&C) Huey (the high ship), another Huey with a door-mounted search light (the Firefly or light ship), and a gunship with rockets (the low ship).

The light ship, the Firefly, is armed with the M-60, a .308 caliber machine gun, and flies at 500 feet above the ground. Above that, at 1,000 feet, hovers the C&C ship armed with a .50 caliber, air-cooled machine gun, mounted by the left door. Below 500 feet, closest to the ground, is the gunship armed with two door-mounted M-21 7.62 mm miniguns and two side-mounted seven-tube 2.75-inch rocket launchers.

The C&C Huey runs the operation by selecting and confirming the targets. The Firefly illuminates the target so the gunship can make the kill. The light operator is the key man. He must be able to maneuver the heavy light, exposed to the air stream, constantly keeping the beam on the target, regardless of which way the chopper turns or twists. The 334th Aerial Weapons Company has three Firefly teams, the Raiders, Dragons, and Playboys. A team can remain airborne for two and one-half hours at most.

Firefly missions have built-in hazards apart from possible enemy ground fire. Each aircraft must maintain strict altitude limitations, flying without lights. The pilot doing the flying (army choppers have two pilots) flies on instruments, being guided by the non-flying pilot. The reason for this is vertigo, as pilots flying circles while concentrating on a single spot of light on the ground are prone to dizzy spells.

Training for Firefly pilots requires a 90-day apprenticeship, flying all three helicopters. Assignment to a Firefly team guarantees an average of 100 hours of night flying each month—earning one's flight pay the hard way. It takes pilots 300 hours of flying to qualify as a Firefly aircraft commander

The captain tells me how to contact the 334th, which I do. I tell them I am the district senior advisor to Trang Bang district and we are on the Cambodian border, where we have a major problem with NVA units crossing the border, at night, in our area. I explain how the area is a main supply route but because we do not know when or where a

crossing might take place—at night it is difficult to be everywhere—
we miss many crossings of NVA troops. I explain that I believe a Firefly
team could help us quite a bit.

The western edge of Trang Bang district is close to the Cambodian border in the area known as the Angel's Wing which separates
South Vietnam from Cambodia's Svay Rieng province. The border is
about six miles west of Trang Bang district headquarters. About three
miles due west of our district compound, between us and the Cambodian border, flows the Vam Co Dong River. This river originates high
in the mountains in Cambodia, wandering its way south and east until
finally entering South Vietnam northwest of the city of Tay Ninh. From
there the river flows generally south. As it flows through the western
edge of Trang Bang district the river is almost 400 feet wide. Into it also
flow many small streams which also originate in Cambodia. The terrain between our compound and Cambodia is strewn with numerous
small streams mostly flowing south and east from the higher areas in
Cambodia.

The area west of us in Cambodia is the terminus of the Ho Chi
Minh Trail, the main supply route from North Vietnam through Laos
and Cambodia, ending in Cambodia northwest of Saigon. Across the
border, one in the Parrot's Beak area and the other just north of the
Angel's Wing (the two points where Cambodia juts into South Vietnam)
are two major North Vietnam Army resupply bases. The one in the Parrot's Beak is Base Area 367 and the northern one is Base Area 706. This
is where all the weapons, munitions, rockets, and other equipment used
to attack Saigon and the U.S. and ARVN military base camps as well as
Vietnamese district and province headquarters come from.

During the darkness of night, NVA and VC transportation units
move weapons and supplies out of Cambodia, into South Vietnam.
Because of the wet terrain around the border and the virtually impenetrable jungle growth all along the banks of the Vam Co Dong River and
the other larger waterways, setting up ambushes is exceedingly difficult. Additionally, the darkness, especially in the jungle areas, makes it
impossible to see engagement targets. U.S. Air Force B-52 strikes, orig-
inating from Guam, are used often to bomb known staging and resupply points frequented by the enemy just inside the Vietnamese side of
the border. While these attacks are not that good at killing the enemy
(except for the first-time strike) they do deny the enemy the ability to
use the same location repeatedly and make resupplying the VC and local
NVA units in South Vietnam a very hazardous and difficult operation.

Water buffalo beasts of burden are most often used to move the
rockets toward Saigon. But that requires at the very least pathways

through the jungle and, in clearer areas, routes that would avoid populated hamlets and villages. The less populated Hau Nghia province is easier to move through undetected by the enemy than is the region closer to Saigon, which is much more populated, even in the rural areas surrounding Saigon.

The major battles along the Cambodian border are in areas known as the Boi Loi Woods, the Ho Bo Woods, the Filhol Rubber Plantation, War Zone Z and War Zone D, all north and east of Trang Bang. The fighting mostly involves major U.S. units against large enemy forces traversing key approach routes to Saigon. This leaves the defense of the entryways between Trang Bang and Cambodia totally up to the local Regional and Popular Forces. Currently the most utilized means of bringing war materials into South Vietnam is via water. Small sampans laden with weapons of war move undetected from inside Cambodia on a small stream, entering the Vam Co Dong or Rach Tram Rivers, which eventually wend their way just west or south of Saigon, and discharging their loads to enrich attacks against Saigon. Most of these waterways cross sparsely inhabited areas where the banks are heavily blanketed with thick jungle foliage, rendering setting up ambush sites almost impossible.

Knowing all of this I convince the operations people of the 334th that we can plan a night operation that will up their kill rate considerably. Working with Major Ai's operations staff, we can set up a section of the Vam Co Dong River where a Firefly team can operate.

One major rule of the land around the border is no one moves after darkness falls. Anyone who does is subject to being killed. This single order makes border surveillance and defense easy. If it moves, it will be shot. All the rural folks know this as well as the enemy. This rule is so well adhered to by the rural people that the only violators must be the enemy.

Our plan is to select a length of the river and, around midnight, take a Firefly team to the area where it can destroy anything on the river. To ensure there will be no problems, I will fly in the command and control Huey, where I can carry a PRC-25 field radio to communicate with the local Regional Force or Popular Force troops on the ground in the vicinity of the river.

An operation is planned for a clear night in late October. Our local troops, in the field, are informed about the operation and it is a go. The Firefly team arrives over Trang Bang a few minutes before midnight. On our small helicopter landing pad just outside of our compound I am ready and, using a flashlight and hand signals, motion the C&C ship down while the gunship and the light ship loiter in the air, over the town.

Using my map, I brief the pilots where we need to go and where we will first intersect the river, upstream from where we would follow down the river. The pilot relays the mission to the other two helicopters and then our ship rises into the dark sky and heads west on a compass heading to arrive at the river.

When the team arrives over the river, the circle of lights is switched on, turning the river into full daylight. And to my amazement, it appears the middle of the river is full of sampans, all heading downstream. They are not supposed to be there. These are not night fishermen but sampans with only one or two people, maneuvering their boats, which are clearly packed to the gunnels with bundles and packs. Spotlighted and scared, the small boats begin to move toward the safety of the banks, but being a couple of hundred feet from the shore, they cannot outrun the fire of the gunship's machine guns.

As soon as the lights go on, I give the pilot permission to open fire, which he immediately relays to the gunship. The light ship, below us, has the circle of lights facing out the right door of the helicopter, so the light ship pilot flies over the left or east side of the river. The C&C ship flies above the light ship, but along the west bank, firing its .50 caliber machine gun. The .50 caliber's tracers ignite the loads of some sampans while the regular bullets shred the people, destroying the packed equipment and sinking the boats. Not a single boat is able to get to the bank or otherwise escape the deadly fire from above.

In a matter of minutes, along a five-mile stretch of the river, many more sampans are detected and destroyed. The command pilot declares his Firefly team got more kills and destroyed more boats this night than the entire company has during the previous 30 days. With our discovery of the Firefly teams, the Vam Co Dong River becomes a riskier means of transporting war goods to Saigon. Because of our continued success with night missions and our high kill rates, whenever we ask for a team, we always get one.

I am flying one to three Firefly night missions a week. The missions are extraordinarily productive, making it more difficult for NVA or VC movement during darkness. Despite the overall success of these night missions, I develop a personal problem. Staring at the spot of light on the ground (looking for the enemy), as mentioned, can cause vertigo, a sensation of being off-balance, resulting in dizziness and/or nausea. For me, after about 20 to 25 minutes of staring at the light on the ground, I became so nauseous that I vomit. Sitting on the right side in front of the open door, it is easy to just lean forward, stick my head out of the aircraft and hurl. After emptying my stomach, I am good again for another 20 minutes or so. Since our missions seldom run over an hour, the most

I ever vomit is twice. Seven years later I became a pilot, and as a passenger in a plane doing aerobatics, I would get nauseated, but if I am the pilot, it never happens.

One way Major Ai tries to run the war in Trang Bang is by having a secret agent living in the small Cambodian town of Krong Bavet, whose only claim to fame is its location on National Highway 22, an off-shoot in Trang Bang of National Route 1 which runs between the capital of South Vietnam, Saigon, and the capital of Cambodia, Phnom Penh. Krong Bavet is about seven miles west of Trang Bang. The town is sort of an international gateway between the two countries. Because of the large contingent of NVA troops in the city and the relationships between the border town and the local Cambodians and the Vietnamese, Major Ai's agent fits in without notice to gather valuable intelligence regarding planned NVA movements.

On Wednesday, 11 November (Veterans Day), a message from the agent in Cambodia is received that a major effort is under way to transport 107 mm rockets to Viet Cong troops within firing range of Saigon. The 107 is a six-foot, 90-pound weapon with a maximum range of six miles. The agent states that the weapons will be moved out of Cambodia at night, by water buffalo, and within three days. We will be told when, later. Because Cambodia is off-limits to us, we can only observe what the NVA are doing, but we cannot touch. So, we wait until they cross the border before engaging in combat.

For the next two days no confirmation of when the rockets are to leave Cambodia is received. On 14 November we receive the information. The rockets will move that night. Major Ai is given the location where the rocket convoy will cross the border and the location where the group will have to cross a small stream about 50 to 75 feet wide. The location of the stream crossing is about 2,000 feet east of the border, on the Vietnamese side. We plot both locations on a map and think if our Firefly team approaches the stream north (upstream) of the crossing, and flies downstream, we can easily spot where the water buffalo have crossed the water because of all the trampling on the stream banks. The crossing spot is about six miles west of Trang Bang. Major Ai has calculated the time the convoy will cross the stream; therefore, we plan to arrive later so we can catch them in Vietnam. I contact the 334th, explain what we know, and they agree to fly the mission.

That night I crouch on the edge of our small landing pad, with my PRC-25 radio. The C&C ship radios me, stating they are five minutes out. Shortly I hear the muted beat of the chopper. Coming in over our compound, the pilot faces the open fields, alert to sniper fire, poised for an immediate departure.

As I climb aboard, the C&C ship quickly moves forward, nose down, picking up speed and then banking sharply away from the black emptiness of the open field, ascending to join the other two. We fly west toward the stream near the border where I hope we will find the rockets. Excitement is beginning to build, just as when I hunted as a teenager.

Firefly Mission

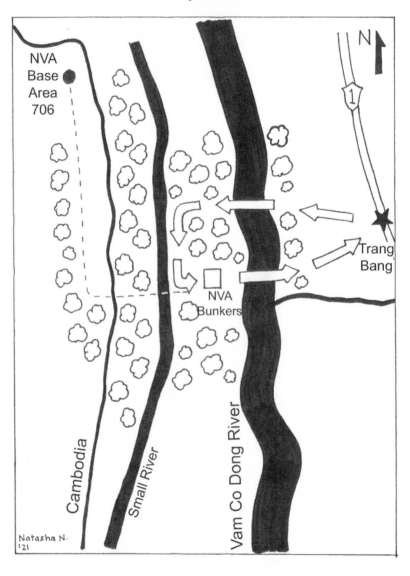

That same feeling returns as Firefly switches on its lights. Following the watercourse, we spot the crossing point.

At 1,000 feet above the ground, I hear the steady whap-whap-whap of our Huey's main rotor blades. The night is pitch-black, moonless. I sit in the open right door cradling my M-79 grenade launcher—a single-shot shoulder-fired weapon, spitting out a 40 mm grenade—in my lap. Over my left shoulder I make out the soft red glow of the instrument panel, and, on the ground below, the soft flickering orange lights of cooking fires pinpoint scattered civilian houses. I am directing a Firefly mission over our target 30 miles northwest of Saigon on the Cambodian border.

Directly below us are unmistakable tracks where several heavy animals trampled the banks on each side of the stream, fading again beneath the dense jungle growth on the near side. We follow the faint trace of an old jungle road where occasional cleared areas reveal freshly matted grass and bushes verifying we are on the right trail. Twisting and turning, we follow the tracks to a small open area.

Eager excitement turns into instant disappointment. The tracks just end in the field—they go nowhere. Maneuvering around the field we cannot see anything to explain what happened. Wondering aloud to each other over the intercom, we curse our luck. The hot trail has evaporated into nothing.

Radio silence is broken by the low ship. Movement is noticed in one corner of the clearing. Quickly the light ship shifts according to the hurried commands of the gunship.

"Swing right ... more ... more ... go to the edge of the tall trees ... hold it ... stop, don't move."

Excitement mounts again as we strain to try and see beneath the foliage. All we see are shadows, but the low ship, down on the deck, is below the treetops and has an excellent view. They have found the water buffalo. Asking what to do, I reply, "Kill them." Moving into position to destroy the animals, the gunship unleashes the first use of our firepower for the night.

We are puzzled, though, as to where the NVA rockets are. Hovering over the field, we don't understand what has happened. The gunship, now hovering a few feet off the ground, sees that what is camouflaged from above becomes visible at ground level—underground bunkers. The gunship is unable to engage the targets. The openings are too low and the clearing too small to allow a proper rocket-run without flying into the shrapnel.

Being armed with the M-79, I carry about a dozen high-explosive, point detonating rounds. The pilots and I agree that the 40 mm grenades are the best we have to shoot into the bunkers. Thus, we switch places with the gunship. The C&C Huey hovers a few feet off the ground next to the bunker opening while I lob a round into the black hole. I engage first one, then a second bunker. Our efforts are immediately rewarded by secondary explosions indicating we have found the rockets.

Moving to the last bunker, I prepare to attack it. The night is torn apart again by the muffled boom of gunfire while shrapnel is bouncing all around. Just before I fire my weapon into the last hole in the ground, I feel a sharp, hot jab in the back of my right thigh, like an electric shock. I ask the pilot if he is flying into our shrapnel. His surprised, negative reply and my sudden realization collide. I tell the pilot I have just been shot.

Now we know where the North Vietnamese soldiers are, and they are not happy about being discovered.

It is sort of like the grand finale at the end of a Fourth of July display; noise, lights, flashes, explosions, all going on at once. Each side trying to outshoot the other. My grenade launcher gains the upper hand, though. I become totally occupied responding to the pinpoints of flame flickering toward us by enemy rifles countering my attack.

It is over quickly. Grabbing my thigh, I pull the twisted copper jacket of a bullet out of the thick muscle. Apparently, a bullet hit the chopper somewhere and it ricocheted up into the back of my leg. The damage doesn't appear too severe; while bloody, it isn't gushing.

We accomplished what we set out to do. The rockets, buffalo and soldiers have been located and destroyed with no serious casualties on our side. Checking the area thoroughly to ensure we have not missed any bunkers; we are satisfied our mission is over. Rising one by one, the helicopters climb out of the field into the black night, lights out, blending once again into the dark sky.

I am dropped off at our compound helicopter pad and limp through the gate, into our house. Most of the advisors are up and playing cards. I explain what happened and ask Sergeant Chesterfield if he would look at my leg. He grabs a bag and we move into another small room where I drop my pants and he examines a large, jagged rip on the back of my right leg, smeared with blood. Because the wound is high, on the back of my thigh, I can't see anything. My medic opens his bag, removing bandages, swabs, disinfectant, and other items and turns me around so he can inspect the injury. The wound is no longer bleeding much. Chesterfield pours some liquid on the swab and then begins to clean out the jagged open cut. Before he starts disinfecting the gash, it feels raw and sore, like a bad paper cut. Jabbing the swab around and into the wound really burns. After pushing and probing and removing cloth threads embedded in the laceration from my pants, he declares the wound clean. Next, he puts more gunk on it and then bandages it. Pronouncing me fit for duty, he retrieves a small tag and fills it out, stating I was wounded by hostile fire while on a combat operation. Upon signing it, he says he will submit this to the province advisory team personnel people, and it will be part of my medical record and be forwarded to MACV headquarters for me to be awarded the Purple Heart.

The next day, the wound hurts even more, like a bruise and a bad cut, at the same time. A couple of days later it is obvious the wound is infected. The injured area looks bigger, is red, swollen, and full of pus, and it hurts more. Sergeant Chesterfield becomes alarmed and arranges for me to ride by helicopter to the Army 3rd Field Hospital in Saigon, where a surgical appointment is made. The chopper picks me up and flies me to the helicopter pad at the hospital.

The Third Field Hospital was activated at Fort Lewis in Washington in March 1965 and transported to Tan Son Nhut, being set up in the buildings of the American Community School just southeast of the airport. Originally created to add support to military medical facilities in the southern part of South Vietnam, it was augmented with other army medical facilities and, by the end of 1965, had become a 325-bed evacuation-type hospital. It rapidly gained a reputation for excellence in the care of combat wounds. It treats combat injuries straight from the battlefield, triaging patients and sending them on to further care and treatment. It is also known for its expertise in the post-operative care of combat wounds, which is why my medic sent me here.

Upon landing, medics come out to receive me and escort me into a building and what looks like a normal hospital emergency room. My clothing is removed, and a hospital gown donned. People come in, look at the wound, mutter some sounds, and leave. Finally, a nurse enters and explains that the wound is infected (of course, I knew that) and debridement is required. I am moved into another room, told to turn over and the procedure begins. Shots are given, the wound is cut open, infected tissue removed, and medicine and gauze stuffed into the now big hole in my thigh (at least it seems big to me, but because of where the wound is, I can't see anything). I am moved again to another room, a small recovery ward. I spend the night, and the next morning the bandage and gauze are removed, inspected, and replaced with new. Some more people bring me my clothes, I am told to get dressed as I am fit for duty and going back to Trang Bang. I am given written instructions for my team medic to follow so my wound will heal. Another person escorts me back to a waiting area, next to the chopper pad. After a couple of hours, my ride appears, and I return to our compound.

14

Being Promoted for
Doing a Good Job as DSA

As the war continues in late 1968, the politicians who will never step into harm's way and the top military leadership struggle to determine what to do and how to do it. This is a complicated war and those running it are not doing a very good job.

The peace talks resemble a clown act. Each side demanding one thing or another. The North refuses to meet if the United States continues to bomb North Vietnam. Operation Rolling Thunder bombing missions began in March of 1965 by the United States to bomb selected military targets in North Vietnam. While the bombing has done considerable damage in the north and killed tens of thousands of people, its military value is questioned by many. The generals advocate for it to continue but the politicians do not. So, President Johnson decides to terminate the bombing at the end of October 1968.

Next is the table controversy. The North wants to talk seated at round tables so everyone will appear having the same status. The South wants a rectangular table to clearly denote two separate factions, opposing each other. By late November, the Government of South Vietnam does not want to recognize the National Liberation Front or the Viet Cong as legitimate entities of the North Vietnamese government, so the peace talks are stymied again.

The politicians demand more information on rural security for the peace talks, which translates to even more reports required by district advisors.

During November large-scale battles seem to decrease but small-scare encounters with guerrilla forces increase. Also acts of terrorism worsen, with more road mines exploding and grenades being thrown into civilian groups.

As we edge into December, my relationship with the 25th does not improve. Our combat operations do not lessen. I have gained back some of the weight I lost to hookworm and the wound in my leg is healing. It is no longer sore, but it is very tender when I sit down on it. The fighting in Trang Bang continues as usual.

During the first week in December, Lieutenant Colonel Bernard pays me a visit, which I think very unusual. He begins inquiring about my health, emphasizing the damage the hookworm and gunshot wound have done to my body. We discuss at length the problems caused by the location of the new hamlets along Route 1 and the Rome Plow strategy. He explains his position in that Vann at CORDS essentially told Bernard to make the problem go away. Yes, Vann agreed, the Vietnamese pacification efforts must be strongly supported by CORDS advisors. At the same time, though, the advisors must get along with the American units operating in their districts and provinces. The heavy lifting in combat and much of the security where we are in Vietnam is because of the U.S. combat forces. Also, Hau Nghia province is unquestionably the most important real estate in Vietnam for the security of Saigon.

The colonel and I share a common background. Both of us have served as enlisted marines, he in World War II and me in the mid- to late 1950s. He openly shares his feelings about the United States being in Vietnam and his thoughts on Westmoreland's vision of how to fight this war.

Being fully aware of the French involvement in Vietnam before us, Bernard is opposed to America being engaged in this war. His background in counterinsurgency leads him to passionately believe that the strategy of employing the military might of the United States (as Westmoreland has advocated) is not the way to go. He describes several incidents in which our military forces destroyed hamlets and harmed Vietnamese people such that we (and by association, GVN) are no longer trusted by the local population. He considers that many actions of the U.S. military (the 25th Division) are arguably the best recruiting arguments the VC have.

He then comments on my short tenure as Trang Bang DSA. He feels I got a raw deal. As soon as I joined the district advisory team, the team leader, Tony Lorenzo, got sick and left, leaving me in charge without a proper orientation. He praises me for being effective under adverse conditions, especially noting my courageous performance under hostile fire, despite all my physical problems.

I now began to wonder, where are we going with this?

More praise on the excellent job I am doing and how successful I am with my Vietnamese counterparts. At this point I feel there is a great big "but" coming. He continues by saying he is genuinely concerned about my health. He insists being in the field as much as I am is not helping my recovery. He indicates that I need better food, better living conditions, and I should be rewarded for the excellent job I am doing as the DSA. He finally announces that I will be transferred in a few days to Gia Dinh province, as a staff officer. Colonel Bernard indicates this is a promotion for me to function at a much higher level, and in much better living arrangements.

Preparations are being made for me to report in to MACV Team 44 in Saigon on Saturday, 14 December 1968. At this point in time my exact duty assignment is unknown. Maybe because no one knows what I will be doing with Team 44 is why I am sent first to stay at John Paul Vann's villa in III Corps Headquarters. Or perhaps it is in regard to my resistance to many 25th Division policies? Who knows?

I am told that an Infantry major, already in-country will replace me, but only after I depart. A week after my surprising visit with Colonel Bernard, I am ready to move. On Tuesday, 10 December, I depart Trang Bang and Hau Nghia forever. I cannot say I regret leaving or will miss Trang Bang. This was a very difficult time in my life and I also experienced considerable physical harm to my body. Life could only get better. A helicopter transports me directly to the helipad next to Vann's villa in Bien Hoa.

At the villa I am met by an Infantry colonel, Elmer Ochs. He is the military senior advisor to the III Corps CORDS, a deputy to John Paul Vann. Ironically, while I have never met Colonel Ochs before, my wife knows his wife as they live near each other in Battle Park at Fort Benning.

Vann's house is a modern version of a typical Vietnamese upper-middle-class educated bureaucrat's home. Large and spacious, it has many rooms. I am ushered into a comfortable guest bedroom. I am shown around the home, where I will eat, and an inviting living room (where I will spend most of my time, reading novels).

Colonel Ochs is only around some evenings, where we pass our time discussing our different military careers. He seems to reiterate Colonel Bernard's belief that I have done a superior job and accomplished more than my predecessors. He echoes Bernard's belief that my new assignment is a reward for a job well done. Toward the end of the week he explains a helicopter will take me to Tan Son Nhut air base Sunday morning, where I will be picked up by someone from Team 44. After reporting in I will meet my new teammates and then learn what my next assignment will be.

I never see John Vann and do not know why. I am just told he is gone. I think he is away on CORDS business. At this time, I am not aware he was reassigned in November to IV Corps, in the same job as

Deputy for CORDS, except now in the Delta, where he first served in Vietnam as an army advisor to the ARVN 7th Division.

Sunday morning, after a short helicopter ride from Bien Hoa, I am deposited next to an admin building at the airport. A sergeant is waiting for me and helps carry my baggage. Inside an Armor major, Pete Mendelsohn, introduces himself. Slightly taller and heavier than me, with short brown hair and a pleasant disposition, he is the Gia Dinh province S-3 advisor for Advisor Team 44. I will be working for him as the Gia Dinh RF and PF advisor, primarily focusing on the security of the bridges around Saigon. He briefly explains about the province headquarters where we work and the guarded villa where most province staff officer advisors live and eat breakfast and dinner. The jeep is loaded with my gear and I climb into the back for the short ride to my new office and assignment.

The Gia Dinh province headquarters is two and a half miles (as the crow flies) east of Tan Son Nhut air base, which is where the province advisors work. It is located on Chi Lang Street, which is about two and a half miles north of downtown Saigon.

Pete takes me inside the province headquarters building to the personnel officer, where I sign in. This is a combined Vietnamese headquarters housing both the province officials and the military responsible for the security of Saigon. Next, we move to Pete's S-3 (operations) office, where I will work. He introduces me to some officers and NCOs, members of his S-3 staff. After showing me around the advisor headquarters, Pete says that he will now take me to the place I will be staying, a house MACV leases for the advisor officers to live in.

Driving out of province headquarters we turn right onto Chi Lang, heading back toward the airport, which brings us to a genuinely nice residential neighborhood. Compared to the better homes in Trang Bang, these are mansions. Halfway up the block, we turn right, again, stopping at a high stucco-covered wall with broken bottles embedded into concrete, sharp edges up, on the top of the wall. Splayed out across the top of the wall is a roll of barbed concertina wire. At the locked gate, on the drive into the mansion, are two ARVN soldiers armed with M-16s. Recognizing the major, they open the gate so we can drive up to the house. The advisor team house is only one and a half miles west of province headquarters and a mile east of Tan Son Nhut air base.

It is a large two-story white stucco oriental cum southwestern style building with several smaller buildings behind it. The grounds are lush with several flower beds and manicured lawns. Pete explains it is a French villa on one acre built for a wealthy French businessman. The advisors just leased it in October. To the right of the main house is a big in-ground swimming pool. I can hear male voices and female giggles coming from the pool. Obviously, it is being used by both genders.

Pete takes me inside house; it is a spacious, grand home. The driver has my baggage and follows us as Pete leads us up the stairs. There is a big hallway with several closed doors which Pete indicates are the bedrooms of province field-grade officer advisors. He leads me into one, a large sunny room with several large windows. The room has four beds (covered with netting to keep out mosquitoes), four chests of drawers with a long place, on the side, to hang clothes (a wardrobe or armoire) with a light bulb at the bottom of the hanging space to ward off mildew by its heat, a small bookshelf and a couple small desks and chairs with lamps on each one. I am sharing this room with three other majors, all on the province advisor staff. I simply cannot believe this, especially as I recall the living conditions at Trang Bang. The driver places my baggage on the floor and leaves.

The entire house has five modern bathrooms (with hot and cold running water) and a total of seven large bedrooms, on both floors. The entire house has electricity and most rooms have ceiling fans. Pete then shows me the rest of the house. He explains about the staff who maintain the building and grounds. There are cooks, maids, groundskeepers and the security soldiers on guard, all day, every day. Some of the Vietnamese live on the property. The kitchen is in a separate building, and on the first floor is a large dining room to seat over a dozen people. There is a large living room with sofas and chairs and a small table or two. A bookcase holds paperbacks and a variety of board games. There is also a formal ballroom which has our bar. Out front, to one side, is a large parking area with a variety of advisor jeeps lined up. Between the pool and the main house is a patio area with outdoor tables and chairs. The entire setup reminds me of an affluent fraternity house.

Pete explains that there are other places like this which house other province officers and enlisted advisors. I have a real problem believing this. In both tours as a combat advisor, I have never seen anything as opulent as this. Pete says that cooks provide three meals, yet most habitants usually eat lunch elsewhere. Vietnamese maids keep the entire house neat and clean and wash and iron our clothes and shine our boots and shoes. The property is guarded by several rotating Vietnamese soldiers who do not live on the property. Two on the front gate, two to four on roaming patrol, and some on the roof, all armed with automatic weapons.

Pete says he will leave me to unpack and get settled in. He asks me to be ready to leave the next morning around 8 a.m. when a driver will pick me up. I will meet the two officers and two NCOs who will work for me. Additionally, I will meet our boss, a civilian Foreign Service Reserve officer who is really an army colonel, promotable to brigadier general. Pete leaves and I begin unpacking and getting settled in. I still can't believe this, in the middle of a war, about 30 miles from Trang Bang and the Cambodian border and I am now living in a mansion, a very, very secure mansion.

15

Duty in Saigon:
What a Way to Fight a War

As promised, my ride pulls up a few minutes after 8 a.m. Fifteen minutes later I am in Pete's office. He shows me my corner of the S-3 operations advisor office and covers what my duties are to be.

Specifically, I will be the senior advisor to the commanders of all Regional Force battalions and separate RF companies in Gia Dinh province that report to the province chief. I will also advise the commanders of Popular Force units that come under province control. If an RF or PF unit is under direct control of a district chief, the district advisors will provide advising, not me. My duties will be to visit the units, monitor their training, assist in any logistical support they need, evaluate their combat effectiveness, and assist the unit commanders and their staff in any way possible.

Saigon has dozens of bridges crossing the rivers, streams, and canals that flow through or by the city. The entire east side of Saigon is flanked by the Saigon River. Because of its size and depth, there are no bridges from the city across this river. North of the city, though, there are bridges crossing this river. On both the north and south limits of Saigon are several waterways and smaller tributaries, all flowing from the west, emptying into the Saigon River. All these water courses have several bridges which must be guarded against VC attacks. Security is provided by RF and PF units. The number of Vietnamese territorial forces securing Saigon and the province add up to the same number of soldiers found in a military division.

Additionally, I will supervise the NCOs and officers of the 23 Mobile Advisory Teams assigned within Gia Dinh province. The official team roster calls for a captain and a lieutenant and three NCOs (one sergeant first class and two more either SFCs or staff sergeants). However, many teams only have three or four members. All the teams in Gia Dinh add up to between 90 and 100 men.

To support me as the RF/PF advisor I have two officers and two NCOs assigned to me. Because of my experience and background, I prefer to work directly with the Vietnamese, so my staff handles all the administrative paperwork and works with the MAT teams. For the next five weeks I spend most of my time with the RF and PF units guarding the bridges and their commanders. I rarely spend any time in the S-3 advisor office at province but accompany Vietnamese commanders as we visit the bridges they are guarding. I see my job as helping my Vietnamese counterparts to become better and to have the resources needed to accomplish their missions. I despise the continuous demand for more and more information to support or justify the advisor effort in this conflict. I think of myself as a warrior, not a paper pusher, and therefore resist, as much as possible, fighting this war by filling out forms and creating reports.

Later that morning I meet Colonel Herbert. A large stocky man with a good-looking broad face and a pleasant smile. In his mid–40s he is balding with sparse gray hair. Currently he is the province senior advisor as a civilian Foreign Service officer yet is awaiting promotion to brigadier general. His is not an uncommon status. While a full colonel in the army, he is working as a civilian U.S. government employee.

A 1945 West Point graduate, he is a Korean War hero as the commander of a Ranger company. He is one of the army's first Airborne Rangers, co-founder of the Ranger Department at Fort Benning and an unconventional warfare expert. He has served several years in Vietnam and today he is dressed in civilian slacks and a short-sleeve shirt.

Shaking my hand, he warmly welcomes me to Team 44. He says he is familiar with my background and is glad to have an experienced combat officer on his team and especially one who is fluent in both French and Vietnamese. He begins to tell me about Saigon and Gia Dinh, and as he speaks it is obvious he is an expert on Vietnam, based on his considerable time in-country.

Saigon is an autonomous capital city. Vietnam has 44 provinces, of which four are just cities: Hue, Da Nang, Delat, and Saigon. Saigon is divided into eight districts; they do not have names like other districts but are numbered. Actually, Saigon is two cities melded into one. In the fifth district is Cho Lon, which means "big market." This is essentially the Chinese section of Saigon and the part of the city where many shops, stores, and other retail establishments are located.

Cho Lon is also the headquarters of the U.S. Support Activity, Saigon. This military activity provides all the lodging and feeding for the thousands of U.S. military assigned to the city. Over 40 Vietnamese

Gia Dinh Province

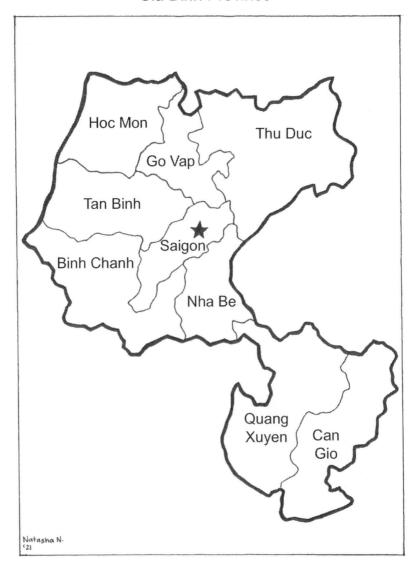

Natasha N.
'21

hotels have been leased and turned into housing quarters and mess facilities for enlisted and officers serving in the hundreds of various U.S. military offices scattered throughout Saigon. There are over two hundred other properties which the Support Activity manages as well as all the personnel and equipment, storage facilities, and almost 2,000 vehicles necessary for the Support Activity to function. Additionally, it runs the Post Exchange in Cho Lon, the busiest in the world.

The city is a hodgepodge of political and legal divisions. Colonel Herbert explains that while Saigon technically is not in Gia Dinh province, physically it is. The security of the city is partly the responsibility of the province. For example, province RF and PF units guard most bridges in and just outside the city. But Vietnamese regular military also guard various U.S. and Vietnamese headquarters. And top-level Vietnamese politicians and senior generals have their own guards from elite Airborne, Ranger, or Marine units. Also, of course, American military, embassy, and Foreign Service facilities additionally have U.S. troops providing security. Furthermore, there are the National Police providing security and manning checkpoints throughout the city. Advisor offices and living quarters are often guarded by Vietnamese soldiers, selected by either the Vietnamese province or district chiefs.

"I am telling you this," Colonel Herbert says, "to make you aware that you are an advisor assigned to Gia Dinh province, but your duties will have you interacting with a variety of various military commands and you must make sure you do nothing to upset any of them."

"South Vietnam," he continues, "is smaller than half our state of California. In several areas it is less than 50 miles wide, as you know from being in one of those areas in Hau Nghia and Trang Bang." He notes this country has a population of 14 million with around 11 million living in rural areas. Saigon itself has some 2 million residents but because of the war about 700,000 of its residents are homeless. During Tet this past January, in Saigon, alone, over 33,000 homes were destroyed leaving 200,000 people homeless.

"In Vietnam, many people perceive two classes of people; those who work with their hands, laborers, or unskilled workers such as farmers, fishermen and woodcutters and the educated people who use their intellectual skills for employment. These are doctors, lawyers, teachers, and other professionals such as those who run the government. Your job will bring you into contact with both classes. In this province you will interact with educated professional people (the Vietnamese people classify American military officers in this category) as well as the laborers and homeless. Treat all with respect and dignity.

"As Pete told you, your primary responsibility is to advise and support the province RF and PF units securing the area bridges. Your experience and language capabilities should serve you well. We welcome you as an excellent addition to our team."

He asks if I have any questions, and I do not so we are dismissed.

During my eight months serving under Colonel Herbert we will become friends (not like drinking buddies but as mentor and mentee) and I will come to admire him greatly.

Pete then introduces me to the province advisory staff and the administrative staff which support the advisors. Colonel Herbert as PSA has two deputies. One is his military advisor, an Infantry lieutenant colonel, and the other is a civilian CORDS officer, a Foreign Service member. On the administrative side, Herbert's team executive officer is an Air Defense Artillery major. For me, I report and take my orders from Pete, the S-3 advisor. Next up my chain is the team executive officer and

GIA DINH PROVINCE
ADVISOR TEAM

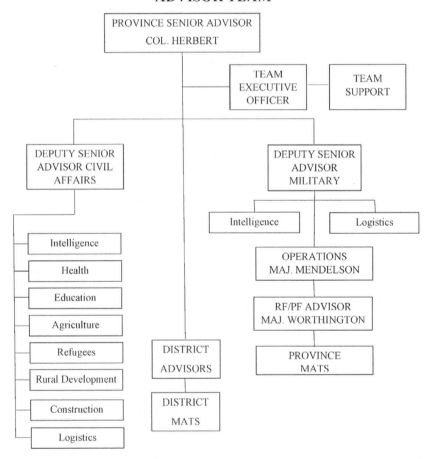

then the military deputy advisor. Undoubtedly, the Gia Dinh province advisory team is one of the largest in Vietnam.

Shortly after my arrival, some of the province advisors are gathered in our conference room to receive some info from the civilian CORDS deputy advisor. After his talk, several of us are discussing our past and how we ended up in Gia Dinh. When I describe how I was sent to Saigon to recover from my hookworm and the leg wound, I mention how I was told the reassignment was to be a promotion for the good job I was doing as the Trang Bang DSA.

As I am talking, the civilian CORDS deputy and the team executive officer look at each other and their eyes roll. Upon completing my story, I ask them what they know that has escaped me. The two men look down, hem and haw, and finally the civilian deputy speaks.

"Bob," he says, "you were fired!"

Not comprehending what he is saying, I ask him what he means. I explain what Colonel Bernard told me and the time spent at Vann's villa and my posting to Gia Dinh.

Then the civilian explains what he and the adjutant know. Apparently the 25th Division saw me as a thorn in their side. Since I am leaving the army, threats to my career had no impact on me. My insistence on supporting the Vietnamese pacification missions was at odds with the combat missions of the 25th. Pure and simple, I was in the way. The generals of the 25th had sufficient influence with the CORDS commander who replaced John Paul Vann to create a reason for me to be replaced.

My rapport with the Vietnamese was excellent. As a DSA, I could not be faulted, therefore I could not be relieved for not doing my job. So, someone produced the idea of transferring me to a higher-level staff assignment somewhere in Saigon so I could recover from my parasites and wound. I was then told the transfer was for doing an excellent job and concerns for my health. The truth was, I was being canned because the 25th Division wanted to get rid of me.

I am told by the adjutant my replacement was a major from the 25th Division staff who had already established his loyalty to the division missions. He became the Trang Bang DSA. Learning this just reinforces my decision to leave the army. My being fired for doing my job was another reflection on the poor leadership found at the top levels of the army. Wow, was I totally conned!

On reflection, though, learning this is not unexpected. I was a thorn in the side of the 25th. Also, I was particularly good as the DSA for Trang Bang. Therefore, the pretext of me being transferred due to my health did seem plausible, but maybe I could have been more aware while being parked at John Paul Vann's villa until another job was decided for me. At any rate, this new job should avoid any more conflicts between me and regular U.S. military units. Now, knowing I was fired for doing my job makes no difference to me. I am looking forward to the new challenges ahead.

What I Actually Do in Saigon: Life in the Big City

One of the first things Pete sets up is a briefing by the Vietnamese RF officer in charge of all the province RF and PF bridge security forces. Shortly after I arrive Pete and I travel to a Vietnamese headquarters building, old and smallish, where we are ushered into a snug briefing room. I am introduced to the RF officer-in-charge (OIC) and several other RF officers, the Vietnamese commanders of the troops guarding the bridges. All of us are conversing in English, in which most Vietnamese officers are very fluent.

As we are chatting, I hear a couple of PF officers and their NCOs commenting (in Vietnamese) on providing a briefing describing the bridge security mission of the PF and RF units and how they are configured to achieve their assigned tasks. They indicate some disdain for having to do this in English as they feel their advisor should learn their language. Apparently, they have not encountered a province advisor who is fluent in their language. The RF OIC then invites us to sit down for the briefing and he introduces the Vietnamese briefing team. As the briefers stand to begin, I ask the OIC, speaking in Vietnamese, if his briefers could give the briefing in Vietnamese. The OIC and the briefers look at each other, obviously astonished because an American is articulate in their language.

I explain to Pete what I have asked, believing I will get a better briefing and more accurate responses to my questions if it is in the briefing team's language. He agrees and tells the OIC it is fine to continue in Vietnamese, which they do.

During the briefing I interrupt several times asking questions about areas of the mission I don't fully understand. The briefing becomes more of an informal discussion of what they do and how than a formal briefing. It is evident I am not a new advisor fresh from the United States but an experienced combat veteran. In our back and forth discussion questions arise about my background and how I know so much about PF and RF units. Upon learning I just came from Trang Bang in Hau Nghia, my stock with the Vietnamese rises higher and higher. As I am interacting with the bridge commanders and the briefers, the OIC explains to Pete what we are talking about. The briefing concludes with me asking if the various commanders could escort me to their bridges and introduce me to their troops so we can discuss any supply problems they have and I might be able to provide some insight on how to improve their defensive postures. They agree to this.

As we express our goodbyes, I recognize I made a very favorable impression with them, most notably with my fluency in their language. I realize that Pete is also enthralled because of the positive relationships I have established so quickly. While he knew I could speak Vietnamese, he was not aware of how fluent I am.

Over the next several weeks I spend most of my time visiting various detachments guarding the bridges with their commanders, mostly lieutenants, some warrant officers, and a couple of captains. I ask questions regarding fields of fire or how they would detect an underwater demolition swimmer wanting to destroy supporting pillars and how they would thwart him. Sometimes, but not very often, I can offer suggestions to improve their defensive positions. Their greatest problems relate to a lack of ammo, equipment, or supplies, primarily logistic in nature.

I become acquainted with the supply advisors who arrange for me to speak directly with the province supply people. This allows me to improve the distribution of some supplies to the guardians of the bridges. Two things are accomplished: first, the morale of the RF and PF soldiers increases; and second, my acceptance as an advisor increases significantly.

Occasionally I will interact with the MATs assigned throughout the province, mostly in the districts surrounding Saigon. Can Gio District in the Rung Sat Special Zone (RSSZ) I never visit. The RF and PF units there function under the Vietnamese Navy, which controls combat operations in the RSSZ. Therefore, my input is not needed or expected.

As I visit various bridge sites, I also receive tours of Saigon along with a narration on what I am seeing. I never leave our advisor house without being armed. I carry my service pistol, the 1911A1 .45 caliber semi-automatic. It is in the standard dark-colored leather military holster on the standard web pistol belt. Also on the belt is a magazine pouch holding two full magazines and my medical pouch containing a bandage and medicine for a wound. Depending on where I might be going, I will add a canteen to the belt. If I am going to visit a bridge in a more dangerous area, I will also carry my .30 caliber M-1 carbine with extra magazines in the lower pockets of my jungle fatigue pants.

I cannot recall ever seeing Colonel Herbert armed with a weapon. But then almost every time I see him is in the advisor headquarters.

Sometimes I am invited to a more formal Vietnamese function such as a play or a dinner or some work-related social function. In most instances I wear my jungle fatigue uniform, without my .45 and the pistol belt. But I am still armed. On my regular belt I have a small leather holster holding my stainless-steel Smith and Wesson model 60 .38 Special snub-nose revolver. I would distribute loose cartridges among various pockets. Because the jungle fatigue shirt is worn over the belt (like a jacket), my holstered revolver is not visible. Thus, I appear unarmed, though I am not. In fact, I do not go anywhere in Saigon unarmed.

Pilots have an old saying about dangerous weather. It is better to be on the ground, wishing you were in the air, than up in the sky, wishing you were on the ground. In Saigon, I would rather carry and never need to use my weapon than not have it if I need it. As it turns out, I never have to draw or use a weapon, ever, in Saigon.

In 1965 the war in Vietnam transformed from an advisor war to the commitment of American combat units. Beginning in March 1965, two U.S. Marine combat battalions entered Vietnam. That was followed by more marines, then in May the army's 173rd Airborne Brigade, then the newly created First Cavalry Division (Airmobile). In 1966 the war became one with several U.S. units in combat. And as the war changed, so did Saigon.

My initial introduction to Saigon was in January 1966, when I began my first assignment to Vietnam as a combat advisor. Saigon (referred to as the "Pearl of the Orient" or "Paris of the Orient") was a beautiful city of broad boulevards flanked by leafy trees providing shade and some breeze to temper the hot tropic sun. Streets were lined with open-air cafes while hotel rooftops embraced bars hosting live music and dancing. Duong Tu Do (Liberty Street), formerly Rue Catinat, was like a Paris street featuring the latest in clothing boutiques, fine dining in French restaurants, shops, along with nightclubs and theaters for evening entertainment. At its south end, a block from the Saigon River and the park including the statues of the Troung sisters—national heroines for their resistance to the Chinese domination of Vietnam in AD 40—is the distinguished Caravelle Hotel. A modern air-conditioned hotel built in 1959, financed by French investors. This ten-story building is home to the Saigon bureaus of ABC, CBS, and NBC, as well as the embassies of New Zealand and Australia. The rooftop bar is as famous as the hotel. During the evenings, patrons can sip drinks, listen to the music, and safely observe the tracers of firefights in the countryside, just a few miles away.

In the center of Saigon is the Cercle Sportif, a country-club-type facility for the elite, rich and famous of Saigon and foreign visitors.

The main structure is a yellow two-story building with a red tiled roof. Second-story balconies line the back side, upon which umbrella-covered tables are randomly positioned. Boasting a large swimming pool and several tennis courts, it functions as a playground for the wealthy.

In January 1966, I could readily see why Saigon was referred to as the "Pearl of the Orient."

Today, three years later, Saigon is vastly different. Many of the splendid shade trees have been cut down so they won't offer conceal-ment or protection from fields of fire. Alleys are crowded with card-board boxes covered with worn plastic sheets where the homeless live. Hundreds of thousands of Vietnamese have traded the destruction and deaths of their rural homelands for the safety of Saigon, only to find starvation, and disease (plague and tuberculosis) their enemies now. The city was originally constructed by the French to house a little over half a million residents. Now that it is home to four times that many, the city public works cannot keep up with removing the refuse, or provid-ing enough electric power, water or sewage. Walking the streets now, it is common to see children and adults defecating and urinating in the streets and gutters.

Any lot that was vacant has now become a shanty slum consist-ing of dirt floor hovels comprised of wrecked lumber, rusty sheet metal, jagged crumpled aluminum, cardboard, and plastic sheeting. From the air, by helicopter, sometimes the area covered by these pathetic homes seems to stretch forever.

There are still areas where the top 5 percent of the city's wealthy live in fine old French villas or more modern homes. There are very few fine (and expensive) restaurants in Saigon, today.

The streets, by day, are packed with pedicabs (both pedal and motorized), bicycles (again both pedal and motorized), vehicles of all shapes and sizes, military jeeps, trucks, buses, and the ubiquitous blue and white small Renault taxis. While at some major intersections the flow of traffic is monitored by policemen, it is mostly regulated by the "he who dares, goes" aggressive driver mentality. Pedestrians are every-where. Most noticed are the pretty, dark-haired slim young women in their flowing and tight bodice ao dais. Many men only wear undershirts and underwear shorts, while others wear Western slacks and sport shirts. Military uniforms run the gamut from worn and bleached jungle fatigues with scuffed boots to green utility fatigues with polished boots to khaki, short-sleeved uniforms with black polished low quarter shoes.

The docks along the Saigon River are full of workers unloading ships from across the oceans or filling them with Vietnamese goods and products. The ports are extremely busy as most of what Saigon needs and uses comes via ship. Every month over 100 ocean-going vessels arrive.

At night, the city can become dangerous, so traffic and people seldom roam about. The downtown bars offer music, dancing, alcohol, and females and are mostly frequented by younger military who have access to a vehicle or live nearby. When I first arrived in Saigon in 1966, some officers who were staying at Koepler Compound took me across the street to a couple of bars to show me what was available. One bar even had a live pet tiger.

Saigon at the beginning of 1969 is so different than what I had seen three years before. While I am shown much of the city by the RF and PF officers during the day, I almost never venture out of the team house after dark. I don't believe it is safe.

During the 1950s and early '60s, American advisors and Foreign Service staff in Vietnam could be accompanied by their families. Because of the increasing combat in the war, in May 1965, President Johnson ordered all American dependents to depart Vietnam. There were many complete families of the military, embassy, other federal agency staff, and civilians living and working mostly in Saigon. Most families returned to the States, while others just moved to another nearby (and safer) country. For example, Colonel Herbert's wife lives in Thailand and she visits him in Saigon. Various times I meet her when she visits. He has his own quarters elsewhere in the city.

For about five weeks I advise the bridge security units and live in the team house. During the days, usually Monday through Saturday, I am visiting RF and PF units. Most nights, during the week, I spend with various RF or PF units guarding the bridges. At night (when staying at our team house) or on Sunday I seldom venture beyond the advisor villa. Occasionally a Vietnamese officer who lives in Saigon will invite me to visit his home and family on a Sunday.

Throughout the city are bachelor officers' quarters (BOQ) with small officer messes, like a miniature officers' club. Sporadically, if I can find other officers to accompany me for security purposes, we go to a nearby mess for dinner. There is a U.S. Army company grade BOQ that has a nice mess not too far from our team house. Next to that is a USO club which offers a variety of services and game rooms. What I enjoy best are the latest in magazines, newspapers, and books but also a snack bar which sells American-style hamburgers, French fries, and milkshakes. Unfortunately, my tenure at the team house is so short I only am able to visit the officers' mess a few times and the USO only once. During my first tour I visited the downtown USO every chance I got to visit Saigon because of the excellent American food at the snack bar.

In the evenings I spend time working on a university correspondence graduate education course I am taking via mail or reading novels. The younger, single officers living in the team house somehow always seem to have young, pretty Vietnamese women visiting them and using the pool. I never use the pool, but many evenings can hear the gaiety, laughing and frolicking coming from the pool area. For some unknown reason I never ask where these girls came from, so I never know who or what they were. I suspect that they work in various American offices where the officers made their acquaintance.

Wednesday, 25 December 1968 ... Christmas Day

We have the day off, so I sleep in. I have some wrapped Christmas presents from my family and the Roxbury, Connecticut, Congregational Church on my desk, waiting to be opened. The package from the church is mostly filled with home-baked food such as cookies, fudge, and cake. Anita and the girls sent me typing paper (for my homework), felt-tipped pens, a couple of novels, and food including pancake mix, syrup, cheese, and candy. After opening my gifts and writing thank-you letters, I go to one of our officer messes for the magnificent Christmas dinner. It begins with shrimp cocktail and crackers. The main course is roast turkey and gravy, corn bread dressing, cranberry sauce, mashed potatoes and glazed sweet potatoes with buttered mixed vegetables or buttered peas, assorted relishes, and hot rolls with butter. Drinks are iced tea or fresh milk and desert is fruit cake, mince pie or pumpkin pie with whipped topping. Without a doubt, this is the most sumptuous meal I have ever eaten during my two tours in Vietnam. After enjoying the meal, I return to the team house to read a novel.

Christmas passes into the new year. I continue to work with the bridge security units but realize that, as nice as it is, Saigon duty is not my cup of tea. It is becoming boring. I am a warrior, not a chairborne ranger. I want out of the city to return to the field. All the six districts surrounding Saigon have district advisor teams like mine in Trang Bang. As the Gia Dinh RF/PF advisor, I never fire a shot in danger or ever find myself in harm's way. In my mind, I am no longer participating in a war but only seeing it from afar.

I learn that another Dartmouth graduate, a Captain Edward P. Stafford, who graduated in 1965, is assigned within the district. Stafford is the great-grandson of the famous U.S. Navy admiral Robert Peary, noted for his late-1800s and early 1900s exploration of the Arctic region.

Operation in Rung Sat Special Zone

On 15 January I fly down to visit the district advisor team in Quang Xuyen in the Rung Sat Special Zone (RSSZ). That night the district chief learns the location of a VC arms cache. He immediately plans an operation using U.S. Navy small landing craft to transport the RF soldiers. I go on this mission and it brings back memories of my first combat amphibious assault in Lebanon, in July 1958, when I was a Marine private first class.

After our landing we still have a way to go to arrive at the hidden weapons. The swampy ground sucks the feet deeper; it's like walking in glue. As I move around bushes and duck under jungle growth, I somehow step into an area of quicksand, I cannot reach the bottom but by grabbing branches of a short bush or tree, I manage to pull myself out.

Much of the Rung Sat has been destroyed by defoliation using Agent Orange. Vast areas of this swamp are nothing but dead trees, dead brush, and burnt-looking grasses. Ironically, 46 years later I will undergo emergency open heart surgery to repair a heart severely damaged by exposure to Agent Orange.

We continue our quest and ford several small streams until we reach one where we must swim across. Unfortunately, there are some soldiers who can't swim who have to be helped, and those men who are carrying radios also need help.

Finally, we reach our objective and it is empty. We take a break and then reverse ourselves, repeating the arduous journey back to our landing craft. This operation is clearly one of the most strenuous I have ever been on. Moving through this godforsaken terrain is bad enough so how do you fight under these conditions? I am sure glad I am not assigned here. At the end of the day I am back at the advisor team quarters, waiting for my helicopter ride to return to province. This operation has totally wiped me out.

While I do enjoy working with the Vietnamese troops and spending time with them, I feel that I am not really contributing to the war and just killing time until I leave the army. I describe my plight to Colonel Herbert, asking (almost begging) to return to a combat unit, to return to the war. I am not happy with duty in Saigon. I want out.

Additionally, letters from Anita clearly reveal her feelings that my the decision to leave the army was made without her input, and she does not want me to quit the military. During the next four months her dissatisfaction regarding my determination to depart the service becomes a building source of contention between us. It is clear she is very unhappy with this.

I am beginning to question what is happening with my life. I hate the army, my job is boring, and my wife is not happy with our future. Twelve years in the military, which I am quitting, but to do what?

Hoc Mon

On Saturday, 18 January, Colonel Herbert calls me into his office. He says he understands my frustration, not being back in the field. He asks what I think of going to Hoc Mon district as the temporary DSA for a brief time, until the major assigned to the position arrives.

Before answering I consider the pros and cons of the assignment. It would only be a fleeting respite from my current job, but I would return to the field. What do I know about Hoc Mon?

Hoc Mon is one of the eight districts in the province. I know Gia Dinh (and Saigon) are often referred to as the industrial center of South Vietnam. Thu Duc district is home to much heavy industry such as an electric power plant, a water purification plant, a cement factory. Throughout the province are plenty of light industry facilities doing boat and vehicle repairs, food processing, and making various building materials. The province has a population of one and a quarter million people with about 800,000 living just outside the Saigon city limits. Much of the rural land is used to grow rice, tobacco, vegetables, and fruit and to raise livestock. The tank farms in Nha Be belonging to Cal-Tex, Esso, and Shell provide most of the nation's fuel. The roads in this province are good.

For most of the districts, security is not a major issue. Hoc Mon (with just under 140,000 residents) is seen as very secure, while Binh Chanh, which lies in the path from Cambodia used by the VC and NVA to bring troops and weapons to Saigon, usually has enemy contact somewhere every night. Thu Duc also has some security concerns in some areas of the district.

Two of the districts, Quang Xuyen and Can Gio, are in the RSSZ, which is under the control of the Vietnamese Navy for combat missions, yet under the province chief for administrative support. Currently it appears these two districts are encountering difficulty fighting the VC. It seems like they seldom engage any enemy in their operations. Also, the American advisors have acquired a less than stellar reputation. Rumors are that the senior advisor spends most of his time in Saigon and the other advisors seldom accompany district troops on combat operations.

The weather from November to April is the dry season. Temperatures run from the 50s to the 90s, but it is dry and dusty outside of

Hoc Mon all-female Popular Force platoon, Bob in back row, middle left, facing camera.

Saigon. Hoc Mon is a relatively safe location with most likely few combat operations, so the job of the DSA would probably focus on CORDS functions, mostly administrative duties and working on civic projects.

I need something different, and this sounds better than what I am doing in Saigon, so I agree to do it.

I quickly pack up and move to Hoc Mon on 24 January. I meet with the advisor team in place (minus the senior advisor) and learn some things about the district that I do not know. It is, by comparison to other districts I have been in, relatively affluent. It has a much higher standard of living than most other districts. Because of a lack of active combat encounters, the district focuses on making itself a better place to live, with an emphasis on the physical such as improving schools, medical facilities, village and district offices and buildings and repair of roads and bridges. Additionally, I learn that the district production of food crops and livestock far exceeds what the district consumes, thus it sells the surplus in Saigon.

Clearly Hoc Mon is a very industrious and, by comparison to Trang Bang, prosperous district.

In Trang Bang, my focus as the district senior advisor was on combat, defeating the VC, locating, and destroying the enemy. In Hoc Mon, my focus is not on security, as the local RF and PF units are doing an admirable job of this. The captain on my team (my deputy for military affairs) spends most of his time working with the local Vietnamese military forces. My other deputy, a foreign national working in Vietnam sort of like the U.S. Peace Corps volunteers, is assigned as the CORDS civil affairs advisor and works with the district administrative staff for the operation and maintenance of the district.

My job is to oversee/monitor the work of my two deputies and the officers, NCOs, and civilians as part of the district advisor team. My work will take me from the District Intelligence and Operating Coordination Center to visits with the district agriculture advisor to schools and medical facilities with the proud district chief to territorial military range firing exercises with my military deputy. This is quite a reversal of my duties as Trang Bang DSA.

I have mentioned several times, I never go anywhere in Vietnam, unarmed. In Hoc Mon, though, so many of the district officials I work with or go on district visits travel unarmed that carrying my .45 in a holster on my web belt seems sort of inappropriate. So, I carry my Smith & Wesson .38 snub-nose revolver, holstered on my regular pants belt, under my jungle fatigue shirt. The weapon invisible to most, I feel safer.

One unique PF unit I enjoy visiting is a village all-female PF platoon combat unit made up entirely of women and young girls. They wear a dark field uniform of long pants and shirts with white hats that sort of look like a mix of the old-time straw boaters and wide brim, flat-topped cowboy hats. The platoon has 51 females ranging in age from pre-teens to women in their early 40s. All the women are trained as medics.

The social aspects of Hoc Mon are plentiful and immensely fun. Most events have some sort of patriotic flavor, some much more than others. Beginning in the early evening, the event usually commences with various short speeches by district officials. Because of my Vietnamese fluency, I am often asked to give a talk about something. I introduce myself, explain what my role in the district is, and then talk about things we are doing; or I am a master of ceremonies and describe what the entertainment for the evening will be. Typically, I say how honored I am to be serving the district and how much I enjoy working with the Vietnamese. My ability to speak their language and to talk to them in Vietnamese always increases my credibility and honestly engages their belief in my desire to help them.

Often the district obtains professional actors or singers from Saigon who put on patriotic shows for the local people, working with the military. In lessor entertainment events, the musicians and entertainers are talented soldiers. The Hoc Mon shows present actors who play

Bob giving speech to villagers in Hoc Mon with district chief on Bob's right.

historic Vietnamese men and women depicting ancient and notable events of older times in Vietnam history. Male and female singers, with anywhere from a couple of electric guitar players to small bands, keep the audience clapping as popular Vietnamese songs are vocalized. These entertainment sessions often last all night long, and usually by 2 or 3 a.m. I leave to sleep.

Another aspect of the district social events are dinners for a large gathering of people; sometimes the guests are wealthy educated economic leaders in the district while at other times the gathering is for the military officers or various district and village officials.

If weather permits, these dinners are served outside by the senior official hosting the meal. One time the district chief holds an outdoor early evening dinner in the courtyard in the district compound, between the advisor team house and his living quarters. I am invited along with my two deputies, the captain and the civilian, neither of whom speak Vietnamese or have ever attended a dinner party like this.

As the tables are being set up, I am able to look at the printed menu (a copy is at the place setting of each attendee). Having participated in these events before, I am looking for one item typically on the menu: chopped raw chicken necks, covered with fresh chicken blood. The first time I was served this, my host encouraged me to partake and I threw up, into my napkin, after just a few bites. This delicacy is on the menu about third of the way down the list of servings.

I corner one of our NCOs to give him explicit instructions for what he is to do. I tell him to watch out a window in our team house as soon as we begin eating. When I reach up and scratch my head, vigorously, he is to come running out and tell me (so everyone could hear) that Colonel Herbert is on the radio and he needs to talk to me, now! The local dignitaries know who the colonel is and that he is my boss.

As the second course dishes are being removed, I can see the servers holding the raw chicken necks in blood. I begin scratching my head robustly, and the sergeant comes running out with his message. I ask my host to please excuse me, which he does. Running into our house, I peek out the window until I see the chicken neck dishes being removed and return to my seat. Glancing at my two deputies I see them looking sick and consuming great quantities of the very potent rice wine. I have avoided a very unpleasant portion of the dinner while my two deputies are worse than I was during my first time having to ingest the chopped-up chicken necks and fresh blood. The rest of the dinner is pleasant and the remaining food very tasty.

The next morning, standing outside by our jeep, the captain and the civilian are very hungover from drinking too much rice wine. They lament the fact that I had to leave when the worst course was served (and each had to leave the table and vomit away from the diners). Their heads hurt and their stomachs threaten to erupt again. I am amused at their very apparent sickness and ask them how the rest of the meal went. Each indicates the main entrée was delicious. I ask them if they know what the meat was?

The captain thinks the meat was chicken and it was excellent. The other man thinks the meat was pork, but he agrees it was incredibly good. I look at each man, leaning against the jeep, head bowed with their bellies churning and boiling. I say I am glad they liked the entrée meat because many people have a problem eating rats. Both turn toward me, asking what was that meat? I explain it was field rat, not a diseased garbage rat. Field rats eat grain and become big and fat and so tasty when properly prepared. Both men immediately throw up all over the outside of the jeep.

As I begin to settle into this vastly different job as an advisor, I develop favorable feelings about both the job and especially the Vietnamese I am working with. I readily see the positive results of what my team is doing. While it takes a lot of effort and attention, it is not dangerous. Yet the work is enjoyable and our accomplishments visible. I ask Colonel Herbert if I can stay here permanently. Even the district chief voices his approval of me and, via the province chief, requests I remain as DSA for Hoc Mon. But it is not to be.

Toward the end of January, the permanent district senior advisor arrives, and I return to province headquarters.

16

Moving to the Rung Sat
Special Zone

The day after returning from my temporary duty as the DSA in Hoc Mon, I am told to report to Colonel Herbert. In his office he asks me to sit down. He explains he is aware how much I wanted to remain in Hoc Mon but he has a much more important job for me if I will accept it. Looking puzzled, I am at a loss for what he has in mind.

He explains that in the southern part of Gia Dinh province are the two districts of Quang Xuyen (where I once went on an amphibious assault) and Can Gio. This area, the Rung Sat Special Zone, has 485 miles of tidal swamp with over 3,000 miles of interlocking streams. Due to the harsh living environment, the entire area only has about 18,000 inhabitants, mostly fishermen and woodcutters, with some farmers.

He continues to describe the unusual military-civilian arrangement in which the logistical and administrative support for the districts are the responsibility of Gia Dinh province. All military activity is controlled by the Vietnamese Navy, based at Nha Be, about five miles south of Saigon. The RSSZ is bounded by the South China Sea on the south and southeast, the Soi Rap River on the west, Phoc Tuy province on the east and Bien Hoa province on the north.

In 1962 the RSSZ was created as a military district to control the Long Tau shipping channel, and in 1964 the Vietnamese Navy was given military control of the region. The major U.S. support for this area is the U.S. Naval Support Activity Base at Nha Be, on a point of land at the junction of the Soi Rap and Long Tau Rivers. The U.S. Navy base is a major logistics complex to support the navy's Mobile Riverine Force, various riverine fleets, and helicopters (the Seawolves).

Colonel Herbert describes the friendly military forces operating in the Rung Sat. He says there are 13 Regional Force companies and various U.S. Navy forces at Nha Be. On the enemy's part, the RSSZ is called D-10 or Doan-10 meaning Group 10. There is a regimental size NVA unit operating within the Rung Sat. This group is split in two with half operating in each district. Each district has a battalion with three sapper/infantry companies with the total force at about 500 men. There are also local Viet Cong squads and cells scattered in the Rung Sat with a total enemy force approximating 1,000 men.

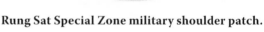

The Problem

Looking right at me he says there is a major problem in the RSSZ right now. "The VC and NVA have been attacking the ships traversing the shipping channels with small arms fire, rockets,

Rung Sat Special Zone military shoulder patch.

and mines. So far, none have been sunk but they have suffered casualties, on-board fires, and ship damage. Part of the problem is that some of the Vietnamese military leaders have been taking bribes to look the other way and have not been taking the fight to the enemy.

"The Vietnamese have removed all these men and they will be court-martialed. All the U.S. Army advisors are being transferred elsewhere. The Vietnamese are bringing in new military officers. The plan by the Vietnamese Navy is to take an RF company and train it to conduct commando-type raids and go after the enemy in the Rung Sat. To do this the U.S. Navy needs a seasoned infantry combat advisor to train the RF unit. Currently the navy does not have such a person, so this job is yours if you want it. This is your chance to return to combat."

The colonel further explains that the advisor team would be assigned as the Quang Xuyen district advisor team, but the focus would be on combat operations. He notes I have over 18 months' experience as a combat advisor, I am fluent in both French and Vietnamese and all my interactions with the Vietnamese in Gia Dinh have received high praise from the Vietnamese. He points out that my combat record is

Quang Xuyen District

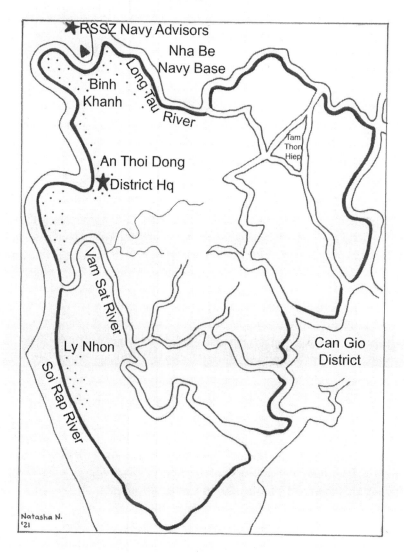

exceptional, with decorations for valor, so I would be the ideal choice to take this assignment.

He also explains that while I would be the DSA under his command, I would also be working for and taking orders from the U.S. Navy advisory command for the RSSZ regarding military operations, as the Vietnamese Navy controls all combat missions in the RSSZ. Then he asks me if I want the job. I can't say yes fast enough. For me this would be a dream job. Training a commando unit, then going out on operations with them. Having my own team of combat advisors again. Life could not get better.

The Advisor Team

For a while we discuss what I would need in terms of a team. I indicate that I have no in-country preferences and the colonel says he will get me a team. I explain all team members must be physically fit to endure combat operations, recalling my recent operation in the Rung Sat. Each must be qualified in their area of expertise. I need an infantry officer with experience in squad, platoon, and company combat operations. I need an intelligence officer who is trained in the Phoenix program as well as how the Vietnamese District Intelligence and Operations Coordination Center functions. I need a senior combat arms NCO who can handle all the administrative aspects of the team and also manage all of the team housekeeping chores such as food, supplies, security, radio communications, and assist me with the logistical support advising the district administration. I need another experienced infantry NCO to share the training responsibilities and to go on combat operations. Since the only means we possess for travel is by boat (the team will have two Boston Whalers, outboard 40 and 50 hp motor–driven 16-foot fiberglass open boats) we will need someone who can maintain our boats. We also need a medic.

Over the next few days, I begin my preparation to move to the RSSZ. First, I need to meet the navy commander I will be working for. Commander Clarence "Jerry" Wages, Jr., has two offices because he holds two jobs. He has been personally selected by the commander of U.S. Navy forces in Vietnam, Admiral Elmo Zumwalt, Jr., in March 1969 to become the senior navy advisor for the Rung Sat Special Zone.

The U.S. Navy advisor team office is at the Vietnamese Nha Be headquarters in an old French building. Additionally, Wages is the commander of the Rung Sat Special Zone River Patrol Group CTG 116.9 (U.S. Navy) stationed at the Nha Be U.S. Naval Support Activities Base, where he has an office and his tactical operations center.

One day I meet Commander Wages at his advisor headquarters, where he clarifies exactly what I will be doing and from whom I will take orders. As CO of the Riverine Group he commands over 70 minesweepers and PBRs (patrol boat, river); HA(L)-3, a helicopter detachment called Seawolves; minesweepers; and some SEAL teams.

As the senior advisor he has several navy personnel and marines on his staff.

Commander Wages is close to a decade older than me, having served in the Merchant Marines at the close of World War II. He enlisted in the Navy Reserves in 1947 and was called to active duty during the Korean War. Released from active duty he enrolled in Louisiana State University, graduated in 1957 and was commissioned in the navy. A man about my size, he has no distinguishing features that I note. He is factual but concerned about the command structure. As he puts it, I report to a full colonel in Gia Dinh and even though I am to work for Wages, he is not legitimately my boss.

This is officially rectified in August when I am ready to rotate back to the States. On 7 August I receive orders from MACV placing me on temporary duty with the U.S. Naval Forces effective 1 June 1969. The date is interesting because I actually report for duty with the navy on 8 February 1969. None of these dates match the dates on my OERs.

Wages expresses his concern over his role as an advisor because the Nixon administration now places emphasis on "Vietnamization," where we are to train the Vietnamese and require them to assume a stronger role in combat operations. He has praise for the RF companies in the Rung Sat but is not that keen on the higher level of command within the Vietnamese in the RSSZ. He wants the RF units to be better trained for combat and raids in the RSSZ. He specifically points out one company, the 117th RF company, which has been selected for us to train for commando-style raids.

Commander Wages is a true warrior who has been promoted early to his present rank. During his two years in Vietnam he will be awarded the Silver Star, the Legion of Merit for valor, the Bronze Star for valor, the Navy Commendation Medal for valor, the Purple Heart, and the Air Medal with 13 flight awards as well as two Vietnamese Crosses of Gallantry for valor. He is to be an excellent leader to serve.

During the first week in February, the members of my team began arriving at province advisor headquarters. My second in command is First Lieutenant Jim Pellman. A big man, the infantry officer has about three years' active duty. Standing six feet two inches, weighing around 225 pounds, he was a college football player from Oklahoma. In his mid–20s, single, he is very muscular. In fact, while on the team, he will fill large tin cans with cement and a pipe to make barbells, which he works with every day. His face is long, and his dark hair cut noticeably short, he wears the ubiquitous black-framed army glasses. His background is all infantry as a platoon leader and staff assignments. He excels in small unit tactics and operations. He has experienced a continuing problem during combat operations, though. While the Vietnamese soldiers, half his size, seem to glide over the wet, swampy ground, Pellman sinks in halfway to his knees, making it difficult to maneuver and very tiring for him. Despite this handicap, he never falters or slows us down.

Third in the leadership functions is First Lieutenant Adam Springer, an intelligence officer. Slight of build, he is five feet eleven inches tall, weighing about 160 pounds. His light-colored hair is cut short, and with wire-rimmed glasses he looks as intelligent as he is. In his mid–20s, single, he completed the Army Intelligence Officer's course and was trained in-country in District Intelligence Operations and Coordination Center functions as well as the Phoenix program. His main duty is to help create the district DIOCC and its Phoenix program to establish systems to gather information regarding the VC and NVA within the district and to establish a highly functional intelligence program in the district.

The senior NCO on our team is Master Sergeant Harry Harris. A seasoned infantry NCO, he is highly skilled in all matters administrative. Short at five feet eight inches tall, but a compact 150 pounds, he wears his dark hair in a crew cut. In his late 30s, married, Harris is extremely competent and will handle all the administrative functions of our advising of the civilian district officials, leaving me to focus on the infantry training and combat operations.

Next is Sergeant First Class Sam Olden, a large bear of a man at six two weighing around 240 pounds. His face is ruddy and round and he has short brown hair. In his late 30s, he is married. Trained and experienced in infantry from light to heavy weapons, small unit operations, Olden has already been in Vietnam six months with a U.S. Army unit before he requested advisor duty. A loud extrovert who smokes a pipe, he is nice to the Vietnamese women working for the various district offices or medical clinics. Unlike Lieutenant Pellman, Olden somehow will seem to avoid sinking in the swamp on operations. And I can never understand how he is able to do that.

The youngest member of our team is our medic, Specialist Fourth Class Tim Dickson. Single, in his early 20s, his short, dark hair is parted. About six feet tall and muscular, he is a qualified and friendly person who favors cigarettes. Most of his duty is serving as the advisor to the district medical clinics, working with the RF company medics and taking care of any health issues the team may have.

This team functions very well together, and we all get along. We do have one glaring issue, though. I am the only advisor fluent in Vietnamese. This is a widespread problem throughout the advising corps

QUANG XUYEN DISTRICT
ADVISOR TEAM

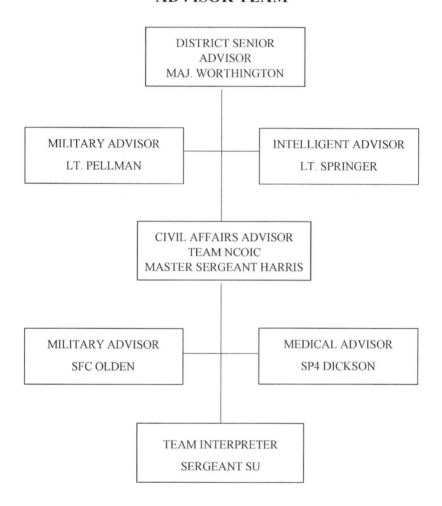

DISTRICT SENIOR
ADVISOR
MAJ. WORTHINGTON

MILITARY ADVISOR

LT. PELLMAN

INTELLIGENT ADVISOR

LT. SPRINGER

CIVIL AFFAIRS ADVISOR
TEAM NCOIC
MASTER SERGEANT HARRIS

MILITARY ADVISOR

SFC OLDEN

MEDICAL ADVISOR

SP4 DICKSON

TEAM INTERPRETER

SERGEANT SU

in Vietnam. Most advisors are unable to speak the language of the people they are advising, and they know almost nothing of the history or culture of the country they are living in. The Vietnamese people truly admire those Americans who have taken the time and effort to learn their language. Most Americans must rely on Vietnamese interpreters who are fluent in English. Fortunately, most of the Vietnamese officers, especially captain and above, have various degrees of English knowledge. For us in the Rung Sat, all the officers we work with have some

Entrance to Quang Xuyen District headquarters compound.

English-speaking ability. Our team will also be assigned a Vietnamese interpreter.

Our Counterparts

One day Colonel Herbert calls me for a meeting with the province chief, Colonel Nguyen Van Ton, to meet some of the district leaders from Quang Xuyen. We meet ARVN Major Nghiem, a slight 140-pound round-faced officer who is a short five feet two inches tall; his neatly pressed fatigues suggest a dapper individual. He is a new appointee who wears a black leather belt and holster for his .38 Special revolver. He is well versed in English. With him is First Lieutenant Cam, commander of the 117th Regional Force company, which is stationed at the district headquarters. Also competent with English, Lieutenant Cam is a little over five feet tall, of compact build with black hair combed straight back. He appears friendly and eager to begin his unit's training with the Americans.

Major Nghiem spends some time describing where we will be living. The district headquarters is located in a compound in An Thoi Dong village on the western edge of Quang Xuyen about eight miles south of Nha Be on the Soi Rap River. The village has a population of about 4,600 people. The district is bounded by the Long Tau River on the north,

Quang Xuyen district chief, Major Nghiem, with Bob.

several different named rivers on the east, the South China Sea on the south and the wide-flowing Soi Rap on the west. He says the district is about 90 percent mangrove swamp with no roads, no bridges, and only two helicopter landing sites, one at district headquarters. Some form of boat is the common mode of travel in the Rung Sat.

Within the district compound are the various district offices, the district chief's living quarters, soldiers' barracks, military and intelligence offices and the advisor team quarters. Within the district are eight RF companies and eight PF platoons, with the total RF force being well under 900 soldiers. The National Police presence in the district numbers 34 men. The only means of communications in the district is by radio as there is no telephone system. Most of the local troops are assigned defensive missions where they live.

The district chief says the advisor building is ready for us to move in. I explain that most likely we will move in on Thursday, 8 February 1969.

Specific Team Duties

To prepare our team to function as a district team and military advisors we must define our administrative and housekeeping duties. Lieutenant Pellman is responsible for the team security. Lieutenant Springer is our liaison with the district chief's staff, Vietnamese DIOCC and their Phoenix program, the intel people of the 117 RF company and the National Police who will keep us informed on what is going on in the district. Master Sergeant Harris is responsible for managing our team housing and food. He is to ensure we do not run out of food, and arranges for local people to clean our quarters, cook our meals, and wash our clothes.

Sergeant First Class Olden is responsible for our team weapons to ensure they are clean, and function and that we have ample ammo. We have one M-60 7.62 mm (.308 caliber) machine gun and a couple of M-79 Grenade launchers. Each of us has our individual issued weapon (a .30 caliber M-1 carbine) and I also have my .45 1911A1 service pistol. Because of his expertise with engines he is also responsible for maintaining our Boston Whalers and ensuring we always have plenty of fuel (which is provided by the district headquarters).

Specialist Dickson is our signal chief, responsible for acquiring the province advisor signal operating instructions (SOI), which are changed periodically. This set of instructions details the province advisory radio net providing call signs, frequencies, codes, and other information necessary to utilize the province advisor radio net as well as providing information on other U.S. assets operating in the area. The signal chief must also procure the SOI for both the U.S Navy advisors and the U.S. Navy assets at Nha Be. Additionally, he obtains the standing signal instructions (SSI) from the three headquarters. The SSI is a set of technical instructions which details the operation of the radio net and explains how to use the SOI. The SOI would normally change monthly but can change whenever it is suspected to be compromised. When a unit's in combat its SOI is changed daily.

Sergeant Harris is responsible for arranging our movement to Quang Xuyen by helicopter. We need to transport our personal belongings, our food, weapons, ammo, radios and batteries, Dickson's medical supplies, and other team equipment.

Vietnamese Court-Martial

Shortly after we move to Quang Xuyen, I am asked to participate in the Vietnamese courts-martial of the several former district leaders who are being charged with dereliction of duty, failure to obey orders, and other charges relating to their accepting bribes to allow the VC to function. At the various military trials, I am a witness for the prosecution. My testimony focuses on the state of combat readiness in which I found the district headquarters and territorial military units upon my arrival in the district.

I explain that the district has no functional DIOCC for gathering intelligence and the military units have little recent experience conducting combat operations. In my experience working with RF and PF units, it seems that in Quang Xuyen they concentrate more on defensive postures where they are located than on performing offensive actions. Obviously, I have no knowledge of the Vietnamese officers being charged, but my comments on the district military units appear helpful.

I have no experience with the Vietnamese military legal system, but the proceedings are like those of the U.S. Army. I am assigned an excellent Vietnamese interpreter to assist me in understanding the legal aspects of what is happening. I can take the stand and understand the questions asked of me in Vietnamese and my responses are also in Vietnamese.

My tenure as a witness is truly short: I go, I testify, and I leave. I think this experience highly unusual and quite different than any other of my experiences with the Vietnamese. The officers charged were found guilty of most of the accusations.

When we set up in Quang Xuyen, we discover the team actually has three boats. An 18-foot Miami Surfer with an 85 hp outboard engine, a 14-foot boat with a 40 hp engine and one 16-foot Boston Whaler, also with a 40 hp engine. Unfortunately, only one motor runs so we need to get the other two fixed and operational.

The day after we arrive a PF outpost (OP) is attacked and one soldier wounded, very badly. A U.S. Navy PBR takes me to the OP so I can assist with the soldier's evacuation to an American medical facility at Nha Be for the emergency care he needs.

Life in our advisor quarters is really comfortable. Because there is no potable water in the Rung Sat, we receive our drinking and cooking water from the U.S. Navy, delivered to the district dock, as needed. We have a team gas generator which Sergeant Harris maintains. The generator provides sufficient electricity for our quarters, especially our big freezer. Our refrigerator is propane powered as is our cooking stove. Thus far I am enjoying my new assignment.

Toward the end of February, in one of the Air America helicopter supply and mail runs, I receive a package from MACV Headquarters. Inside is a blue box, about four inches by nine or ten inches, which opens from the top like a clamshell. Attached to the box is a set of orders and inside is a Purple Heart Medal. The orders, dated 25 February 1969, are for the award of the Purple Heart for wounds received in action in the Republic of Vietnam on 14 November 1968. The Purple Heart certificate was made out to Major Elliott R. Worthington, 05011335, Infantry, United States Army, and signed by General Creighton W. Abrams, Commander, MACV.

Training RF Company 117
for Commando Raids

Our new home is a large, long building with a corrugated aluminum roof and wood sides. The entire front is a very large screen-enclosed porch strewn with a mishmash of couches, comfortable chairs and tables and metal shelves. There are rolled-up cloth shades to pull down in case of rain or to block out what we are doing at night. There is a kitchen, a dining area and several small bedrooms. In the middle of the building is a small room where we keep our radios, team weapons, and a lock box for classified items such as our SOI and SSI.

We collect rainwater for washing and our potable drinking water is brought in by boat. I have a BOQ (bachelor officers' quarters) room at the Nha Be U.S. Navy base, where we keep our assigned advisor jeep. The BOQ is where I keep most of my clothes and other personal items I don't need or want at Quang Xuyen.

The mission subscribed by Colonel Herbert is very clear. While we are the new Quang Xuyen district advisory team, our primary focus is to train the 117th Regional Force company as a commando unit and then crush the Viet Cong in our part of the Rung Sat Special Zone. I am back in my element again, returned to warrior status.

The Vietnamese government of each district is divided into two functions, one being the civil administration of the district and the other being the military operations of the sub-sector (the district) military forces protecting the district. Typically, the district and sub-sector chiefs are the same person, who reports to the province/sector chief. In the Rung Sat, though, things are different.

The administrative side of Quang Xuyen district reports to the Gia Dinh province chief. But all combat operations in the Rung Sat are controlled by the Vietnamese Navy and the Vietnamese chief of naval operations, Rear Admiral Tran Van Chon, a highly decorated combat officer. As such, his American counterpart is the senior U.S. naval officer in

Advisor team house at Quang Xuyen District headquarters compound.

Vietnam, Vice Admiral Elmo "Bud" Zumwalt, Jr., commander of U.S. Naval Forces, Vietnam.

The RSSZ has always been a bone of contention during the Vietnam War, and since 90 percent of all supplies coming into Saigon are by ship, the security of the waterways from the South China Sea into the ports of Saigon (about 20–25 miles of twisting rivers through the Rung Sat) became very important. As combat operations escalated after the 1968 Tet battles, so did the attacks on shipping lanes into Saigon. In 1964, the Vietnamese Navy took charge of military operations, but the fighting forces were local militia, commanded by assigned Vietnamese Army officers, reporting to the province chief. Unfortunately, the Vietnamese officers were reluctant to conduct combat operations against the Viet Cong, and thus they were court-martialed, and their American advisors reassigned.

In Quang Xuyen the army district advisors become an exception. For district administration, they report to the province advisors. For combat operations, though, they report to the senior RSSZ senior advisor, Commander Clarence "Jerry" Wages.

The district is not big in terms of people (14,732), villages (only 4) or hamlets (12). The population subsists mainly on local crops and what

Quang Xuyen district officials (left to right) Captain Minh, district deputy commander; Major Nghiem, district chief; a district official; Bob.

Quang Xuyen District headquarters building with district chief's bodyguard.

they can catch in the water. The only industry is a small local rice mill. The main district emphasis on providing for the local people is in areas of health and education. The primary mode of transportation is motorized sampans. The military uses outboard motorboats and helicopters. There are no fixed wing airports in the district.

From my point of view, our mission is very simple, train the company in the conduct of small unit operations (tactics, weapons, planning missions based on intelligence, and executing combat operations) and then start hunting VC. In addition to training the 117th RF company, we also must set up a viable District Intelligence and Operations Coordination Center and the Phoenix program. We must gather intelligence while creating networks and make them work.

This is going to be fun.

Commando Training

To start, my team and I begin to brainstorm what any combat troop unit would need to engage and win in combat against the enemy. First it needs an intelligence system to gather information on the enemy. It must have a network of spies, agents, or common folks to inform on enemy activities and locations. Then we want well-trained, disciplined combat soldiers to seek out and destroy the enemy.

These troops would need to be competent in sneaking up on the enemy, and then capable of overtaking them. This means knowing how to close in on the enemy using small unit tactics such as fire and maneuver, ambushing, raiding, establishing blocking positions, employment of crew-served weapons, leadership, fire control, unity of command and demolitions. We also place emphasis on good scouting techniques and anti-ambush tactics. We never want the enemy to have any advantage over us.

We advisors acknowledge that these soldiers have been fighting all their adult lives and they know the Rung Sat like the backs of their hands. Collectively they have much more combat experience than we have. Going to the 117th and saying, okay, we are going to teach you how to fight is not a good idea.

Instead, we ask Lieutenant Cam, the 117th CO, to look at our list and decide what would be best for his company. He asks if first we would like to inspect and evaluate his company and see what we think about the soldiers, their equipment and the weapons. We do so and we feel his company is in great shape. Working with his officers and key NCOs we draw up a list of the most needed training.

1st Lieutenant Cam, commanding officer of the 117th Regional Force Company.

Lieutenant Pellman and Sergeants Harris and Olden conduct most of the training. I do the demolitions training and discover the soldiers have a deathly fear of using C-4 to destroy bunkers or mold shape charges to burst through steel or concrete.

Composition C-4 is a military grade explosive. Made of explosives, chemicals, binders and motor oil, it is like modeling clay. It works via an explosive device (blasting cap) creating a massive hot gas expansion so fast it is a very deadly explosion. As a solid block of explosive, it is rather inert and safe. Dropping it or even shooting a bullet into it will not set it off (though the Vietnamese do not believe this). In fact, often on combat operations I would take a pinch of C-4, place it on a rock or the ground and set it afire with a match or lighter and a dab, the size of a fingertip, will have an aluminum canteen cup of water boiling in seconds.

For my training I explain how C-4 works. I cover the three items necessary to ignite the C-4. In a chunk of C-4 is placed a blasting cap (an explosive device) by punching a small hole in the C-4 and pushing the blasting cap in the hole. Then a section of black (military) fuse is attached to the blasting cap. When ignited by match or lighter it burns at a steady rate until it reaches the blasting cap, then it explodes.

When obtaining a new length of fuse, we cut off a foot, ignite it and then time how long it takes to burn. The length of the fuse is used to create time between lighting the fuse and its reaching the blasting cap, allowing the demolitions guy time to torch the fuse and get far enough away to escape the blast. The more C-4 used, the greater the explosion, so the further away one needs to be, thus the longer the fuse.

I take the soldiers out in a field where we have a large dirt berm to hide behind during the demolitions training. We use steel plates, chunks of concrete, and massive wooden structures to place charges, insert a blasting cap, and then attach a length of fuse, long enough to allow us to safely move behind the berm. Despite the training and showing how safe C-4 is, the Vietnamese are still afraid to use it. And I can never understand their fear of using explosives. While they would carry the C-4 on operations, more often than not, I would set and ignite the explosive.

Intelligence Training

Lieutenant Springer is responsible for the intelligence training. Within the district there are Phoenix agents, military intelligence officers and NCOs, National Police, the Chieu Hoi chief (the person operating the district program to convince disgruntled VC to defect) and several civilians working in the District Intelligence and Operations Coordination Center.

Our DIOCC is the hub of where intelligence information is collated and analyzed to plan combat operations. Part of the DIOCC is the Phoenix program, or in Vietnamese, Phung Hoang. The Phoenix is not a unit or an organization, but a strategy designed to collect and examine information on the local VC political infrastructure and then devise a plan to capture or destroy the members.

Because the information collection involves primarily Vietnamese people, any direct American interaction would stand out like a sore thumb. The U.S. advisors do not look like Vietnamese, nor do most even speak the language. With the emphasis of these intelligence operations and programs mostly functioning at the district level, the control must be retained with the Vietnamese, which it is.

Lieutenant Springer's role is to help set up the entire intelligence gathering network of soldiers, local civilians, police, and adjacent U.S. forces and to assist in record keeping, mapping and evaluating enemy sightings, contacts, or movements, and developing files on various identified VC leaders and known VC infrastructure members. The DIOCC aims to create a list of every identified VC political leader and VC military leaders and to initiate a substantial dossier on each person, so as added information comes in it can be compared to other data in their file. Eventually enough information can lead to either capturing, turning, or eliminating that person.

Springer shows how to plot enemy sightings on a large map and try to predict what their intentions are. Part of his job is to coordinate with other intelligence agencies and assets such as the U.S. Navy and province command, and he must know how to properly disseminate information for immediate exploitation. He also trains the Vietnamese intelligence workers (both civilian and military) on what information is needed from their network of informants, such as the number of VC seen, their clothing and weapons, physical condition, supplies carried, location and direction of movement.

A major tool Lieutenant Springer possesses is money. CORDS and the CIA provide funds to pay for information. While the money is in Vietnamese currency, it is controlled by Springer. But as to who gets paid what, Springer must work closely with the Vietnamese DIOCC people and the military. Basically, the better the information provided and the greater the prize (VC found, weapons captured, size of unit identified), the more money given out. Springer and his Vietnamese counterparts create a rough sliding scale so money paid out is on a uniform basis according to the value of the info received. This incentive goes a long way to helping the DIOCC function.

Prior to our moving in as advisors, there was no DIOCC because the Vietnamese leaders avoided the enemy and the U.S. advisors were not trained in intelligence gathering or how the Phoenix program operated. Lieutenant Springer is part of a new concept. In 1969, the U.S. Army began to train intelligence lieutenants to function as intelligence advisors, especially at the district level. Springer is one of these lieutenants.

Additionally, Springer works very closely with the Vietnamese Chieu Hoi (Open Arms) propaganda program designed to get VC and VC political leaders to desert and give themselves up to the South Vietnamese government. Leaflet drops, helicopter-borne loudspeakers, word of mouth, and other means of reaching the enemy are employed to convince the enemy to quit the VC. Many see this program as a success. During the war 160,000 enemy switched sides, and many Chieu Hois joined the ARVN as Kit Carson scouts and, with their knowledge of the local VC, became very useful to the ARVN. On the other hand, some Chieu Hois would switch sides many times. Some VC would defect to get a rest, food, and to learn more about their enemy. When fed, restored, and full of intel, they would rejoin their old units.

By mid–March our training is completed and the DIOCC is operating at full capacity. Intelligence networks have been established. The word is out that we pay for good information. The local VC have been preying on local people. Sometimes the VC will raid a small hamlet demanding food. Other times fishermen or woodcutters, encountering some VC, are robbed of their fish or wood, boats and tools. Knowing there is now a fundamental change, where the RF and PF soldiers are after the VC, local people have begun to provide useful information. Much of it is time limited, so exploitation must be swift. This is where the commando training comes to fruition. The 117th always has a platoon on stand-by as a quick reaction force, ready to deploy at a moment's notice. Motivation and morale are both high and we are ready to go to war.

Most of the time we move by boats with motors. We disembark far enough away so our engines will not be detected and approach the enemy on foot. In most instances this works fine. Sometimes when we arrive on foot, the enemy has vanished into the swamps—where, we do not know.

Our operations are inside the district, along narrow waterways, streams, or small dry patches of land. We do not have any operations on the sides of the major rivers. These are typically covered by the Vietnamese Navy or the U.S Riverine Forces using boats such as the PBRs and Swift boats. Most of our operations are in the interior and often not easily accessible by larger navy boats.

A major disadvantage our team has is I am the only advisor fluent in Vietnamese. While most of the Vietnamese we routinely interact with

Deputy District Chief 1st Lieutenant Thoi and the advisor interpreter, Sergeant Su.

speak varying degrees of English (the majority were adequate to excellent), the members of my team are unable to converse in Vietnamese. Therefore, we are assigned a Vietnamese Army interpreter, Staff Sergeant Su, of average height but very gangly, thin to the point of being skinny. Sergeant Su accompanies Lieutenant Pellman and our two sergeants during most of our training. I do not need to use him when I am conducting training. Seldom does Lieutenant Springer need an interpreter in the DIOCC because normally there are present at least a couple of Vietnamese (military or civilian) who are fluent in English.

By late March I am notified that our army advisory team will be replaced by U.S. marines sometime in June. Life in Quang Xuyen is easy and relaxed. Raids on our compound never happen. I am not required to compile and submit nearly as many CORDS reports as I had to in Trang Bang. Also, almost no CORDS officials ever visit Quang Xuyen so we do not have them breathing down our necks demanding all sorts of worthless information. Additionally, I begin teaching English again, as I did at the beginning of my first tour in Vietnam. Through some province advisors I acquire English language textbooks from the U.S. Information Agency and begin classes for any interested Vietnamese. Most of my students are either military or civilian district workers, with an even mix of both men and women.

My First Ride in an Oscar Deuce

I assume part of my responsibility in training the RF company for raids in the Rung Sat is to become very familiar with the territory of our district, which is sort of heart-shaped with the large portion at the top of the district, tapering off to the south. The entire district perimeter is defined by major rivers. The land within the district is continuously split and divided by dozens of smaller rivers, streams, and canals. Even though the defoliant Agent Orange has turned much of the flora into dead scrub brush and trees without leaves, considerable area is still covered with new growth or old growth the chemical has not yet destroyed. From the ground, visibility is quite limited as the land is flat and growth from a few feet up to tree height of 20 feet or so blocks any forward viewing other than a few feet. Also, the terrain is, in many places, a tidal basin swamp, almost undoable on foot as the wet gummy soil grabs boots like glue, and ambulation requires extraordinary effort. If you are big and heavy, crossing these swamps becomes almost impossible.

Quang Xuyen district comprises around 60 percent of the Rung Sat Special Zone, or about 137 square miles. Almost 90 percent of the district is mangrove swamp. leaving only 10 percent habitable with villages and hamlets surrounded by rice fields. Within about 123 square miles of swamp and foliage live several small hard-core Viet Cong units of about 15 soldiers each. The total VC combatants within the Rung Sat probably number around 150 at the most. Added to this are another 60 or so village VC political leaders. Most likely most of these VC operate within Quang Xuyen district. The lack of fresh water makes it very difficult for the swamps to support humans attempting to live off the land. The primary mission of these small VC units is to act as guides for the larger company-size VC or NVA units passing through to attack and harass shipping in the Long Tao River.

One goal is to use aerial recon aircraft to become thoroughly familiar with the waterways and the land. To orient myself to the lay of the land and its water courses, I contact the province operations advisor and make a request for an aircraft to do the recon. Later that day I am told an Air America chopper will pick me up early the next morning. It will take me to the Bien Hoa Air Base (about 15 miles northeast of the province headquarters in Saigon) to the operations office of the U.S. Air Force 19th Tactical Air Support Squadron (TASS), where my recon ride will be an air force O-2 Skymaster, the military version of the civilian center-thrust twin-engine Cessna 337.

The day of my flight I rise early and have a big breakfast (because I am not sure when my next meal will be). Grabbing my gear, I have my pistol belt with my .45 semi-auto service pistol, ammo pouch with two eight-round magazines and my first-aid pouch and a canteen, also in a pouch on the belt. Four more magazines drop into my pockets and my topo map of the Rung Sat, covered with plastic and a couple of grease pencils. I board the CIA Huey and we make our way to Bien Hoa and the 19th TASS.

The 19th has an interesting background. It was activated at Bien Hoa in 1963 to train Vietnamese Air Force (VNAF) pilots to fly as Forward Air Controllers (FACs) in the O-1 Bird Dog single-engine fixed wing aircraft. In mid–1964 it was deactivated, and its assets turned over to the VNAF so they could do their own training. Two and a half months later the USAF resumed control of the school and the 19th became activated again. Apparently the VNAF was unable to conduct the proper training. I had heard, though, that the trained VNAF pilots, would not fly combat missions but instead somehow ended up flying transport missions, not combat. In 1965 the 19th began to fly FAC combat missions, working in both II and III Corps. In 1968, the O-1 was replaced with the twin-engine O-2 plane. The primary mission of the 19th is now visual and photo recon, in addition to its original FAC missions.

Approaching Bien Hoa from the south, one encounters it as a massive aviation complex. Twin 10,000-foot east-west runways define the airfield. On the south side of the runway is a long single taxiway. From the air, it looks like three runways instead of two. On the south side of the taxiway are dozens and dozens of buildings, hangars, maintenance facilities, offices, housing for the airmen stationed there, mess halls and numerous other administrative and storage buildings. Additionally, away from where people live, work, and eat are large fuel farms, tanks holding aviation and jet fuel for the aircraft. The Air America helicopter dropped me off on a parking ramp adjacent to the 19th flight offices.

Inside the ops shack I meet my pilot, an air force captain. He explains a little about the Cessna O-2, in military terminology, referred to as the "Oscar Deuce." I pull out my Rung Sat map as he pulls out his, which is like mine. The previous day I met with the district intel NCOs and marked several possible positions on my map where the VC might be hiding. The pilot notes my map positions on his and then does some calculations. He explains the Rung Sat is about 22 miles south and once airborne we will be there in less than 15 minutes. We will cruise there above small arms fire, around 3,000 feet. Once over the Rung Sat he will fly all over the area for me to see how it appears from the air. Then we will seek out the possible VC target areas and go down low for a closer look. Picking up his survival equipment, weapons, and flight bag, we leave the building to walk to his plane, parked nearby.

On the ramp is the high-wing O-2. A dull gray in color except for the top of the cowling, which is black. It has two large doors, one on each side of the front with the USAF Stars and Stripes insignia with the white star in the blue circle on both sides of the plane, just aft of each door. The plane is almost 30 feet long, with a wingspan of 38 feet, and the top of the twin tail booms are almost ten feet tall. The civilian version seats six but the military version only has the two seats in front, with all the room in the back loaded with radio equipment. The plane has two normally aspirated, air-cooled six-cylinder 210 hp engines, one on the nose and the other on the rear of the fuselage.

Most twin-engine planes have the engines on the wings, creating excitement for the pilot if one engine fails. With only one engine running, the pilot must immediately identify which engine failed and instantly apply corrective action. The reason is the operating engine, being off center wants to turn the plane toward the dead engine, making a crash eminent. With both engines being in the center of the plane, there is no asymmetric thrust, only a reduction in power, making recovery much easier.

The civilian Cessna 337 came on the market in 1964 with fixed gear (meaning the wheels of the plane do not retract). The next year it was produced with retractable gear, with production ceasing in 1980. The USAF in the 1960s was using the two-seat Cessna, high-wing, single-engine L-19 for recon and FAC operations. While visibility was excellent with tandem seating, the small aircraft lacked power and enough fuel capacity for loitering over target areas for extended periods of time. The air force wanted a more powerful plane with longer airborne endurance.

In 1967 the air force contracted to purchase 532 O-2s, which came in two models. The A model was for recon and combat air control support, while the B model was configured for psychological operations such as having loudspeakers or dropping leaflets. Actually, the military version of the 337 is only a makeshift interim model until the air force can develop a totally new military FAC aircraft.

The military airplane has many areas reinforced for hard landings and other forms of abuse, and employs heavy-duty brakes, self-sealing fuel tanks and larger cowl flaps for increased cooling of the rear engine. The instrument panel is standard military, including an armament panel and a gun sight for the weapons. Under each wing are two hard points to attach either rocket pods (each pod holding seven 2.75-inch rockets) or 7.62 mm mini-gun pods.

Inside are two side-by-side pilot seats, with the back of the plane holding a metal shelf rack loaded with four stacks of radio and navigation equipment, thick wiring harnesses, and other paraphernalia for communicating on aviation and ground combat radio nets. Both door windows have small openings for cooling the cockpit.

The plane holds 122 gallons of aviation fuel and is capable of staying aloft just over seven hours, cruising at 144 mph. While the gross weight of the civilian plane is 4,630 pounds, the military version can go as high as 5,400 pounds.

I walk with the pilot as he does his preflight of the plane. As he moves around, his hands testing the movement of the elevators and the rudders, he visually inspects the aircraft and runs his fingers over the leading edges of the propellers, checking for pits, cracks, or indentations on each blade caused from debris on the field while taxiing. Fuel and oil levels are inspected. When finished, he opens the right door and ushers me inside, showing me how to hook up my seat belt and chest straps. Handing me a spare helmet, he shows me where the push-to-talk button is on the yoke, in front of me. I am good to go.

Climbing into the left seat, the pilot places his helmet on and grabs his knee board (a small clipboard pad of paper strapped to a pilot's leg to write on). From a box between our seats, he pulls out a checklist. Clipping the checklist to his knee board, he prepares the plane for start-up.

As he pulls on both seat belts and chest straps, his feet test the foot brakes and his hands begin to move switches on the instrument panel. Master switch on, voltage regulator on setting number one, landing gear down and locked (green light), cowl flaps open, and fuel selector switches set with front engine on left main tank, rear on right main, and confirm radios and electric equipment off.

Mixture is moved into rich, propellers set to high RPMs, throttle is pushed in and then moved out one inch to prepare the front engine for starting, auxiliary fuel pump on low. The pilot looks around the outside of the plane to ensure no one is near, shouts, "clear" through a small open port in his door window, switches the starter and the front engine comes alive. He repeats the process for the rear engine. As both engines purr smoothly, he checks the gauges and turns off the aux fuel pump.

Pulling out his map, he makes some notes on his knee pad, grabs an airport diagram (which also has all the airport radio frequencies). He obtains the altimeter setting, the wind, and the runway in use. Ground control provides taxi instructions to get to the active runway, while he makes notes on his knee pad. Glancing around for safety, he begins his taxi to the runway.

On the taxiway at the end of the runway, he does his engine run-up to ensure all is functioning properly. Setting 1,800 RPMs, he moves the yoke forward and aft, then sideways to check the flight controls. Doing the magnetos checks, he scans the gauges again, switches his radio to the tower and requests permission to move onto the runway to take off.

Moving onto the runway, lowering flaps, he pushes both throttles full forward to 2,800 RPMs, tweaks the mixture levers and moves down the runway. Around 70 mph, he lightly pulls back on the yoke, allowing the plane to gently become airborne on its own. As we rise above the airport, the gear is retracted, flaps raised, and the O-2 climbs at about 115 mph. In a few minutes we are at 3,000 feet and he levels off. Power, trim, and mixture are adjusted to fly at 140 mph to the Rung Sat Special Zone.

Airplanes with more than one engine should have all engines running alike or synchronized. This means that both propellers are rotating at precisely the same speed. The O-2 has an electric prop synchroscope that will help do this. The pilot adjusts one engine to what he wants, adjusts the second engine to match this and the synchroscope provides a visual indicator of when both engines are synchronized.

A twin-engine plane not in sync means the engines are running at different RPMs, which can cause a plane to not fly straight and create excessive vibrations.

Over the Rung Sat in less than 20 minutes, the pilot explains what he will do. First, he will fly down the eastern edge of the district, then move up along the western edge (this flight path will always keep the district to the right of the plane, where I am sitting), then head south again, but down the middle of the district. All of this takes about 45 minutes. Now he indicates we will go down lower to examine the areas where our intel thought some VC might be living.

Thus far I am feeling okay, but it is getting very hot in the plane. At this point the O-2 shows its limitations. For one to properly observe the ground the plane must turn into steep banks of 30 to 60 degrees. While the plane has two engines, it is not as nimble at slow speeds, especially with two husky men aboard and the entire back of the plane crammed full of electronic gear. With full fuel, the plane is almost maxed out with its useful load. With full flaps and level with the ground, the plane will stall just above 70 mph. At 60 degree bank the plane must fly at 100 mph to not stall.

Usually each side door window has a small opening for air, but mine is jammed, so no air. Twisting and turning a few thousand feet above the earth, in a hot and humid cockpit, finally gets to my full stomach. I tell the pilot I am going to throw up. His face lights up and he searches the cockpit for some fashion of a container, but none exist. He hands me his glove and I promptly fill it. His window port is open, so he gingerly grasps his glove and pushes it out the opening to disappear into space. I thank him and we continue to explore the Rung Sat. About 20–25 minutes later I tell him I need his other glove and immediately fill it and it joins its mate through the open side port. With no more gloves, we both decide it best to return to Bien Hoa.

As we approach the air base, the pilot slips into the pattern, on downwind reduces power, sets flaps, lowers the gear, sets the proper fuel selectors, and makes the turn onto short final. Moving across the ground around 95 mph, we gently touch down with twin chirps as the main gear tires sweetly kiss the runway, slowing; the nose gear also touches down and we taxi back to the 19th TASS ops office.

I make several other O-2 recon flights over the Rung Sat but never eat anything before a flight. I also carry a dozen plastic bags in the leg pockets of my jungle fatigues. I never want to embarrass myself by ruining a pilot's Nomex gloves again. And guess what? I never did get sick on any other O-2 flights.

In the past the Viet Cong have dominated the Rung Sat, using terror and bullying tactics to retain control over the local people. Under the prior leadership, friendly forces tended to avoid contact with the VC. This led to the VC becoming complacent with lax security around their base camps.

The 117th RF company is well trained and equipped for combat. The intelligence operations are beginning to pay off. The advisor team has functioned as a single, effective unit and we are proud of our accomplishments. We have achieved quite a bit in a brief time and now we are ready to see just how good we all are at the demanding work that lies ahead.

18

Combat Operations
Against the Viet Cong

Our First Contact with the VC

Over the past few weeks, we have received reports on VC sightings. Loading up in our boats we would land near the area where the VC were sighted. But every time we arrived, there was no enemy. They move often, during the night when the chance of being spotted, either by boat or aircraft, is very slim.

Late the night of Wednesday, 6 April, an NCO from the DIOCC comes to the advisor house requesting the major and Lieutenant Springer come immediately to the DIOCC. We both go with the NCO. At the DIOCC are several intelligence officers and NCOs and the district chief, Major Nghiem, as well as the 117th commander, Lieutenant Cam.

Cam takes charge to explain why we are meeting. Earlier that day a local woodcutter had been gathering wood along the Rach Don Creek, about two miles due south of the compound we are standing in. The woodcutter was sitting in his sampan, taking a break, when he heard several men, which he realized were VC, moving north on a trail about 20 yards away from him. The heavy brush and trees hid him from the VC. He thought there were about six to ten VC who were complaining about carrying so many weapons. The apparent leader told the men to quit bickering as they were almost at the base camp where they would hide the weapons in a concrete bunker. As the woodcutter remained quiet, the VC soon moved out of sight and hearing.

The woodcutter moved a distance away from where the VC passed by and continued to gather wood to take back home in An Thoi Dong village. That night the woodcutter came to the district headquarters to report what he had seen and heard. Because a map is foreign to the local people, the woodcutter is unable to use a map to pinpoint where

Bob in district boat with district officers.

he saw the VC. But the local people and most of the RF and PF soldiers know the Rung Sat like Americans know the neighborhoods where they live.

Major Nghiem has assembled some PF soldiers and some local men, in the military conference room, along with the woodcutter. The major, Lieutenant Cam, and some intel specialists continue to debrief the woodcutter. His descriptions as to where he was are further interpreted by the other locals. The soldiers and the intel people begin to use the map of the Rung Sat to identify exactly where the woodcutter was when he saw the VC. The woodcutter had used the sun to determine directions, so it wasn't too hard to locate on the map where he had been. Some of the locals are aware of the trail and the woodcutter knew the VC were moving north so they could identify a spot on the trail where it is dry and could make an excellent, well-defended base camp.

The intel people have calculated that there is at most a VC platoon (20–25 men) or perhaps a reinforced squad (maybe 12–15 men). The major and the lieutenant discuss how many men the area could support and 30 is deemed as too many. To be safe three lean platoons of the 117th will conduct the attack. A lean platoon is about 20 fighting men instead of the full platoon of 25 to 30 soldiers. Now the concern is how to get there. Walking directly there is impossible as the Rach Don Creek is too deep to ford and the base camp is on the south bank, across the stream from the district headquarters.

As the discussion ensues, I become more aware of the difficulties of mounting a three-platoon-sized operation in the Rung Sat. Many of the streams and waterways are too deep to ford so boats must be used, and the RF company does not have enough boats to transport the entire company. Straight line distances are certainly the shortest, but in the Rung Sat that may be impossible so the curving and twisting water-ways must be utilized. While this VC base camp is only a couple of miles south of us, because boats must be used, the distance on the water is about nine miles, and even then there would be movement, on land, through the swamps, of about a half mile.

More questions are asked of the woodcutter and the local men regarding the terrain, trees and brush covering the area, and how best to approach the base camp. The local people are then dismissed (but the local PF soldiers remain because they know the area).

Lieutenant Cam talks to the major about needing more boats to transport the force, about 70 men. The major nods and speaks to a couple of NCOs. Telling them to talk to some locals who have larger motor-powered boats, junks and large sampans, enough boats to

One of the junks used in the raid where 98 weapons were captured.

transport all the attack force (which includes the Vietnamese command group and advisors). I ask Springer to get Dickson to send a coded message to Commander Wages explaining what we are planning and our need for at least one armed Seawolf (call sign for the U.S. Navy Huey helicopters at Nha Be) to be available, on standby, for our operation.

It could sit on the district helipad and be available in minutes, whereas if it flew above us during the approach to the VC base camp, it would alert the VC and they would run away. Wages acknowledges my message and replies the Seawolf will be available as requested.

With the VC camp located on a map, we consider the best way to get there. With enough powered large boats, we could depart district before daylight moving south on the Soi Rap River for about seven miles. By daylight we could enter the mouth of the Vam Sat River, moving up stream another two miles. Just beyond the beginning of the Rach Don River we could disembark to begin our movement toward the VC camp, about a half mile northeast of us. It is a very valid plan which should allow us to raid the camp without being detected.

We have one major advantage which was sorely lacking when I was in Trang Bang, on the Cambodian border. In the Rung Sat, the VC have not been challenged for some time. They use intimidation, terrorism, and the bribing of district officials to get their way. What little information we have suggests they believe themselves to be invincible. We are about to change that.

Lieutenant Cam calls for his platoon leaders and sergeants to go over what is now called "Chuong Duong 1/69." Springer and I return to the team house to go over the operation with the other advisors. It is decided that Lieutenant Pellman will go with me, Lieutenant Springer will stay in radio contact with me and be with the Seawolf on the chopper pad while Dickson will be the radio relay between me and Commander Wages, back at Nha Be. Pellman will remain with Lieutenant Cam in the company command group because he doesn't speak Vietnamese and Cam speaks very good English. I will accompany the attacking platoon because I do speak Vietnamese. When we initiate the attack, Lieutenant Springer will release the Seawolf to join us. Sergeant Su, our interpreter, will remain with the advisors at the district headquarters.

For weapons, I will carry my .45 pistol and my MACV issued M-1 carbine. None of my other advisors are interested in a handgun, probably because it is not an easy weapon to be accurate with and most soldiers are not proficient with the .45, whereas I am. Therefore, they carry their issued carbines, and we all carry extra loaded magazines. The RF soldiers have their M-1 carbines, 40 mm grenade launchers, hand grenades, and a couple of crew-served machine guns.

Chuong Duong
1/69 Operation

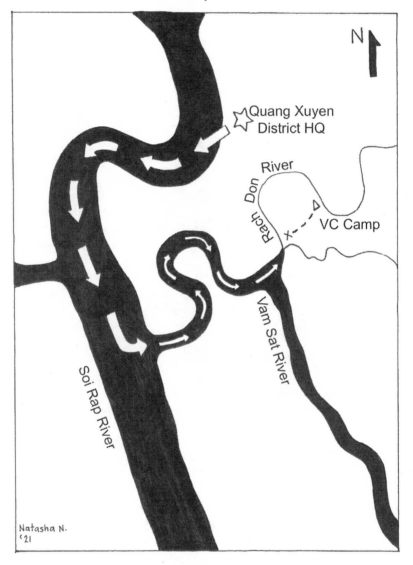

It is an excellent plan and hopefully we will see just how good the 117th is in combat. I return to the DIOCC to tell Lieutenant Cam what the advisors will be doing and arrange when and where we will meet in the morning. Then we advisors go to bed.

Chuong Duong 1/69

At zero-dark thirty all the advisors are up, eat and move to the docks to board our boats. It is quite a flotilla, comprised of several large sampans with outboard motors, a large junk, and two command Boston Whalers. Both Pellman and I are assigned RF privates to carry our PRC-25 radios (and spare batteries). The radio checks have been done before leaving the district compound because en route we want radio silence. The ride down the Soi Rap is swift and uneventful, as is the trip up the Vam Sat. As planned, it is daylight as we disembark and start our forward movement.

Cam's two scouts move ahead of us to locate the base camp and return to report to him. They leave as we begin our trek toward the VC camp. Because of the swampy land, movement is slow and Lieutenant

Quang Xuyen dock at district headquarters where most operations begin.

Pellman has the most difficulty due to his size. I am with the first (attacking) platoon. Lieutenant Cam has directed the attacking platoon to spread out when we are near the camp. The second platoon is to set up blocking positions while the third platoon is held in reserve. An hour and a half later the scouts rejoin us and describe the VC camp. There are about a half dozen VC soldiers in the camp and what looks like a small concrete bunker off to one side. The scouts describe the VC as not doing much and no guards or any outposts were detected.

Lieutenant Cam calls his platoon leaders up and lays out how the attack will proceed. For the last fifty or so yards the company will move very quietly and slowly. At a prearranged time (to allow the attacking and blocking platoons to get in position), the attacking platoon will begin its sweep across the VC camp.

And that is exactly what happens. The lead platoon, in line, begins moving forward and shooting. Lieutenant Pellman radios Springer to send the Seawolf. As the VC, stunned, realize what is happening, a couple return fire while most drop their weapons and run toward the Rach Don to escape. I am with the attacking platoon as we sweep across the VC camp, our soldiers yelling, shouting, and shooting as the VC who are not running away return fire at us before they too, flee. Springer releases the Seawolf, and by the time it appears overhead the fight is over.

It took several hours to arrive at this VC camp, but the fight is concluded in minutes. After a minor skirmish, all the VC have run away. One RF soldier suffered a minor flesh wound and is quickly repaired by the company medic.

We estimate that seven VC escaped. Their camp is not very much, almost like an overnight campout. Then we check out the concrete bunker. It is placed mostly below ground, about five feet long, two or three feet wide and four to five feet deep. What amazes us is it had a little water in the bottom but holds dozens and dozens of weapons.

As the RF soldiers remove each weapon, I radio the Seawolf hovering above us, what we have. The radio transmissions go like this, "...two AK-47s, an SKS-56 semi-auto rifle, a couple of World War II–style bolt-action rifles, three AK-47s..."

Then I hear a bunch of grunting, some cursing (in Vietnamese) as three soldiers are quickly thrashing around in the bunker. Then cheers by all the soldiers removing and stacking the weapons.

As I radio what is coming out of the bunker I say, "and an iguana." The Seawolf pilot asks me to describe the iguana as he is not familiar with that weapon. I reply that it is about a foot long, with a long tail, a big mouth with sharp teeth, it's like a lizard and it is alive. Apparently,

Ninety-eight weapons captured in raid.

the VC found a large lizard and placed it in the bunker as a guard to persuade the curious to stay away. The soldiers will kill it, cook it and eat it.

Next to the bunker, covered with a canvas tarp and camouflaged, are two 20 mm anti-aircraft guns. In total we capture 98 weapons. The operation is a success with just the one slightly injured friendly casualty. Some smaller boats come down the Rach Don to join us at the VC camp, and after several trips the soldiers and 98 weapons are transported to where we disembarked. By the end of the day we are back home, and Commander Wages is ecstatic.

As I reflect on our first big combat operation, I cannot help but consider how the war in the Rung Sat differs so much from fighting on the Cambodian border. In Trang Bang the enemy was vicious, never yielding any quarter. In Quang Xuyen, though, the VC have prevailed for so long, facing a dominant adversary appears daunting to them. Now instead of continuing the fight, after their initial resistance, they run away.

Our Various Duties in the District

As we enter our fourth month in the Rung Sat both the advisors and the 117th are functioning as a well-oiled team. Lieutenant Springer has the DIOCC operating as if it has been doing this for years. The intelligence provided by the local fishermen and woodcutters is paying off. Springer's money being paid for good information is also a huge incentive to convince people to tell us what they are seeing or hearing.

Additionally, the fact that the district military is responding and beating the VC makes a difference. Because of this information we have conducted more operations against the VC than the district did over the previous two years.

Lieutenant Pellman and Sergeant Olden normally accompany many platoon-size operations. Sergeant Harris takes care of all the household tasks and works very closely with the civil side of the district, overseeing CORDS supported construction projects. He also assists the district administrative staff in the proper submissions of paperwork to obtain funding, building materials, and food to sustain the upkeep and maintenance of our two refugee camps, housing over 750 families totaling over 5,000 people. The VC have raided many smaller collections of people, stealing food and whatever possessions they can use, prompting the people to flee the swamps and move into district refugee settlements for safety.

Quang Xuyen District medical clinic with staff outside.

Specialist Dickson focuses on the medical facilities located in four villages. At the district village there is a large dispensary with the district health chief, a midwife, two nurses, and one laborer to care for the building. Another village has a dispensary with three health workers, and a third village has an aid station with two health workers. The last village has one health worker in an aid station, still under construction. If there are any district military forces co-located in a hamlet, and if the PF platoon has a medic, he would also assist the village health workers. Since the largest dispensary is co-located with the district headquarters, I can easily visit that facility. Because the district health chief spends much of his time visiting the other medical facilities, the dispensary is mostly managed by a young midwife in her 20s. She is extremely capable, as Dickson and I have seen her manage complicated births, treat patients with lockjaw, sew or splint serious wounds, dispense the very limited medicine available, and soothe families experiencing sick children. It is amazing watching a very talented and dedicated young person, out in the middle of nowhere, devote her life to helping her fellow countrymen. This is just another reason I enjoy my job so much. The men and women of Quang Xuyen are so devoted to their jobs, my team and I will bend over backwards to do whatever we can to help them. We honestly feel our presence is making a positive impact on the local Vietnamese.

The entire district has many, many, trained, motivated young people, doing their best to make the district function, fight the VC, and give their all to make Quang Xuyen a better place to live. As an advisor who speaks their language, I am proud to be able to do what I can to improve their lives. And all the members of my team also feel this way.

The team is involved in several civic projects within the district. We obtain funds to improve the latrines for six schools in the villages, repair three schools, and renovate some district administrative buildings. One major project I am pleased to begin is to build a separate small building next to the district dispensary. The young midwife now sleeps in a storeroom in the dispensary. The new building will be a house for her to live in.

The HES Report

During the first week of each month I need to complete my monthly HES report. Ah, the ubiquitous Hamlet Evaluation System report. I say "ubiquitous" because it is my third time since 1966 where I have been responsible for determining the safety of all hamlets in whatever district I am assigned to. The HES report was initially designed in 1964 as a numerical means of evaluating the degree of security in just the pacified hamlets. Vietnam has 11,729 hamlets in its 242 districts. That is a lot of hamlets to be evaluated, so the report became a monthly chore for most men assigned as district senior advisors. In 1967, the report was changed to cover all the hamlets in a district.

The purpose is to establish, monthly, a measurement representing the security of the hamlets in each district. The form has several pages, looking at multiple aspects of security (terrain, hamlet, its people), as well as estimating the strength and capability of the enemy. My method of completing this report is to sit down with the district chief or his deputy and assess a rank based on how safe we felt in the hamlet, the amount of security we needed to enter the hamlet. Quite often my responses on the report are more of a guess than based on first-hand knowledge. Another example of how the politicians want to fight this war ... reduce everything to numbers (à la McNamara?).

From 1961 until 1968, our Secretary of Defense, a number-crunching statistician, believed that the best way to analyze situations, people, and events was to rate everything numerically and then analyze the numbers to measure progress. I have no idea who created the HES report but am sure that Robert McNamara certainly had a hand in it. Numbers are the yardstick generals and politicians use to evaluate how the war is going and who is winning. Numbers of tons of expended ammo and bombs, numbers of soldiers fighting, and the ever-present tally of body count, how many VC were killed today.

Often the numbers are meaningless on the ground; after all, in combat, dead civilians could always be counted as dead VC. But at the top echelons in Vietnam or the politicians' offices in Washington, D.C., these numbers are used to support sending more troops, or to declare that now the Vietnamese can take charge of the war and Americans can go home. I do not see the HES report as any valid indicator of how the war is going or how secure the countryside is. In Trang Bang, for example, during one week, Vietnamese soldiers could be charged with protecting a hamlet and therefore most residents would be pro–GVN. The next week the soldiers depart and now the hamlet is pro–VC. So how does one rate a location that changes hands so often?

Regardless, it is a required part of my responsibility as the DSA to complete the report as honestly as possible. In my mind, and that of many other DSAs, it is not a valid measure of what is really happening, just another administrative function of the job.

And the HES report was only one document required of district advisors, when many different reports were required to assess how well the war was going. My opinion: the time spent generating these reports was wasted, as they did not accurately reflect what was really happening.

Some advisors, wanting to look good, would submit inflated security data to indicate they are doing a superior job. Others may have little knowledge of security throughout their district, so guesses are made. Yet all these reports, at the top levels of command in Vietnam, are used to justify the conduct of the war and for politicians to proclaim how we are winning the war.

Problems with Whom I Tell What

Upon entering Vietnam, at least with MACV, one is asked if they want anyone notified if they are injured or wounded. My records indicated that no one would be notified of me being harmed, for any reason.

My letters to Anita become more frequent and contain more details regarding what I am doing. Yet, I have never revealed my eight days in the hospital due to the hookworm or being shot on the Cambodian border, nor have I told my parents. Despite my attempt to not worry Anita or my parents, I did screw up, big-time.

I have a fraternity brother from Dartmouth whom I would occasionally correspond with regarding my job in Vietnam. John Ferries is an account executive with Benton and Bowles Advertising agency in New York City (later he became in charge of all of Benton and Bowles European operations). In my letters to him I have described the hookworm episode and being shot. Not thinking, I did not even consider the fact that my youngest sister, Diane, also worked at Benton and Bowles, although not in the same area as did John. Apparently one day, John and Diane were together, and the conversation became about me. John revealed he knew about the hookworm and me being wounded and Diane expressed her astonishment as she knew nothing about these.

Diane lived in an apartment in the city and our father managed a bank on lower Wall Street. While our parents live in Connecticut, Dad commuted daily into the city. Occasionally, Diane and Dad would meet for lunch or talk on the phone. Sometime after Diane learned about my adventures in Vietnam, she discussed this with our father, who told our mother.

I had not informed my parents about these events but eventually did share with them more information about what had happened. Knowing that eventually Anita would hear about my adventures, I decided it best for me to come clean and inform her of my hookworm and being shot. I tried to soften this news by downplaying the actual details, so my explanations suggested what happened was no big deal, the hookworm was a parasite that was quickly treated, and the gunshot wound was just a scratch.

19

Attack on a Major
Viet Cong Base Camp

By the afternoon of 5 May (my thirty-second birthday) the Hamlet Evaluation System report is done, and Lieutenant Springer comes bounding into our team house, looking extremely excited. He very enthusiastically explains that we have finally located a major VC base camp with a large VC unit. He says that Major Nghiem has asked me to join him in the District Intelligence and Operations Coordination Center, which I do.

Our Big Raid

In the DIOCC are several intel specialists and Lieutenant Cam, commander of the 117th RF company. The major describes what is going on. Early this morning a woodcutter reported seeing a large group of heavily armed civilians moving along a trail into a heavily wooded area. They all had packs, as if they had been on the move for some time. He estimated at least two dozen men, whom he figured are Viet Cong. Later today a fisherman came to the DIOCC describing a fortified camp near the La Be River with many, many VC soldiers. DIOCC members, after questioning each man for some time, have concluded it is the base camp for a VC company. Now is the time for a decisive raid.

Major Nghiem has some RF soldiers present with the fisherman and the woodcutter. The soldiers think they know where the VC camp is. Next to a small stream which runs into the La Be River, on a higher piece of ground (higher meaning maybe six feet above the stream). They describe the place as 30 or so yards square, surrounded by brush and trees. Small firing holes could be scrapped out of the ground for cover to defend the camp. The major thinks it should be a one-company operation.

The location of the camp is almost four miles south of district head-quarters. The only way to get close is by boat and sampans, but even big ones could not transport one full company, around 100 fighting men. Looking at the topographical map of Quang Xuyen, the major and the RF company commander calculate how to approach the VC. By now all the other advisors have joined us. It appears that the best way to attack would be to disembark on the east bank of the Vam Sat River, about a mile and a quarter west of the VC camp. The company would move east, toward the camp. The 117th would move into position just west of the camp and attack, one platoon blocking on the camp's south side with the lead platoon attacking from the west, toward the La Be. No streams would have to be crossed, but from disembarking the boats to get there would still require crossing over a mile of swamp in heavy foliage. The major asks my opinion at every step of his planning. I just concur because the plan of the operation seems solid.

Because we do not discuss upcoming operations over the radio, I call Commander Wages and ask if he could fly down to our district headquarters, now. I say it will be worth his time and we need his help. He says he can be there in an hour, which he does, with his deputy and his Vietnamese Navy counterpart. We need enough boats to move about 100 soldiers and he can make that happen.

Now the major, his Vietnamese boss and Commander Wages are discussing stream widths, depth, and the vegetation around the streams. Can the commander provide enough U.S. crafts to move the RF company?

The tides vary with the phase of the moon each month. High tide can vary between ten and 12 feet. At high tide almost 85 percent of the lower swamps of the Rung Sat can be under water. During low tide, many smaller streams can be empty. There are two high and two low tides each day, roughly about six hours apart. So, if operations are not planned to complement the exact tide tables, boats can find themselves in deep water at the beginning of an operation but a few hours later high and dry, sitting in mud. During high and low tides water in the streams can become too swift to cross on foot with the water gushing in or out at over 9 mph. Often if an operation is executed that will take several hours where the transportation is by boat, pickup by boat cannot be accomplished for 6 to 12 hours after the operation begins on land.

Commander Wages, talking with the Vietnamese Navy commander, his deputy advisor and the operations NCOs, calculates that the tides will allow a morning landing with the boats departing to return about 12–13 hours later. Operation Chuong Duong 23/69 becomes reality.

We discuss the strength and capability of the enemy. Since we began our combat raids in April we have agreed that the VC are complacent, not very vigilant, as they have controlled the Rung Sat for some time. Yet we doubt if this engagement will be that easy; most likely they will have guards posted beyond the periphery of their well-defended camp. We know they will have dug in fighting holes so we presume they will defend their camp. It is our contention that when attacked, they will fight.

The plan is to sneak up on their camp and attack hard with two platoons of the 117th, with the third platoon immediately behind to add more strength where needed. Our attack should force the VC against the La Be, a wide and deep stream on the east side of their camp, which would be outflowing fast due to the upcoming low tide.

Commander Wages discusses boat transportation with his deputy and his counterpart, and they conclude the U.S. Navy will provide enough assault support patrol boats (ASPBs), normally referred to as "alpha boats," to move the RF soldiers. Wages tells Major Nghiem the boats will arrive at the district docks and load the soldiers at 0700. Major Nghiem will be the operation commander. Lieutenant Pellman will accompany the blocking platoon, Sergeant Olden will remain with Major Nghiem in the district command group, while I will accompany Lieutenant Cam for the attack. Commander Wages also places two Seawolf gunships on standby at Nha Be, if needed.

The ASPBs are the only military boat designed for the navy specifically for Vietnam. With a one-quarter-inch-thick steel V-hull, the 50-foot boats are powered by twin 430 hp General Motors diesel engines and look like huge speed boats. Mid-ship is a square cabin; the forward deck is covered with twin .50 caliber machine guns in a turret. Aft of the cabin, the rear of the boat is open like a pickup truck. It also has a pedestal with an 81 mm mortar. With a draft fully loaded of under four feet, the ASPB is a heavily armed shallow water boat used for carrying assault troops, patrols, escorts, and minesweeping. Therefore, it is fast for its size (16 mph), maneuverable, well armed and manned by a crew of five.

Now all that remains to be done is for the troops and the advisors to prepare for tomorrow's raid.

We Fight the Viet Cong, Again

The ASPBs are waiting as promised. The ride down the Soi Rap River is speedy, but as we enter the Vam Sat, the boats slow down to reduce the diesels' noise. By 9 a.m. we are at our drop-off point. The

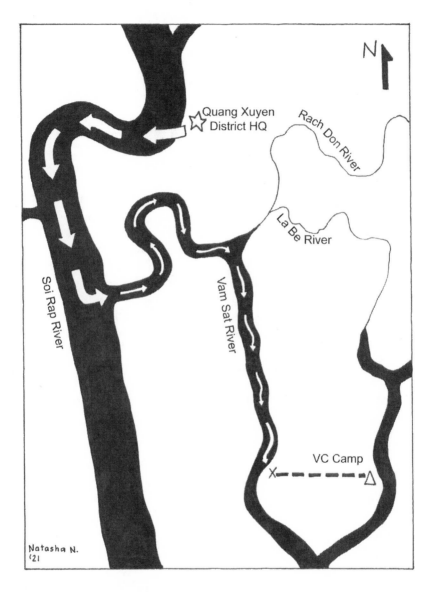

trek through the swamps takes over two hours. Our scouts report we are about 100 yards away from the VC camp, which is heavily guarded. The scouts tell us there are no enemy outposts to provide any early warning of an attack. A major mistake on the VC's part.

The 117 moves into position. The blocking platoon moves south of the VC camp while the offense platoon lines up for the assault. Lieutenant Cam and I are with the attacking platoon. At Cam's signal we initiate the charge. Rushing forward, we fire at every person we see in the camp. We are immediately countered by heavy returning fire as many VC quickly dive into their firing holes and unleash AK-47 automatic fire as well as RPGs (rocket-propelled grenades). Our forward movement is promptly slowed under the withering fire. Cam and I begin rushing from position to position, encouraging the soldiers to continue to move forward. I am barely conscious of the AK bullets ripping through the leaves surrounding us as they also smash into the trees spraying my face and upper body with splinters and sharp pieces of bark.

The fire discipline of the 117th is remarkable. Hunkering down, they return fire more accurately than the VC. I persuade several soldiers to rise next to me (I am crouching above them), yelling to others to move forward. Our line of soldiers rises, and their extreme firepower convinces the enemy to abandon their firing holes to escape. Our fire and maneuver turn the fight in our favor. Moving forward, shooting as we go, we sweep across the camp, firing to our front in a massive outpouring of death. We continue to push the VC toward the La Be River as the fire of the blocking platoon forces the VC into the jungle consisting of swamp, Nipa Palms, mangrove, and brushwood. The VC separate individually and disappear into the heavy brush and ferns along the banks of the La Be River.

Lieutenant Cam halts the platoon and we turn around to make a return sweep through the camp. As we clear the heavy jungle growth and re-enter the camp, we come under aggressive enemy fire again. Many VC have returned to their firing holes and engage us, as we return. I grab a squad of men, and we maneuver around to the side of the camp to attack the VC in their firing positions. As the rest of the platoon continues its frontal assault on the VC, lying in their deep firing holes, the squad I have hijacked initiates our attack from the side as we exchange fire with the VC. Our exacting accuracy overwhelms the enemy as they abandon their positions and weapons, again running into the jungle. The camp is now ours. The blocking platoon moves in and sets up our perimeter guard in case the VC decide to return.

As in previous encounters with the local VC, while their initial resistance was fierce, it quickly gave way to fright as they rapidly faded into the swamp

The base camp held over 40 VC. The weapons we recover fill three pages of a report. We find ten individual weapons (seven Chicom machine guns, one U.S M-I carbine, one B-41 grenade launcher with 19 RPG rockets, and one French submachine gun), 1,000 grenades, four 81 mm mortar rounds, 10 Claymore mines, three cases of AK-47 ammo, 4 sampan motors and five large (15 to 18 feet) boats, 330 pounds of rice, tools and clothing and considerable enemy documents and maps. There are several dead VC and, miraculously, no RF soldiers were wounded, let alone killed. It was quite a coup for the district.

With the amount of blood trails exiting the camp we figure we have wounded several VC. This must have been a semi-permanent camp as we uncover several bunkers reinforced with heavy wood from felled trees. We destroy the bunkers and the firing holes, conduct another sweep of the area to ensure we have not missed anything and prepare for the march back to where our boats will meet us. The U.S. Navy provides a couple of smaller boats to get to the VC camp to retrieve all the captured weapons, equipment, and food.

Back at the district compound, we are greeted by cheers and praise because we have engaged and defeated a major VC force of a large-sized, heavily armed unit. The documents on the mission are quickly evaluated by DIOCC officials and then sent to the Vietnamese Navy officials at Nha Be.

This operation again reveals that the Viet Cong in the Rung Sat have spent too long not being challenged. Their security and discipline under fire have seriously eroded. While their initial opposition was strong, it

Some soldiers from the 117th Regional Force company returning home after a combat operation.

quickly diminished, and they ran away. The vastly superior 117th company has proved, time and again, they are relentless fighters.

On the night of Sunday, 11 May, Major Nghiem sends a runner over to the advisors informing them there will be a district awards ceremony for the recent operations. District officials will be present as well as the 117th RF company. Would the advisor team also please participate? The soldiers will begin to line up at 0830 and the ceremony will begin at 0900. The uniform will be clean combat uniform (jungle fatigues for the advisors). I tell the runner all advisors would be honored to participate.

Medals Awarded and Then Taken Away

The next day, Monday, 12 May, we have some very unexpected visitors. The soldiers of the 117th RF company and the three advisors who accompanied the raid are all in formation. Apparently, the district chief is aware of what is happening because when a U.S. Navy helicopter touches down just before 0900, a district honor guard is in formation at the helipad when several men jump out. Two Vietnamese are in gray cotton uniforms with military brimmed caps. Two more men are in khaki uniforms, also with the military, brimmed cap, both Americans. Last out is Commander Wages, wearing jungle fatigues. The honor guard presents arms, while Major Nghiem salutes. As the group approaches, the deputy district chief, Captain Minh, calls the assembled troops to attention. Myself, Lieutenant Pellman, and Sergeant Olden are placed in front of the assembled 117th RF company along with Lieutenant Cam, the attacking platoon leader, his platoon sergeant, and several RF soldiers, including the one who had been wounded in the commando raid on the weapons cache.

One of the two Vietnamese men stands in front of us soldiers, all at attention, and calls out, "Parade rest," in Vietnamese. He then begins to praise the company for their valiant conduct and the successes of Chuong Duong 1/69 and Chuong Duong 23/69. He refers first to the 98 captured weapons. Then he comments on the enormous success of the raid on the VC camp and everything recovered. He also refers to the bravery of the wounded soldier. The speech is short but powerful, acknowledging the company's excellent conduct in battle, their outstanding training, and how their actions go a long way to rid the Rung Sat Special Zone of the Viet Cong. Additionally, he gives praise to the American advisors who trained the 117th Regional Force company and their courage during the battle. The man then announces that awards will now be given out.

At this point in time I am neither aware of who the two Vietnamese in gray are nor who the two American officers in khaki are. But I am about to find out. As the group of men who exited the helicopter line up, the district chief, Major Nghiem, leads them in front of the end of our short line where I am standing.

I recognize that one of the two Americans is a U.S. Navy admiral whom I do not know. Nudging Lieutenant Cam, I whisper to ask who are the Vietnamese and he replies, "Commodore Tran Van Chon, commander of the Vietnamese Navy." I think, wow! The head of the Vietnamese Navy coming down for a ceremony for our RF company. Our operations must have been a big deal.

Commodore Chon is a stocky man, short, with close-cropped black hair, wearing dark-framed glasses, his round face belying his age of 40. A black plastic name tag over his right pocket displays his full name, while over his left pocket he wears eight rows of ribbons. I recognize he has several Vietnamese Gallantry crosses (he was awarded nine) and the U.S. Purple Heart. He certainly does not look like the warrior his decorations identify him as.

As the line moves forward, Major Nghiem, at the head, introduces each soldier to Commodore Chon. When Chon stops in front of a man,

Major Worthington being decorated with Vietnamese Cross of Gallantry by Admiral Tran Van Chon, Chief of Naval Operations for Vietnam (the award was later taken away).

he salutes and Chon returns it, then shakes the man's hand. The Vietnamese officer trailing Commodore Chon, carrying a case, takes out a Vietnamese medal, hands it to the commodore, who then announces what medal he is pinning on the soldier's chest. The soldier salutes again, the salute is returned, and Chon moves on. Stopping in front of me, he explains the advisors are being recommended for Vietnamese Crosses of Gallantry for bravery in battle. He continues to say that since we are not navy, he cannot give us the medals today, but they will be sent to us.

Reading the American admiral's plastic name tag I now know who he is, Elmo Zumwalt, commander of all U.S. Navy forces in Vietnam and senior advisor to the Vietnamese Navy. He is average in size, his face angular and sharp. His black hair is cut short, and he has very dark and bushy eyebrows. Following the admiral is his aide, a navy lieutenant (same as an army captain) whose nametag reads Kerr, who is carrying a briefcase. As the admiral stands in front of a soldier, the lieutenant opens his briefcase, extracts a medal, hands it to Zumwalt, who pins it on the soldier next to his Vietnamese award. This is my introduction to Admiral Zumwalt's impact awards.

The admiral says the U.S. Navy has recommended me for the Navy Achievement Medal with Combat "V" for the operation where 98 weapons were captured. He continues to tell me that for the raid on the VC camp last week, the Navy has also recommended me for the Bronze Star with the Combat "V" for my heroic actions during that raid.

But because I am in the army, neither award can be presented to me now. Zumwalt explains that the recommendation must be offered to the Secretary of the Army, and if he accepts, the award will eventually be presented to me. Both the commodore and the admiral apologize for me not being able to receive any awards during this ceremony, but both insist that, eventually, in the future, I will be honored. After all awards have been presented, the entourage returns to their helicopter and departs. All in all, the ceremony was uplifting, and for me to be recognized by the two top Navy officers in Vietnam is a distinct honor that renders our advising efforts very worthwhile.

Later I learn how this ceremony really came about. Admiral Zumwalt felt that morale would be heightened if shortly after a heroic battle, the participants were recognized by the awarding of medals for their combat success by a senior flag officer (a general or admiral). Thus, the impact awards.

Admiral Zumwalt and his aide, Lieutenant Kerr, will hop into the admiral's helicopter and fly to where the combat troops are. The Navy is not known for providing enlisted or officers with sufficient weapons training to know how to shoot. Both the lieutenant and the admiral

District Chief Captain Tri and his son.

have admitted neither knows how to shoot a rifle, so the admiral travels unarmed. Inside his briefcase, Kerr carries several different navy commendation medals, some Bronze Stars, and some Purple Hearts. Additionally, he has in this briefcase a loaded .38 caliber revolver.

Kerr later explains that the impact awards can become an administrative nightmare. Admiral Zumwalt would pin a medal on a soldier or sailor and move on. Kerr had to keep a list of who got what. Then the medal, already presented, had to have paperwork prepared indicating why the medal was presented. Sometimes Kerr wasn't sure, so the admin people had to contact the unit commander or the involved American advisor to ask what the recipient did to get his medal.

New District Chief

In mid–May Major Nghiem is replaced by Captain Tri as the new district chief. Tri is of small stature, slim, in his late 30s with his hair combed and parted. His soft-spoken manner reminds me of that of a lowly clerk in some insignificant administrative position. Looks, though, are deceiving, for while he does not resemble a warrior in any sense of the word, he is one. A good listener, agreeable, easy to advise, he is

Bob with daughters of 117th Regional Force Company soldiers.

an excellent counterpart. Working with Captain Tri is enjoyable and productive.

When he is assigned as district chief, he moves his entire family to Quang Xuyen; wife and three children, two girls and a boy. The youngest girl is two, and reminds me much of my daughter, Julie. Like my own daughter, she is very stubborn, but loves to walk around the compound with me, grasping my big hand with her small and delicate fingers. When I would visit the family, she would climb in my lap and want to play games. My ability to talk to her in her own language made every visit a bright spot in this war-torn world she would have to grow up in. Her future is another reason I want to help the Vietnamese as much as I can.

20

R&R in Hawaii

On Friday afternoon, 23 May 1969, several team advisors and I pile into our Boston Whaler for the trip to Nha Be navy base. Upon landing we go in separate directions. For me, I am headed to Hawaii to meet my wife for R&R (rest and recuperation). I leave with them wishing me a safe trip and a good R&R. The other advisors go their way, to visit various navy supply offices. They have an assortment of VC combat souvenirs and intend to trade them for things we need. I go directly to my BOQ. That evening I eat on base, and the next day, Saturday, province headquarters arranges for transportation to the R&R processing center at Camp Alpha on Tan Son Nhut Air Base. I change from jungle fatigues into the short-sleeve khaki uniform with my combat infantry badge and three rows of ribbons including my new Purple Heart and Air Medal. I carry a small bag with civilian shirts and slacks, underwear, and toiletries. Anita will also bring some of my civilian clothes.

Camp Alpha began in the early 1960s as a small tent compound to in-process army personal (not MACV) into Vietnam. As more troops arrived, Camp Alpha grew. In mid–1969 it is a large, sprawling collection of masonry, white one- and two-story buildings, mostly barracks and admin offices. It is the home of the 90th Replacement Battalion. My vehicle enters the large metal and mesh wire main gate but must stop there. I continue inside through a walk-in gate manned by several guards. My orders are to report in at 1400 hours (2 p.m.).

Anita's travel to Honolulu is more complicated than mine from Vietnam, yet Peckham Travel Service in Columbus, Georgia, makes it happen. She begins with a Delta regional flight from Columbus to Atlanta, next another Delta flight to Los Angeles, and then a United flight to Hawaii. The entire round trip (both ways) costs $349.83. She arrives on Thursday, the 22nd, and is waiting when I arrive on Saturday.

In one sense I am apprehensive about our getting together again. Our letters reveal her reluctance to leave the army career way of life. For our entire time together, I have been in the military. I met her while a Marine private first class. When we married, I was an enlisted man in the Army Reserves and an Army ROTC cadet. Upon graduation from college I was commissioned and entered active duty as a second lieutenant. Now I am a field grade officer and quitting the army, much to her dissatisfaction.

After checking in the R&R processing center I board Military Airlift Command (MAC) mission P208, Saigon to Honolulu. Following our landing at Hickam AFB in Honolulu, we quickly board old olive drab painted buses for the 20-minute ride to the U.S. Army Fort DeRussy R&R center on Waikiki Beach. Right away we see each other, run together, and hold each other for an awfully long time. Anita has made us reservations at the Surfrider, a Sheraton hotel, about six blocks from Fort DeRussy, also on the beach. We taxi directly to the hotel.

This trip we decide not to do again what we did during our R&R visit on my first Vietnam tour. I want to avoid rich foods and simply take it easy and relax.

Later that night, Anita is sitting on the bed and I am sitting in a straight-backed chair nearby. She stares at me, cocking her head, looking puzzled. Finally, she asks why I am sitting so awkward? I ask what does she mean? She answers me that I am not sitting down squarely on both cheeks of my butt. Instead, my weight is more on my left cheek and my right leg is positioned so the back of my right thigh is off the seat.

I explain to her that after I was shot in the back of the right thigh, it become infected. I describe that I sit the way I do is because when the unhealthy tissue was cut out, it left a thick plug of scar tissue (about the size of half my little finger). Now, when it presses into my sensory nerve, it puts the leg to sleep. Consequently, I have adapted by sitting sort of sideways, so the scar tissue does not press into my thigh.

Once I finish relating about that escapade, I move on to another. I tell Anita that last fall when I made my MARS call to her is when I was in the hospital recovering from hookworm. I try to keep talking so she will not get more upset. My tactic is to assure her that since I am no longer on the Cambodian border, the danger where I am is reduced to almost nothing. I brag that I am now in admirable shape. I have regained the weight I lost, am tan and muscular so I am the image of the young man I want to be, in perfect health.

Two caveats about my "perfect health." First is that Anita does not hear me past "regained the weight I lost." That leads to a detailed and somewhat lengthy discussion. The other is a requirement that soldiers entering Hawaii from Vietnam must carry a U.S. Public Health yellow card. This is a Health Alert Notice identifying the card holder as a person who has been exposed to serious communicable diseases, specifically cholera and plague. So, maybe I am not quite as healthy as I think.

I explain to Anita that the army advisor team will be replaced in June by marines. My boss, Commander Wages, has asked me to stay on at his advisor headquarters, helping his team understand what to do in Quang Xuyen until I depart Vietnam in August. I tell her I have agreed to do so. This will remove me from combat, which makes her happy.

Mostly we spend hours relaxing on the beach, which is out the hotel back door. Many local excursions are by foot, ventures just a few blocks from the hotel.

Our hotel is across from the International Market Place, so we spend a lot of time there shopping. Anita buys a bikini and light jacket at Tahitian Beachwear for $19.66. At the Overseas Wig Warehouse, she

Bob relaxing on R&R.

buys a fall for $37.70. We buy monkeypod wood carvings from Woods of Hawaii and other items from various other shops. Behind the market is Waikiki Wee Golf, the largest and newest miniature golf course in Hawaii, with two expansive 18-hole layouts. We play several times and Anita wins every round but one; that one we tie.

One day we get a rental car and visit the U.S. Army post Schofield Barracks, located almost in the middle of Oahu. Schofield is famous for being the setting for James Jones' novel *From Here to Eternity*. The 1953 movie starring Burt Lancaster, Deborah Kerr, Frank Sinatra, Cliff Montgomery, and Donna Reed won eight Academy Awards. Driving around the base, it seems like we are in the middle of the movie set. That evening we dine at the Schofield Barracks officers' open mess. Most days we eat at the Fort DeRussy officers' club.

We devote a lot of time to discussing our future. It seems like we are finally on the same page once again. In three months, I will out-process from active duty. Anita will arrange to have our Battle Park household goods packed and placed in storage until we move three small girls, two vehicles, and a travel trailer from Fort Benning to Flagstaff, Arizona, acquire a new home and move in. Then get the kids registered in school (and me, too) and I either get a scholarship, work-study or a job. I am eligible for the G.I. Bill, which will help quite a bit, but first I must apply for the benefit.

We decide that with almost 13 years of military service (ten years' active duty and almost 3 years' reserve), it will not be wise to quit the military altogether. I plan to remain active in the Army Reserve when we get settled in Flagstaff.

I need to let Northern Arizona University know I will be on my way. We have already collected quite a bit of information on schools, real estate, and various housing areas during our visit to Flagstaff last summer. We look at when we can move out of Georgia and when school starts and make several tentative plans on what needs to be

Anita on R&R.

completed by what dates. We lie in the sun, we talk, we plan, and we dream about our future. We are happy, optimistic, fully believing that we are making the best decisions for our forthcoming adventures. We hope everything will turn out okay.

While we avoid sumptuous, rich meals, about three blocks away from the Surfrider is the House of Hong, one of the nicest Chinese restaurants in the world. We eat there our last evening and find the following in our fortune cookies: Bob's reads "Romance is yours tonight." Anita's reads "A new home is in your future." Both are certainly true.

Too quickly, our six days together end. My return flight to Vietnam is scheduled for early morning so we get a cab to the DeRussy R&R Center, say our goodbyes and I board an ancient olive drab bus to Hickam, back to the Rung Sat Special Zone and the war again. Later that day

Ice drink stand in market outside Quang Xuyen district headquarters.

Anita checks out, paying the final hotel bill for eight nights, laundry and valet fees, for a total of $165.

My return flight takes 13 hours, arriving at Tan Son Nhut in the afternoon. Arriving back at Nha Be later that day, I spend the night in my BOQ. The next day, I hitch a ride on a U.S. Navy vessel that drops me off at the village dock. Carrying my overnight bag, I make my way through the village to the district compound. The local people know I have been gone for a week and as I pass people I know, like our barber, or the staff of a small restaurant we would go to, or the huts belonging to local soldiers, I ask what has happened during my absence. They all have some important piece of gossip or news to relay to me. The VC have attacked a small fishing hamlet, a fisherman's boat has sunk, someone's home has caught fire and burned, a soldier was shot, but is doing okay. And the stories continue, so the short walk to our compound takes a long time as I stop to chat in Vietnamese with our neighbors.

When I arrive at the team quarters, I am greeted by all and questioned about my R&R. Shortly later we all sit down for the evening meal.

Children playing in back of Quang Xuyen market.

I then ask what has happened during my absence. Any VC situations, any enemy contact, any good or bad things happened to the civilians? My advisors glance at each other and then, getting back to me, respond no. It was a quiet week, and nothing happened at all.

Their response just reinforces my deep opinion that all advisors should be trained in the host country's language to be most effective in their roles.

In less than 90 days I will be a civilian and a grad student.

21

Chieu Hoi

A Chieu Hoi Candidate

As we move into June 1969, we continue our combat operations as we obtain worthy intelligence. One day Lieutenant Springer and the district Chieu Hoi chief come to me and say they want to talk about a potential Viet Cong defector. This is not a run of the mill VC but a VC officer. The Chieu Hoi chief wants to talk to me about converting this officer in Chieu Hoi (open arms), the program designed to locate, identify, and convince VC members to defect and give their allegiance to the South Vietnamese government. Together, we move into the DIOCC.

Apparently, this VC lieutenant has become unhappy with the demands the Viet Cong are placing upon him. He is a poor fisherman with a wife and three children, one a baby. He lives in a very small collection of huts in the Rung Sat, sort of like an unofficial hamlet. This small "hamlet" consists of probably not much more than a dozen homes, very crude huts made of thatched palm leaves, scrap aluminum for roofs, and bits and pieces of wood for walls and stability. Most are a single-room abodes. The homes are strung around a small bay, maybe 50 to 75 yards wide, at the end of a waterway. The bay is circular, with the homes backing the small bay, facing a small footpath and then another row of huts, across the footpath.

One might ask, why live here? First the residents are very poor. Second the residents are either woodcutters or fishermen and where they live is in the Rung Sat, where dead wood is abundant and the fishing is excellent. Chopped wood and fresh fish are readily sold in nearby hamlets and villages. Third, their small housing area is protected from harsh weather by the very thick jungle growth surrounding the bay. The shoreline around the bay is lined with all manner of small fishing boats, sampans, and bigger boats to carry chopped wood.

The interiors of the huts have a very crude semblance, with coarse handmade tables and chairs, shelves to hold cooking utensils, clothing,

Corner guard tower with .50 caliber machine gun at Quang Xuyen district compound.

and food, with rough wooden beds covered with woven mats for sleeping. In the middle is a fire pit for cooking and, during the rainy season, for warmth. Most of the residents are apolitical, having no need for any form of government or government benefits. These people just want to be left alone to earn a living (albeit, just barely) and raise their family. In fact, their very limited existence is the opening the Viet Cong use to recruit them into the communist cause.

VC Coercion

VC leaders in the Rung Sat would locate these smaller communities scattered around the Rung Sat and begin their quest to convert the

Rung Sat Special Zone swamps.

residents to communism and the VC cause. At night the VC would surround the small collection of huts and collect the residents outside so the entire group could be addressed at the same time. The propaganda speech would go like this.

The VC would draw attention to the barely sustainable conditions of living these people are forced to endure. Their scarcely livable existence is because of the illegal and corrupt government of South Vietnam. Just look at the place where the Quang Xuyen district chief lives. He lives in a mansion (a mansion only by comparison to where these people live), protected by soldiers conscripted by the GVN. He and his family live in luxury paid for by the illegal collection of taxes by more GVN officials who take from the poor citizens of the district to enrich the crooked and corrupt GVN leaders.

This talk rings a bell for these people. They are aware of how the district chief and his assistants live. They are very attuned to the spiel on taxes because they must be licensed to fish or cut wood to sell. And their licenses cost money. Sometimes when they are fishing or gathering wood a boat of National Policemen (with soldiers for security) demands to see their proper identification and their licenses. If they fail to produce either one, they can be arrested.

These people are poor, uneducated, and often fearful of their own government leaders. This the VC exploits by offering a much better way of life, one in which everyone contributes but also shares in the benefits reaped by hard work. The communist way of life is without the corrupt government taking everything, where both land and communal effort rewards everyone. It is not hard to convert people who have nothing with the promise of everyone sharing all the better aspects of life.

This is how our potential Chieu Hoi lieutenant became a VC. Beginning as a common soldier, he quickly rose to a leadership position. But as the demands by VC higher-ups increased, he saw no improvement in his existence or that of his family. It became harder and harder to serve as a VC leader and at the same time find time to fish to sustain his family. When he argues that he needs more free time to care for his family he is resisted by his leaders, who explain he needs to give more to the cause, and that includes suffering for everyone until they win this war.

Frustrated, angry, and not knowing what to do, he came across a Chieu Hoi illustrated leaflet offering him a way out, a way to save his family. One day, while in An Thoi Dong village, he surreptitiously began to collect information on how the Chieu Hoi Program works. He would discuss this with his wife, and they have decided to pursue it in more depth.

Using a trusted friend, the VC lieutenant has learned what it would take for him to Chieu Hoi. The program offers several ways to convince the VC to defect. They can be offered money, family protection, or the entire family being relocated to where they could enjoy a much better life. To make this happen the Chieu Hoi chief must know what exactly he is getting and negotiate with the VC for his defection. It is at this point where the advisors come in. To make this work, we must work with the province Chieu Hoi program to get money (used to pay VC to defect), secure protection for the VC and his or her family, and work out a relocation plan. The VC would have to tell us what information he or she will give us, such as the organization makeup, its members, weapons, future VC plans, or whatever would be worth our while.

Planning the Chieu Hoi Raid

The VC agrees to defect, and plans are laid to capture him. To ensure the safety of his family we will set up a raid on his house and then pretend to capture him and whatever weapons he might have. We will take him away, leaving his family behind. A few days later his wife would leave, telling everyone she needed to take her children and go to her mother and family, because she has lost her husband and is unable to provide for her children on her own. Instead of going to her family, though, she goes to the province headquarters to meet with the Chieu Hoi chief and, if all has gone well, be reunited with her husband, to begin a new life somewhere else.

Arrangements are made to make the snatch. Because he lives in a VC area, we will need to sneak in silently, grab him as he makes a show

Rung Sat Special Zone swamps.

that he is resisting, then get out quickly, before any VC can react to save him. It is decided we will go in with a small squad of heavily armed RF soldiers and some intel NCOs and the VC's trusted friend, who will guide us to the VC's house. I will also go on this raid.

We can use motorized sampans to get close to the collection of huts where the VC lives. Just beyond range of hearing our subdued engine noise, we can shut off the engines and paddle the rest of the way in. Departing with our VC and weapons, though, could be too dangerous in our small boats. This is where the U.S. Navy comes in.

The navy patrol boat, river, is a 31 foot-long fast (33 mph), shallow draft (2 feet), heavily armed fiberglass open boat. It has twin .50 caliber machine guns in a tub in front, with 7.62 mm machine guns on the sides and a 40 mm grenade launcher on the stern. In the middle is an open cabin, covered by a canvas tarp, so the boat resembles a World War II PT boat, less the torpedo tubes. Powered by two 180 hp diesel engines, it moves by jet water propulsion (no propellers to get caught in weeds) created by the Jacuzzi hot tub company.

I have arranged for two PBRs to follow us in but remain beyond hearing of the people in the area we plan to raid. After we capture the VC, I will radio the PBRs to enter the small bay, pick us up, and take us out. Our sampans can be tied to the PBRs and they can be towed out of the bay. Everything is set up to conduct the raid. It is a go.

Executing the Raid

The next morning the raiding party assembles at the village dock, where we meet the two PBRs. Using our map, I go over the plan with the petty officer in charge. I explain our raid to capture a VC lieutenant but fail to disclose he is a willing participant. I make it clear that we all will be in VC territory and the probability of having to fight our way out is very high. Therefore, we need the power, speed, and firepower of the PBRs to diminish the risk. Because the PBRs are so much faster than our small sampans, the petty officer says they will remain in the main channel until we reach the point where we will kill our engines. Then as we paddle to the bay, the PBRs can come to their holding point and wait for me to radio them for our pickup.

We depart alone, leaving the PBRs behind us as we began the journey to the VC collection of huts. Upon reaching the "kill-engine" point, I radio the PBRs where we are, and say we are going in.

As we enter the bay, one intel NCO asks our guide where the VC hut is. The guide replies that it is the last hut on the right, so we paddle the sampans to the right side of the bay. Beaching the sampans, we charge the last hut, half the squad taking up defensive positions around the hut, with the rest setting up blocking positions facing the rest of the huts to protect us. The intel NCOs, the guide and I storm inside the hut. We are met by an older couple who challenge our entrance. The guide immediately realizes we have raided the wrong hut. We retreat outside quickly, and I ask the guide what he was doing. His face and eyes instantly reveal he is scared, confused, and he begins to shake. He stutters as he explains that he doesn't know what happened, he always enters this place, turns right, and walks down the footpath to the VC's hut.

Then I realize what is wrong. The guide previously entered from the front, having walked some ways to get to this place and turned as he described. We entered from the back so the VC's hut must be on our left, not our right. I speak to the senior NCO and he agrees, so we all climb back into our sampans and paddle across the bay, beaching like before, and initiate our second raid of the day. The RF soldiers deploy as before, securing the hut as we stage our second theatrical act of rage and anger against the VC. Inside stand the lieutenant, his wife, holding a small baby, and his two other children. While the VC and his wife know what is happening, the children do not, so, scared to death, they begin to cry and scream. Now our acting commences. Two intel NCOs swing at the lieutenant, pushing him to the ground, yelling and cursing, as they would smack their fists into an open palm, sounding just like they are beating him up as I stand and watch.

The lieutenant is pushed and shoved as the NCOs yell at him, saying they will shoot his kids unless he tells them where any weapons are hidden. In lower voices they ask where the weapons are and he points to a mat on the floor of the hut, under a crude bed. More acting, more yelling by the NCOs, more smacking of fists, and the entire scene sounds so real but looks like a batch of keystone cops play-acting. The small hut is torn apart as an NCO finds a box buried under the bed, holding a few shoulder weapons. The NCO calls in a couple of RF soldiers to collect the rifles.

When the lieutenant is identified, I radio the petty officer to come as soon as possible, as we have the VC. A couple of minutes later the PBRs back up to the shore next to our sampans. Now the VC lieutenant is being held and shoved by the NCOs as they rough him up for the benefit of any onlookers. The wife with her screaming kids is left in the torn-up hut as we retreat to climb into the PBRs. RF soldiers move backwards to cover our escape as the lieutenant is hurriedly tossed in a PBR as I jump in with him.

As soon as we are in the boat, two sailors, who most likely have never seen a live VC before, attack the lieutenant. One swings a fist at the slight man, and I leap between the VC and the sailors, pushing him to the deck, covering him with my body so they can't hit him again.

The weapons are loaded on a PBR, our sampans tied tight to the rear of the PBRs, the RF soldiers jump aboard, and we speed off out of there. The two sailors try to get around me to pound on the VC again as I tell them to back off. Luckily, we never encounter any other VC and get away without any fight. It is a real comedy of errors where we attacked the wrong hut and had to repeat our raid all over again. But it worked—we got our man.

The VC remained at district, being questioned by the DIOCC people for 24 hours, and then the Chieu Hoi chief took him to province headquarters. We heard that several days later he was joined by his family and relocated.

22

Sailors and Hand Grenades

Nha Be Sailors

The U.S. naval base at Nha Be is on a spit of land jutting into the Soi Rap River right across from where the Long Tau shipping channel splits from the Soi Rap. Also, across from the Nha Be naval support activity is the northern tip of Quang Xuyen district.

The base is oriented northwest and southeast, about 550 yards wide and about 800 yards deep. It is a massive combat and logistics complex manned by several hundred navy personnel. In 1965 it was an underwater swamp but in 1966 over 300,000 cubic yards of sand dried up the swamp, creating a large, flat, dry parcel of real estate which sprouted over four dozen buildings to house and feed sailors, store supplies and fuel (there are four 1,000 gallon fuel tanks), and serve as maintenance facilities for both boats and helicopters. On the western edge of the base are two exceptionally large helicopter PSP runways about a couple of hundred yards long oriented almost east and west and north and south. Off the southern tip of the base is a T-shaped pier to tie boats and for boat repairs.

While permanent party sailors are a static number, Nha Be also has a large, but shifting population of transient people. There are civilian boat experts to assist in the maintenance and repair of boats and engines, pilots and aircrews from other services and a host of various combat people, all temporarily stationed at Nha Be. For example, I am not stationed at Nha Be but have a permanent BOQ room and a place to store the advisor jeep we use to drive to Saigon or Gia Dinh province advisor headquarters or the U.S. Navy RSSZ advisor headquarters located at Nha Be district headquarters.

Nha Be is the home of one of the U.S. Navy riverine forces used to patrol and secure the shipping channels and to support American and Vietnamese combat operations in the Rung Sat. Nha Be houses both support and assault helicopters (the Seawolves), a YRBM barge

Aerial photograph of Nha Be navy base (photograph by R. Fries).

(a 260- by 50-foot boat repair barge used to berth and mess its crew of ship repair people), 84 riverine craft (mostly PBRs and Swift boats), as well as three platoons from SEAL team 1.

Nha Be is a large and industrious base, going full-time day and night. Our Sergeants Harris and Olden pay the wives or children of the RF soldiers to make VC flags from worn-out materials, grind them in dirt and then place chicken blood on them. These "combat souvenirs" would then be taken to Nha Be and swapped with sailors for food (steaks), beer, or other supplies we are unable to procure through our regular channels.

While the navy base is now on dry land, in front of the base are mostly thin strips of land with walking paths and Vietnamese homes built on stilts over canals of water. Out the main gate of Nha Be is a

Bachelor officers' quarters at Nha Be navy base. Bob's room is on second floor, middle of the building.

single road which goes north through the Vietnamese homes outside the base, past the major private fuel depots (which store about 80 percent of petroleum products used in Vietnam and are owned by a Dutch conglomerate, Shell, and Esso), through the Nha Be district headquarters and on into Saigon.

Cinderella Liberty

But right outside the main gate are several bars, providing drinks and girls. Typically, the major portion of the front of these two-story buildings is a room with many tables and chairs, where drinks are served. A small portion behind the open bar area are the living quarters of the Vietnamese who own the facility with a kitchen large enough to also provide food for the sailors. The second floor is primarily small rooms with beds for the girls and their customers.

The front of the bars open onto the main street, while the back end of the building is typically built on stilts rising out of the waters in the canals. The operation is a total family affair. Mom and/or dad run the bar itself and manage its customers. Small kids keep the place clean, wait tables, hustling drinks, or food, and assist their parents however they can. The buildings are built so close together that often only a couple of feet separate them. Some have live music while most have some form of recorded music. The front of the second story typically has a balcony, surrounded by a railing where favored customers can sit and drink, while watching the crowds pass by, just like Mardi Gras in New Orleans.

The U.S. Navy allows what is referred to as a "Cinderella" liberty program. The main gate opens at 4 p.m. for all naval personnel who do not have to work. They can frequent the local bars, visit the "B" girls, but at 8 p.m., liberty ends, and all sailors must return inside the base. So, for many of the hundreds of sailors at Nha Be, being allowed four hours of unrestricted enjoyment of girls and booze turns the single street into a massive party every night.

At this point in time, the reader must be thinking, the only way I can know all about the bars and its girls would be for me to partake of the festivities. Well, not quite. You see, many of the businesses are owned by combat disabled or retired NCOs of the 117th RF company. Because of my Vietnamese fluency, I would visit the homes of the 117th officers and NCOs and meet their families. Often this would include mothers and fathers, brothers and sisters who had once been associated with the 117th. When family members who own a bar would visit their relatives at An Thoi Dong Village, I would be introduced to them or a soldier would take me to Nha Be and take me to the family bar. Because I am not stationed at Nha Be and am not navy, I have no liberty restrictions and can come and go as I please. Mostly I visit after the 8 p.m. curfew and spend time with the old soldiers and their families. I am an oddity, an American who is fluent in Vietnamese and advisor to the 117th. None of the Nha Be military personnel who frequent the bars speak Vietnamese, so I am accepted as a friend of the family.

As I have mentioned before, I do not wear any signs of rank or branch of service. I do wear well-worn jungle fatigues (the sailors wear dark blue denim trousers and light blue denim shirts). If I happen to be there before 8 p.m., I am a decade or so older than most sailors and because I only speak Vietnamese, I am suspected of being a left-over French worker at one of the major fuel farms just up the road.

It is interesting to listen to the girls talk in Vietnamese about a sailor, telling him in English how great he is, while in Vietnamese, describing him as ugly, broke, drunk, or other negative aspects about him.

I would attend meetings with Commander Wages or a staff member occasionally. Also, a couple of times a month, Colonel Herbert or some other advisor would want me to attend a meeting at the province headquarters. Sometimes my ride would be in an Air America helicopter, but often by a navy boat or in our team Boston Whaler. If the sessions were either early in the morning or afternoon, I would elect to spend the night in my BOQ room rather than go by boat as night approached. During these evenings in the BOQ, I would visit one of the family bars, usually after 8 p.m., and enjoy a nice Vietnamese supper.

Air America

During combat operations, Commander Wages would arrange for the use of navy assets such as a boat or helicopter. But for administrative aspects of our job such as getting food, supplies or mail or trips to province, we depend on the province advisors to get a helicopter for us. Because we are CORDS, this means Air America, the CIA civil aviation transportation. The kind of flying they do around Saigon and Gia Dinh is referred to as "ash and trash" missions. They haul people, supplies, documents, and mail from one safe heliport to another. Yes, they get to fly their Huey, but on very boring and uneventful flights.

Many Air America pilots are former military pilots, typically ex–combat pilots, who left the service because the CIA pays more. I get to know some of the pilots who support us regularly and they describe how they miss the action of combat missions. Somehow our conversations get around to where I could use more recon flights around the Rung Sat looking for VC activities. The CIA pilots think low-level recon flights would be a welcome change from their routine flights. The pilots are armed (even though the Air America helicopters are slicks, meaning not armed) with various handguns and M-16s. I would go over their topo maps of the Rung Sat and we would set up where I need to scout. I use the Air America helicopters often and they enjoy adding some risk to their normal flying. I never even consider how they can account for a couple extra hours of flight time when on a round trip of about 40 minutes. Regardless, whenever I need a recon flight, they are always ready to fly.

Life Back with the Advisors

In early June, knowing we will be replaced by marines, we decide to host a going-away party to thank our Vietnamese counterparts and those we enjoy working with.

The location is our large screened porch. We invite all the district staff, so we have a mix of Vietnamese military and civilians. There are over 20 people in attendance. Both men and women from the district administrative offices, the medical staff, DIOCC and Phoenix, Chieu Hoi, and the officers from the 117th. Also, we have been working with a couple of marines on Commander Wages' staff, a captain and a gunny sergeant (same rank as an army E-7 platoon sergeant like Sergeant Olden). We are working with the marines because the Quang Xuyen army advisors will be replaced by a Marine advisor team soon.

My team wears civilian clothes and all the women wear the national garment, the ao dai, slacks with a tight bodice with two panels, front and back. Some of the military wear jungle fatigues while others wear civvies. We set up tables filled with food in one of the rooms off the porch. We serve beer and punch. The party lasts over two hours and it appears everyone has a good time, enjoying themselves.

District officials at our party: Miss Mon, district medical clinic; 1st Lieutenant Thoi, deputy district chief, Miss Hanh, local schoolteacher.

Radio Watch

One aspect of being an advisor team is the requirement to maintain radio communications 24/7. At Trang Bang, the enlisted men set up a schedule for a radio watch during the night. In Quang Xuyen, with only a six-man team, an all-night radio watch would be difficult. However, I have the unique ability to be asleep and, when receiving a radio call, I am able to immediately wake up. Therefore, I decide to set up a cot in our radio room. The radio is placed right next to the bed. Each month our call signs change for the province advisor net. So, one month it might be "Red Baron" and the next "Brown Dog"

Each district advisor team would have a number, so we would be, say, Red Baron five. If any other Red Baron number was called, we would not respond, but if the radio transmitted "Red Baron five," the call would be for us and we would reply. Somehow, I can sleep through any of the nighttime radio calls unless it is for us. At night, the province radio traffic is mostly limited to only periodic radio checks, so my sleep is hardly ever disturbed. And the rest of the team really appreciates not having to endure any night radio watch.

Grenades, Grenades, and More Grenades

One day one of the DIOCC Vietnamese officers comes to me to discuss another mission. Apparently, a woodcutter came across an underground storage bunker dug into a berm on the bank of a small river. He said he took off the protective cover and all he saw were hundreds of hand grenades. He described the bunker as being concrete, about two to three feet square. When he explains where he had gone seeking wood, some of the RF soldiers have a good idea of where the bunker is.

The district chief, Captain Tri, tells the 117th commander to take some soldiers, find the grenade bunker and, using C-4, destroy every grenade and the bunker. The lieutenant said that a couple of squads for security would go in a few sampans to arrive around high tide. This is where I come in. I am the advisor team demolitions expert. After all, I trained the RF soldiers.

We go into the DIOCC with Lieutenant Springer, the 117th commander Lieutenant Cam, along with a senior NCO from the RF company. The details from the woodcutter make it easy to locate on the map the general area where he was working. He has described the concrete bunker on the top of a berm on the bank of the small river near where he was seeking wood. The bunker was raised almost a foot above the ground and tightly sheltered from the weather with a wooden cover. While he did not know how deep the bunker was, it was surmised that it was dug on the berm so even at high tide no water could get into the grenades. Not knowing how big the cache is, I tell the 117th NCO to bring his best demolition people, several blocks of C-4, a roll of fuse cord, and several blasting caps. I say I will go along to ensure they set the charge properly to comply with Captain Tri's wishes.

We plan to meet about midmorning to avoid low tide. The DIOCC figures it will take almost two hours to get to the riverbank by sampan. The soldiers believe that the actual berm where the bunker is could be anywhere on a half-mile-long stretch of the river. At least the woodcutter was positive about which side of the river the bunker lay.

We arrive around noon. The area is almost nude as Agent Orange defoliant airborne swaths have sprayed all the area around the river. Grass is growing but trees and the thick brush are nothing but dead branches looking like a forest fire has gone through. The ground is dark brown in some areas and almost wheat-colored in others.

During the Vietnam War around 21 million gallons of various herbicides were used throughout South Vietnam to destroy any growth on the ground. Beginning in the early 1960s, USAF twin-engine C-123 Providers were used for special aerial spray flights, mostly dumping Agent Orange to make enemy observation easier and to deny the enemy food. While the herbicides did their job, it was later discovered that Agent Orange also destroyed humans. If anyone moved or operated in defoliated areas the chance for future problems with soft tissues of the body was almost a certainty. At age 78 I was diagnosed with ischemic heart disease, which destroyed the aortic valve of my heart, assumed to be caused by my extensive exposure to the chemical in the Rung Sat.

We depart the boats at one end of the riverbank and begin our search for the bunker. The bunker is located and, as described, is chock full of hundreds of hand grenades. What I have imagined to be a simple procedure quickly becomes a fiasco.

Calling the two demolition soldiers up with their explosives, I ask them how they would blow it. Confusion seems to radiate from their faces. They are not sure. I ask questions and they are unable to explain how to blow this bunker. Finally, they admit they are afraid of using C-4. I recall that during my demolitions training the Vietnamese soldiers did show a fear of using explosives and were reluctant to do so. I call their NCO and the four of us begin a discussion of what to do. Finally, the sergeant orders the two soldiers to pay attention, set up the C-4 and blow up the bunker. Afraid to challenge their NCO yet equally fearful of the explosives, they begin a disastrous attempt of rigging the demolitions.

One soldier cuts off a quarter stick of C-4, punches a hole in it (but not deep enough to push the blasting cap in all the way). The other soldier never tests the burn rate of the fuse but just cuts off about 12 inches, which might be a 45 second to one-minute burn time. The first soldier just places the quarter stick of C-4 on top of the pile.

I tell them to stop. I ask the first soldier if that is enough charge to destroy a couple hundred hand grenades. He mumbles, he guesses so. I ask if laying the C-4 on top of the grenades is the most effective way to destroy the grenades and again he mumbles he thinks so.

I address the second soldier and ask how long the fuse will burn and he replies "a minute." I ask how he knows that, and he says that is what it did in class. I ask if he had a new coil of fuse and he replies yes. I ask if perhaps it would be best to burn a foot and know exactly how fast it would burn and he mumbles yes. I then ask him if he did use the 12 inches he cut and if it did last one minute, where would he go? Looking confused, it was apparent he does not understand the question. I then ask if, after he lit the fuse, if he is just going to stand next to the bunker to watch it blow. He shakes his head no. So, then I ask where he would go in less than one minute. He looks around, and then mumbles that he is not sure.

Obviously these two soldiers are not even close to being able to use the demolitions.

I turn to the sergeant and say what we need to do is to first determine how far away we need to be to be safe. We decide that across the 20-foot-wide river, lying down behind the high bank, would be best.

I explain I will show these two soldiers how to properly set up the charge. I tell the NCO that when the charge is set up, he and all of his soldiers should get in the sampans, cross the river, place the boats downstream, protected by the bank, and all the soldiers should get behind the berm. I would cut enough fuse to allow me, after lighting it, to dive in the river, swim across, scramble up and over the berm. We think that I should be able to do that in three minutes at the most.

First, we light the 12 inches the soldier has cut and, ironically, it burns one minute. I explain that in the case of this bunker it would be best to overload with C-4 rather than use too little. I also explain that the charge should be placed below the surface of the top grenades as we want the C-4 to ignite as many grenades as possible. We want to destroy all the grenades but also the bunker. Taking the quarter stick and the rest of that stick and a couple more sticks, I tape them all together. I punch a deep hole into one stick and place a blasting cap attached to our four-foot fuse.

We very carefully remove a couple dozen grenades, place the explosives and then just as carefully place the grenades we have removed back into the bunker. It is ready to blow. I remove my web pistol belt with my

.45, ammo pouch, first-aid kit, USAF survival knife, and canteen. I also empty my pockets of a plastic-covered map, my demolition tool, and the LRP rations which I brought for lunch, and unstrap my watch. I remove my jungle fatigue shirt, so I only have my T-shirt, trousers, and jungle boots. I give all this to one of the two demolition soldiers, telling him I will collect it after I cross the river. The NCO and his soldiers leave. After the sampans are stowed with the soldiers behind the berm, I ignite the fuse and, with a bound and a leap, dive in the river.

The twenty feet is swum in much less than two minutes, with soldiers' arms reaching down to grab me and pull me over the berm. I figure the blast will be focused down into the grenade bunker and blow straight upward. I know I overloaded the bunker but that is okay. I peek over the bunker and wait. In about a minute it blows. There is the C-4, immediately followed by the secondary explosion of the grenades. I can see a bunch of stuff blown upwards and then chunks of concrete, smoke, dust, and debris, all round the bunker. We wait a couple of minutes for the smoke to clear and then the sergeant sends two soldiers across in a sampan to determine the damage.

They report all grenades blown and the bunker broken and caving in, no longer usable to hide anything. Mission accomplished.

We decide to eat lunch before returning to district. Placing guards out, we eat. The advisors are issued plenty of C-rations (vacuum-packed canned food) but my sergeants have dickered with the SEAL teams at Nha Be and provide us with the much better LRP (long range patrol) rations. In 1964 the army created freeze-dried dehydrated field rations for special ops troops. The package could be opened and filled with 1.5 pints of boiling water, then closed to let the hot water make food. For combat troops in the field, compared to our C-rats, this is a five-star meal.

The LRP rations come in eight different dishes: hash, beef and rice, beef stew, chicken and rice, chicken stew, chili, pork and potatoes, and spaghetti. All excellent. I first used the LRP rations in late 1966 while on combat operations toward the end of my first tour in Vietnam.

After eating (the Vietnamese have their own field rations, while many just carry rice balls for lunch), I dress, and we head home. The VC have now been deprived of a major cache of grenades.

My Adventure with Our Advisor Boat

Often some advisors would take our Boston Whaler to Nha Be to get supplies or conduct business. One day after our grenade destruction episode, I am piloting our boat to Nha Be with a couple advisors aboard. Normally we would ease up to the large boat pier upon arrival to tie up and go about our business.

Our Boston Whaler has a small console in the center of the boat where the steering wheel and the engine controls are. Coming into the pier the boat driver would pull back on the throttle to reduce the boat's speed to ease in next to a piling on a pier or dock. But today, something goes wrong.

The pier for Nha Be juts out into the Soi Rap River which has a strong flow south. Maneuvering into the dock for the small boat requires a judicious use of power: too much and your forward movement will slam the front of the boat into a piling; too little and the current would knock the side of the boat into a piling.

Doing the same thing every time I dock at Nha Be, I begin to traverse cross-current with plenty of power to keep from being swept downstream or into a piling. Actually, it would appear as if I were aiming at an imaginary point some ten feet in front of the piling, then easing off of the power and our Boston Whaler would smoothly glide next to the piling so we could tie up.

As I approach the pier and the piling I plan to tie on, I move my

Bob piloting one of the advisor team's Boston Whalers.

hand to the throttle to ease off on the power. Instead of slowing down, the engine ramps up to full power and the boat races toward the piling. Jiggling the throttle does no good and the boat crashes into the piling before I can shut down the engine. The sudden stop tosses me forward, where my side crashes into the small console, twisting me around as I heavily trip over a seat and thud onto the floor. One of the sergeants shuts off the motor while the other ties us onto the piling. It is obvious from their looks that they think that I screwed up and pushed the throttle forward, rather than easing it back.

I lie on my back, holding my very painful side. I can't get up so one sergeant helps me up. I explain that something happened, as I did pull the throttle back. One sergeant checks the throttle and it does not move at all; somehow it is binding. At Nha Be is a Mercury rep, whose job is to support all the outboard motors used by the navy, the Vietnamese, and the advisors. Sergeant Olden says he will find the rep and get our boat fixed.

Sergeant Olden and the Mercury rep find the throttle cable has somehow come loose from its attachments and become tangled and caught between the throttle handle on the console and the engine. It is not my fault but a mechanical mishap.

While my side hurts quite a bit, I do not realize the extent of the damage. About a week after the injury, I am in considerable pain and go to the Nha Be Navy medical clinic. My ribs are x-rayed, and several are broken. I am taped up and told that it will take a month or more to be completely healed.

23

Leaving Vietnam

Our Replacements

During June 1969, we spend much of our time training the marines who are replacing us. Sergeant First Class Olden recently returned to the

Binh Phuoc hamlet, across the river from the Nha Be Navy Base.

States. That leaves Master Sergeant Harris, our medic, Dickson, and our two lieutenants. We will be replaced by a Captain Beach, Gunny Sergeant Haysos, Sergeant Milton, and U.S. Navy Hospital Corpsman Shiller.

The captain is about my height but much thinner with dark close-cropped hair, early 30s, eager to assume command of the advisory effort. Haysos, mid–30s, is dark-skinned, tall, muscular, with close-cropped dark hair, like the captain. Milton is young, early 20s, about six feet but muscular, with dark hair, parted, and longer than either the gunny's or his captain's. Shiller is medium size with light-colored hair. The Marine team members all wear dark green berets and the typical jungle fatigues, except for Sergeant Milton, who favors camouflaged fatigues. Eventually most of my team will be replaced by this group. Because of Lieutenant Springer's skill as an intelligence officer, specifically trained in the Phoenix program, most likely he will

U.S. Navy Advisor headquarters at Nha Be. Jeep in front (without top) belongs to the Quang Xuyen advisors.

remain in Quang Xuyen. While this team is under the command of Commander Wages, the relationship of the district advisors serving as civil and administrative advisors to the district is yet to be worked out.

Both the captain and the gunny must understand how the Vietnamese district military RF and PF units function. They also should know how the DIOCC operates and how the DIOCC interacts with the Phoenix and Chieu Hoi programs. Additionally, both men should be introduced to the other three district villages, the civilian offices, agencies, and medical facilities in the villages and hamlets. Air America and our boats spend a lot of time transporting us and Captain Tri, the district chief, to all villages for visits.

I take Captain Beach with me on a few one-day combat operations. Not for a lack of trying, none of the operations results in any worthwhile skirmish with the VC. One drawback Captain Beach's team has is that no one speaks Vietnamese.

Corpsman Shiller spends his time with Specialist Dickson, visiting all the district medical facilities, meeting the district medical officer and the various medical people at each clinic or dispensary.

My last days as DSA at Quang Xuyen end on 24 June. I bid farewell to Captain Tri (and his family) and Lieutenant Cam and the soldiers of the 117th. The marines have joined my advisors and assume control of the advisor team.

My New Job

An Air America chopper takes me to Nha Be, where for the next few weeks I will serve as the Special Projects Officer for Commander Wages, to assist in a timely and smooth advisory transition from the army to the navy. For the next seven weeks I spend most of my days working with the new Marine advisor team covering what it takes to serve as advisors to a district. Additionally, I spend time also training Commander Wages' staff on their duties to support the advisor team. The navy (and the marines) are totally ignorant regarding the enormous amount of reports required by CORDS. They must learn how to complete all the pacification reports and how to requisition supplies for rural development. There is a lot to accomplish so the days pass quickly.

Departing Active Duty

My quest to be released from active duty ends up being a comedy of errors, with one problem after another.

The administrative requirements to depart active duty are unbelievable. The physical exam is expected but everything else is just mind-boggling. Exit interview with a flag officer, counseling with a Veterans Administration official, doing the paperwork to receive the G.I. Bill, and the list goes on. So, during much of July, I am involved in visits to a variety of army administrative and medical appointments.

As part of my release from active duty, I must take a separation physical. On Monday, 21 July, I report in to the 218th Army Medical Dispensary in Saigon. Everything is normal except a high-frequency hearing loss is noted. I have gained back most of the weight I had lost to hookworm. At the physical I am five feet ten inches tall and weigh 164 pounds (normally I weigh ten pounds more). I am found medically qualified for separation from active duty.

As I am a field grade officer, I am required prior to separation to be counseled by a flag officer (a general). I am told to report to the province advisor headquarters and to contact the office of a brigadier general I have never heard of. I call his office and talk to his aide, who wants to schedule an appointment for me to talk to his general. I quickly say no. I explain I am getting out so a talk with anyone is a waste of time. The aide doesn't know what to say. Apparently, the general is next to the phone because he takes the phone and identifies himself. I tell the general I am leaving active duty to attend graduate school but intend to remain in the Army Reserves. I further clarify that my mind is made up, I have been admitted to a grad school and there is no reason for me to see him. He agrees, wishes me luck in school and thanks me for my call. One more item checked off for my leaving the army.

Meeting with the Veterans Administration

Another visit scheduled for me is with the Saigon Veterans Administration office. I am shown to a desk where a man in his late fifties, tall, heavy, with sparse balding gray hair, sits. He greets me, is friendly, and introduces himself. He looks at my paperwork and acknowledges that I am leaving the army. My papers indicate that I first entered the military on 14 February 1957. He notes that I have twelve and a half years' service, so he assumes that includes some enlisted time. I explain my Marine time and my army enlisted Reserve time while in ROTC. He begins to discuss what benefits I would be eligible for such as the G.I. Bill for education, a VA-backed home mortgage, and disability benefits for injuries sustained on active duty.

The only benefit I am interested in is the G.I. Bill, so I explain I am going to graduate school this fall. He has me fill out some papers so that when I get to school the papers for the G.I. Bill will be there waiting for me. With the signing accomplished, I am ready to move on. He tells me he is a retired infantry colonel and when it came time for him to retire, he had no interest in what the VA had to offer. He said he had to suffer through the VA counselor as I am. But his counselor convinced him to think about his later years and to allow the VA to get copies of all his records before he retired; otherwise, all his army records would be filed away and maybe some might even get lost.

I emphasize that all I need is the G.I. Bill and nothing else. He asks if I was ever injured and I say I am in good health, so I need to move on. But he persists and asks if I have the Purple Heart, and I nod yes. He asks if I ever broke any bones? I am ready to say no when I recall my broken hip from jump school and tell him about that. He asks more questions about injuries and I begin to describe what has happened to me over time.

He clarifies that while I feel fine now, in my sixties or so, I could begin to encounter difficulties hearing, walking, or doing other things because my injured body, as I age, will get worse. And if my injuries are identified now (before I leave the army), they will already be documented in my VA file. He convinces me, so I sign the Department of the Army form 664, my official application for compensation due to injuries or wounds suffered while in the service. Additionally, I also sign VA form 21–526e, which allows the VA to access all my medical records prior to my release from active duty (REFRAD).

This is the best thing I ever do regarding my REFRAD and it begins to pay off shortly after my leaving the army.

Problems Leaving the Army

My original plan to depart Vietnam early to attend graduate school never panned out.

In July 1968 I was accepted in the College of Education graduate program at Northern Arizona University in Flagstaff. In August 1968 I submitted a request to be released from active duty on 15 May 1969 to attend the summer graduate school program which began on 15 July 1969. Apparently, my request became lost. In January 1969 I resubmitted everything a second time, expecting to receive a response in a month or two at the most. April rolled around and the MACV personnel office said they had nothing. Lost again? Who knows!

My January request for REFRAD (second time) took almost six

weeks to go from Vietnam to the Pentagon (with no stops in between). It spent another month bouncing around the Adjutant General's Office in the Pentagon before returning to me in mid–April. Request denied. It stated that before being REFRAD, I had to complete my current tour in Vietnam, which was then noted as 17 August 1969. Therefore, no summer school for me.

Angry, frustrated, feeling even more bitter at the obvious lack of concern about my welfare in the army, I wrote, on 3 April 1969, a personal letter to General William Westmoreland, the Chief of Staff for the entire U.S. Army. The letter succinctly explained everything I had done and all my paperwork just getting lost, time and again.

In a personal letter dated 28 April, General Westmoreland replied to my letter. I believe he held a special feeling for Vietnam veterans, especially officers who had served two combat tours, with one under his command. He said he investigated my REFRAD request and it had been received and action taken.

Bob getting into Army helicopter at Nha Be.

He continued by saying I would be released at my point of embarkation (Oakland) upon completion of my Vietnam tour. He said he regretted my leaving the army because it needed combat veterans of my experience and caliber. He was glad I had decided to remain in the Reserves and expected me to make a valuable contribution there. He said it was unfortunate I experienced so much trouble getting my REFRAD processed but hoped I would still have time to enter school.

In mid–June I had received my REFRAD orders from MACV. On 15 August I was to report to Room 106 in the MACV Annex Building at Tan Son Nhut Air Base at 8 a.m. for out-processing from MACV. I would depart Vietnam on 16 August and be transferred from MACV to the U.S. Army transfer Station at Oakland, California. I would at a later date receive orders specifying my exact REFRAD date.

My Last Meeting with Colonel Herbert

With two days left in Vietnam, I take my last chopper ride, from Nha Be to the Gia Dinh province advisor headquarters, where I continue my out-processing. I spend some time with Colonel Herbert discussing my tenure at Quang Xuyen. Both of us will leave Vietnam about the same time.

Two areas we discuss. The colonel says he is recommending me for a third Bronze Star for meritorious service. I then ask him if instead I could receive an Army Commendation Medal (ARCOM). He stares at me, incredulously, and asks why. I explain I am leaving active duty and I already have two Bronze Stars for valor, but I do not have an ARCOM. Leaving the army, I am thinking that quantity (of medals) would mean more than quality. Ironically, after I return to active duty in 1971, I receive a couple more ARCOMs, so I should have just kept my mouth shut. Colonel Herbert indicates he will approve the ARCOM, but the written citation reads like one for a much higher award.

Next, we discuss my officer efficiency report. During my tenure at Gia Dinh (from 14 December 1968 to 15 August 1969), I have already received two OERs. The first covered my duties as the province RF and PF advisor and supervising 23 Mobile Advisory Teams (around 100 company grade officers and NCOs). The overall OER ratings were superior. The second OER was just as good but covered my period as the Quang Xuyen district senior advisor (from 8 February to 6 May 1969) until I officially was transferred to the U.S. Navy as the DSA. On 7 August 1969 MACV Headquarters retroactively placed me on temporary duty with the U.S. Naval Forces at the Rung Sat Special Zone, effective 1 June 1969. I have no idea why my assignment dates on my orders do not match the OER dates, but who cares? Then the colonel explains we have problems.

The U.S. Army Officer Efficiency Report (Department of the Army form 67–6) contains both several numerical ratings in a variety of different categories as well as written narratives. To properly complete my Army OER, Commander Wages had to get a copy of the regulations describing how to properly complete the OER. What the regulations say and what is done, especially for combat OERs, tends to be quite different. One reason the OER form seems to be changed often is because the officers who prepare an OER on subordinates they admire will increase the numerical reports to ensure their officer stands out when the OERs are used for assignments, schools, and promotions. Soon the entire system of OERs becomes so inflated the OERs do not reflect a true picture as required by the regulations. So, if you think an officer is very good, to make him competitive, the numerical ratings must be very high. Commander Wages, not being aware of this, followed the OER regs to the letter. My numerical ratings were nowhere near my other combat OERs.

During my six months working for Commander Wages (yet his OER for me only covered the last three months) my team had turned the 117th RF company into a very effective fighting force and I had been recommended for four combat decorations (two U.S. Navy and two from the Vietnamese Navy). These achievements were noted in Wages' written narrative about my service as a combat advisor. Colonel Herbert went over this glaring discrepancy between the numerical part of the OER and the narrative. Thus, he told me that he would add an enclosure to explain why the difference.

The day before I leave Vietnam, I am handed a personal letter from Colonel Herbert, who has already left.

That night I read Colonel Herbert's two-page handwritten letter to me. It states in part:

"Dear Major Worthington, ... The greatest tribute that could ever be paid to me would be to say that I had done as much for my country in the Advisory Effort for the province as Major Elliott Worthington has done for 'his' district." He went on to continue to praise me for my work as a combat advisor, signing it, "Warm regards, JAH."

As I reflect on my two years as a senior combat advisor, I am proud of the fact that not one of my five different advisor team members was killed or even shot (except for me). On my first tour I did lose two advisors to malaria, but they recovered and were assigned elsewhere.

Departing Vietnam

I report to MACV out-processing on Friday, 15 August, to receive my final REFRAD orders. I will report to the Transfer Station at Oakland to complete my out-processing. I will be authorized five days' travel time (beginning on 15 August) and officially released from active duty on 20 August 1969. I will then be assigned to the U.S. Army Reserve Control Group in St. Louis, Missouri, until further assignment to a Reserve unit in Arizona. Upon REFRAD I will receive a lump sum payment for the 30 days' leave accumulated during Vietnam (essentially my full pay for a month). I will also be authorized free shipment of all household goods and travel costs for me and my family from Fort Benning to Flagstaff.

That afternoon, at 2:10 p.m. I board a Pan Am Boeing 707 for my return to the States. Our first stop is Yokota Air Force Base in Japan for a crew change and refuel. Our next scheduled stop is Alaska and then Travis AFB in California. After departing Japan, the pilot announces he has enough tailwinds, so no stop in Alaska; we are heading directly to Travis. With the time difference and the International Dateline, we arrive at Travis on the day I left Vietnam, 15 August, at 3 p.m.

After several hours completing more paperwork, I am taken to the commercial airport in San Francisco and I board another airline to fly east, destination, Columbus, Georgia. I arrive in Columbus midmorning on Sunday, 17 August 1969, where I am met by Anita and the girls.

I am home.

24

Leaving Active Duty

Back Home

Returning home is wonderful. Susan and Julie are thrilled to have Daddy back home. Karen, though, is doubtful. She is extremely shy around me, not wanting to get close. I am this large, different person her siblings are excited to see. To Karen I am someone she does not know, and it frightens her. I knew I would have to tread lightly to win her approval as a father. She was only four months old when I left, and now she is almost a year and a half old.

On 20 August, I will be out of the army but not yet out of Fort Benning. Anita has made arrangements for shipment of our household goods to Flagstaff. We plan to arrive in Flagstaff no later than 11 September so I can register for the fall semester at NAU, about three weeks away. Monday and Tuesday are spent packing up and with me getting my REFRAD orders. I also learn that the army has a munitions base just outside of Flagstaff. Navajo Army Depot is where I can go to arrange for delivery of our household goods and to voice any complaints for damaged goods.

On the Road

I am again a civilian. We are driving two vehicles and a travel trailer; two parents, three children, and our pet cat. We have made this trip before but—a big but—never with two cars. I will drive the Ford station wagon pulling the travel trailer and Anita will drive my CJ-5 Jeep. My plan is for us to caravan, Anita following me.

We load up the travel trailer with food, clothes, and documents, hook it to our Ford station wagon, and we are ready to go. We decide to fix up the back of the station wagon like a large playpen for Karen and Susan while Julie rides with her mom in the Jeep. Kitty rides in the Ford.

The trip to Flagstaff is over 1,700 miles and takes four and a half days. Anita is not happy driving the Jeep. It is loud, bumpy and without air-conditioning. Its four-cylinder engine is pushed trying to keep up with the more powerful Ford. And Anita has to stop more often for gas, something I did not realize before we started. Anita's biggest complaint is that I do not pay attention to the Jeep in my rearview mirror. When she pulls off the interstate for gas, I unknowingly continue driving. On the highway I keep on pulling away from her, so we are not always in a convoy. After that first day on the road, Anita procures her own set of road maps to follow at her own pace.

Northern Arizona University

When I decided to leave the army and attend graduate school, I confined my search to the Southwest (great people, friendly, not expensive, good weather, and values close to mine). I grew up in a rural community (about 700 people) and went to a small college where outdoor activities were emphasized. So, my search focused on a small university that had a good graduate program in counseling. Northern Arizona University (NAU) was at the top of my list.

NAU was founded in 1899 as a teachers college, located in Flagstaff, a small city at 7,000 feet and the largest community in Northern Arizona, with a population of 48,000. It is a railroad center for the area ranches and lumber. In 1930, at Flagstaff's Lowell Observatory, the planet Pluto was discovered. The city is surrounded by the largest stand of Ponderosa pine in the country. Known for its mild summers and cold winters (with almost eight feet of snow annually) it is an outdoor haven. Our visit last summer was beneficial. We have a good feeling about the city and the university.

NAU has a beautiful campus with impressive professors. At the time of my enrollment it offers bachelor's and master's degrees but a doctoral degree in Education would be approved in 1970. The school has 7,747 students when I enroll. Living in Flagstaff is enjoyable. I love the master's program at NAU and the professors I have.

Our New Home

Arriving in Flagstaff we park in a local campground until we can find a place to live. We meet a real estate agent at an Allstate agency, start looking at houses, and quickly find one we like. It is about a mile north of NAU off state highway 180 in an area called Coconino Estates, or as the locals verbalize, "professors' ghetto" because so many NAU professors live here. The three bedroom, two-bath 1,527-square-foot home with a large fenced-in back yard is for sale for $22,800. It only costs us $5,500 cash plus closing costs to acquire it. We sign the papers on Friday, 12 September, and move in on Monday, 15 September.

It is a nice neighborhood. Our girls' elementary school is right across the street from our back yard. There is a gate in the back fence. Next to the school is the Arizona History Society Pioneer Museum, which hosts many summer activities for children. Up the road is the Museum of Northern Arizona.

Our first night in our new home we do not have furniture, so we all camp in the family room, in front of the fireplace, in our sleeping bags. Shortly after dawn, one of the girls screams about actually being out west because the back yard is full of buffalo. Glancing out our rear windows we can see them. There are no buffalo in our back yard, but across the highway the front yard of the school is full of the large shaggy animals, grazing on the lawn. The girls are overjoyed at being in the real West where buffalo roam, almost in their back yard. Even little Karen, not having a clue about what is going on, is grinning, laughing, and clapping her hands, imitating the pleasure of her big sisters.

Soon we see a couple of fire engines arrive. The firemen move onto the lawn and spread out so they can drive the buffalo back behind the school. We find out later that the school property backs up to a large mesa. This mesa splits the town in half. On top is Buffalo Park. The west boundary of the park is adjacent to the school, so the buffalo breach the fence and wander into the schoolyard to graze. The firemen are always called because there could be a gas leak. Some gas lines are buried underground, and the hooves of the heavy animals have the potential of puncturing the lines. After a few hours, all the buffalo are herded back into their park and the fence repaired. During this whole time, my daughters are fascinated watching the animals and the firemen. We could not have had a better introduction to our new home.

Settling In

I meet with my faculty advisor, and we plan my graduate studies in guidance and counseling. No scholarships or work-study jobs are available. Next, I need to find a job and placement in a Reserve unit.

I locate an employment firm downtown and sign up. I learn there is a new job opening for which I am suited. A large lumber mill in Flagstaff has decided to build a fiberboard plant as it accumulates tons of sawdust and wood shavings annually. The electrical company which has the wiring contract is a union shop from Phoenix. This company needs a part-time person to manage their office, keep track of the timecards, receive and inventory supplies, and do the associated paperwork.

I interview for the job and find out they also need a part-time draftsman. There are no electrical plans for the job, so the electrical contractor agreed to supply the plans for the electrical work completed. The plans will be drawn as the electrical equipment and lines are installed. I tell the project manager I can do that as I had taken drafting classes in both high school and college.

I am hired and my work times are flexible. The intent is for me to accomplish everything I am hired to do. I can do the paperwork and drafting at any time, nights, or weekends, so I can easily arrange my work around my classes. The job will last over a year, which should cover my entire graduate program.

1969 NAU and My First Semester

Classes are going fine. My classmates have one thing in shared competence which I do not have. All have degrees in some form of psychology. Some have been working in various professions, but most are coming straight from earning their undergraduate degree.

My major was not psychology. It was art, so my professors have me attend some of their basic undergraduate psychology classes. While I lack the undergraduate academic background my classmates possess, I have experience in dealing with many different types of people, managing them, ordering them, persuading them, counseling them, dealing with motivations, emotions, different feelings. That is to say, the entire range of human behaviors. Practical experience is what my classmates lack. I am pleased to be asked by the professor, in one course I audit, to teach the section on persuasive coercion (brainwashing), which I do.

The typical course load of graduate students is nine hours or three classes a semester. Some only take six hours. I have just come from an environment where everyone is on the job essentially 24/7. I feel that being a graduate student is not hard. I decide to take 18 hours' credit every semester so I can complete my degree in one year. Given that many of my senior professors are either World War II or Korean vets, we have a common bond.

I receive A's in all my classes.

VA Disability

In the fall of 1969, I receive a letter from the Veterans Administration asking me to contact them for a physical examination to determine if I have any military-related injuries that would qualify me for any disability compensation (i.e., money). I arrange a day to go to Phoenix to a VA medical facility for the exam. A couple of months later I receive a letter from the VA. The exam determinsd that the right hip I broke in 1963 from a parachute jump (my third and last jump at the Army Parachute School) and the gunshot wound (also in the right leg) in 1968 in Vietnam together qualify me for a determination of a 20 percent disability, which pays $46 a month, retroactive to the day after I left the active duty.

Reserve Duty Assignment

I am in school. I have a job and the G.I. Bill. I have a place to live. So now my hunt is to find a Reserve unit to join. In Flagstaff there is only one Army Reserve unit, a Military Police company commanded by a captain. There is no unit requirement for a major and the captain does not want a field grade combat veteran in his unit. There are opportunities in Phoenix but that is 150 miles away, three hours' drive time.

I discover that located at the university is a Naval Reserve Surface Division Reserve unit commanded by a Reserve lieutenant commander. I make an appointment with him and explain that I want to be in a Reserve unit, but the closest possible army unit is in Phoenix. I give him a rundown on my background, and he replies he would be delighted to have me join his unit. Their mission is to conduct initial basic training for new sailors before they go on active duty to receive specialized training. We begin the paperwork so the U.S. Army Reserve administrative headquarters in St. Louis, Missouri, can approve my request to join this navy unit. It is approved. In early 1970, I begin training one weekend a month with the navy.

My duties are varied. One area requested by the navy that I am uniquely qualified for is counterinsurgency training. All branches of the military are still focusing on Vietnam. I develop a tailored program which includes using the documentary film I made during my first tour and create an 80-minute training film for the unit. I oversee small arms training, classroom and range, and conduct leadership training for both new sailors and the unit staff. I participate in many other military functions of the unit.

1970 NAU and My Second Semester

One of my first classes is most enlightening, Principles of Guidance, Education 601. It is a practical course designed to introduce the student to what a guidance counselor does in his or her job. A major class requirement is to create a guidance program at the level you wish to work. This could be as a counselor in an elementary or junior high or high school. Most students turn in around 10 to 12 pages, while I turn in 80. I know I spent much more time on the course than the other students. But then my research shows that high school guidance counselors do little counseling. So—I changed my major to counseling psychology.

On 29 April 1970 ARVN and U.S. forces cross the Cambodian border and begin offensive operations against VC and NVA reinforcements in Cambodia, which, until now, was the units' sanctuary as we could not cross the border. I follow the action using maps and in newspapers about which U.S. and ARVN units are participating. I know that my old nemesis, the NVA 706th base camp, has been attacked. I share with the professors what is going on and why. I said I have been shot defending that same border and how we could not cross to secure it. They understood but many students do not.

Students protest that now the United States is going to war against Cambodia. One of my classmates, an enlisted member of the Naval Reserve unit I am in, loudly argues against this terrible invasion of Cambodia. I try to explain to her that the NVA use Cambodia as a safe haven. They attack inside South Vietnam and then retreat across the border, knowing we cannot follow. Now President Nixon authorizes us to cross the Cambodian border to attack and destroy the base camps and their sanctuaries. She refuses to believe me or even the military of her own country.

My Award from the Navy

One spring day in 1970 I receive a call from the office of the commander of Navajo Army Depot, asking me to attend an awards ceremony (in uniform) in the commander's office. I answer that I will be there.

Anita, daughter Susan and I are present. I receive four decorations for valor. As Admiral Zumwalt promised, the awards went up the Navy chain of command and down the army chain of command to ultimately reach me. I receive from the U.S. Navy the Bronze Star and the Navy

Achievement Medal (both with the Combat V) and from the Vietnamese Navy, two Gallantry Crosses.

Life is good. I am doing well as a graduate student. My assignment to the Naval Reserve unit is enjoyable and worthwhile. My job as the office manager/draftsman for the electrical contractor is going well with the hours flexible enough to match my school classes, and it pays well. Moreover, I receive two checks each month from the VA. One for the G.I. Bill and the second my disability compensation.

Clearly, I am adapting to life as a civilian.

Epilogue

After receiving an MA in Guidance and Counseling from Northern Arizona University, certified as both an Assistant School Psychologist and a School Psychometrist, I worked a year as a counselor at the school's Institute for Human Development, an organization that provides psychological and vocational evaluation services throughout northern Arizona.

In the fall of 1971, I entered a PhD program in Counseling and Clinical Psychology at the University of Utah. Upon entering the PhD program, I was selected to return to active duty in the army (as a student) while obtaining my PhD. After receiving my degree, I was assigned as an army clinical psychologist, which was my profession for the next decade. I also graduated from the Army Command and General Staff College and earned another master's degree, in business administration and management, from Webster University. As a psychologist, I engaged in considerable research, focusing on the adjustment of Vietnam veterans, to include a five-year psychological evaluation program for U.S. Army Vietnam Repatriated POWs (Operation Homecoming), earning an international reputation as a pioneer in PTSD research regarding Vietnam era veterans. I retired in 1981 as a lieutenant colonel, having served as the Psychology Consultant for the U.S. Army Health Services Command (HSC) since 1975. During this time, I was additionally an adjunct psychology professor at several graduate schools.

As an Army Psychology Consultant, my job required considerable travel. Aviator friends suggested I learn to fly, so I became a pilot at the age of 38. I later earned my instrument rating and during 40 years of flying accumulate over 7,000 flight hours, own nine planes, and fly in 49 states (never Hawaii) and three foreign countries.

For the next sixteen years, I was a business professor and a journalism professor, and a nonfiction writer. In 1997, at age sixty, I retired as a journalism professor at New Mexico State University. In addition, over the years, my wife and I have owned several small businesses.

265

Today, I continue writing with over 2,500 publications to date. This includes authoring a regular column in aviation magazines and writing non-fiction books. My first book on my job as a combat advisor in Vietnam, *Under Fire with ARVN Infantry*, earned a Gold Medal for Excellence in Literature. In 2019 I produced the documentary film *Combat Advisor in Vietnam*, with all footage filmed by me in Vietnam. Visit my web site at www.BobWorthingtonWriter.com.

Bob Worthington
Military History

Elliott Robert "Bob" Worthington retired from the U.S. Army in October 1981, three and a half months shy of 25 years of service as an enlisted man, NCO, and officer. His military career began when he dropped out of college to enlist in the U.S. Marines in February 1957.

After Parris Island boot camp and Infantry training, he was assigned to the 10th Marines, an artillery regiment in the Second Division at Camp Lejeune, North Carolina. He ended up in a 4.2" mortar battery and went on a six-month Mediterranean cruise as part of the USMC reinforced Marine Infantry battalion trained for combat assaults as needed anywhere in any countries facing the Mediterranean Sea.

On 15 July 1958, his unit completed a combat assault on the city dump of Beirut, Lebanon, as part of the U.S. Operation Bluebat, to stop the war being fought in Lebanon by outside countries. The war lasted several weeks, and by the fall, Bob returned to the States. While in the Marines, he met Anita Elliott, a Washington, D.C., college student, whom he dated.

As a corporal, he left active duty in February 1959 to return to Dartmouth. He and Anita married in September 1959 as he entered his junior year. During his senior year at Dartmouth, he was employed as a regular, full-time police officer with the Hanover, New Hampshire, Police Department. Majoring in art, he graduated in June 1961 as an ROTC Distinguished Military Graduate. He was an Army ROTC cadet (as well as enlisted in the Army Reserves). Due to a mistake in his ROTC records he was not commissioned in the Infantry, but in the Chemical Corps. After completing the Chemical Corps Basic Officer Course, he remained at Fort McClellan, Alabama, where he became a platoon leader in a smoke generator company.

He requested a branch transfer to the Infantry, transferring to the 2nd Infantry Division at Fort Benning as a rifle company platoon leader in early 1963. That summer he attended Jump School. On his third jump he broke his hip, was hospitalized for two months and then received a one-year medical profile, prohibiting his return to the rifle company. He became the battalion assistant personnel officer. An additional duty was as the battalion OIC for its pistol and rifle team. During the Fort Benning post matches, one of Bob's pistol shooters was unable to shoot so Bob took his place, winning the post pistol championship. This led to his becoming the XO of the Division Marksmanship Detachment, and as a professional pistol shooter, he earned the highest competitive rank of Master. He held this position until his one-year profile expired and he was assigned as the assistant operations officer in an infantry battalion. During the summers, the battalion was trained by a Special Forces team in unconventional warfare tactics and it also trained in helicopter tactics. Bob was promoted to captain in mid–1965 and then received orders to Vietnam as a combat advisor.

Bob attended the Military Assistant Training Advisor Course at the J. F. Kennedy Special Warfare Center at Fort Bragg, North Carolina, and then the Vietnamese language school at the National Defense Language Institute at the Presidio of Monterrey, in California.

He served in Vietnam as a combat advisor in 1966–1967. After Vietnam, he was assigned to the Armor Officer's Career Course at Fort Knox, Kentucky, and next attended the army classified Nuclear Weapons Employment Course. Then he was assigned to Fort Benning to command a Basic Combat Training company, which became the worst job he ever had because of his overbearing battalion and regimental commanders. The assignment was so bad he decided that if these men represented what he would become, he wanted to get out and attend graduate school, which required money. He knew if he returned to Vietnam as a combat advisor, he could save a lot of money. He was promoted to major, which ended his command tour, and he returned to Vietnam as a combat advisor from August 1968 to August 1969. At the end of his tour he was released from active duty and began school at Northern Arizona University. He received his MA in counseling and psychology in August 1970 and joined the university as a staff counselor. After a year he entered the University of Utah Counseling Psychology PhD program. At the same time, the army was anticipating difficulty with senior officers and NCOs when it transitioned from a conscript force to an all-volunteer force. The solution was to locate former combat arms officers and return them to active duty to receive doctoral degrees in the behavioral sciences to help the army move into an all-volunteer force.

He graduated with a PhD in counseling psychology and a minor in clinical psychology in August 1973 and received a one-year post-doctoral fellowship in community psychology at William Beaumont Army Medical Center, in El Paso, Texas. While in the Army Reserves and on active duty, Bob attended the reserve Command and General Staff College, graduating in the fall of 1974.

Assigned as the clinical psychologist for the Army Hospital at Fort Polk, Louisiana, he had only served about nine months when he was selected to become the first Psychology Consultant for the Army Health Services Command, a flag command at Fort Sam Houston in San Antonio, Texas, overseeing all health care, health facilities and personnel in CONUS, Hawaii, Alaska, and the Panama Canal Zone. During this time Bob became a member of the DOD Operation Homecoming, a five-year project following up on the adjustment of all military Vietnam repatriated POWs, and a member of the Center for POW Studies (where he headed the program to do the psychological evaluation of all army Vietnam POWs). He served as a sports psychologist with the Army's Olympic Modern Pentathlon Team and became a pioneer researcher on the adjustment of Vietnam veterans. Because of his considerable traveling to work with army medical facilities and personnel in the States, Bob became an instrument rated pilot and the army paid him to fly his own plane. This led to him becoming an aviation psychologist, working with army aviation. Because a lot of his work required management consulting within and outside the army, Bob earned a master's degree in business administration from Webster University in 1978. He ended his army career as the chief of the Fort Sam Houston Army Mental Health Service (while also serving as the HSC Psychology Consultant). Bob retired from the army as a lieutenant colonel in October 1981.

His military decorations include the Combat Infantryman Badge, the Legion of Merit, seven decorations for valor, the Purple Heart, an Air Medal, three Army Commendation Medals, and the USMC Combat Action Ribbon.

Bob became a university business professor, a full-time writer and then a university writing professor, retiring in 1997. As a writer Bob has over 2,500 publications, including several authored or co-authored books, and journal and magazine articles. This book is the second of a trilogy depicting Bob's military adventures. The first is *Under Fire with ARVN Infantry* (McFarland, 2018). Anita passed in July 2021. Bob lives in Las Cruces, New Mexico.

Index

Numbers in **bold italics** indicate pages with illustrations